AMERICAN
FOREIGN POLICY
OPPOSING VIEWPOINTS®

Other Books of Related Interest in the Opposing
Viewpoints Series:

AMERICAN
FOREIGN POLICY
O P P O S I N G   V I E W P O I N T S®

David L. Bender & Bruno Leone, *Series Editors*

Carol Wekesser, *Book Editor*

OPPOSING VIEWPOINTS SERIES ®

Greenhaven Press, Inc.   PO Box 289009   San Diego, CA 92198-9009

Library of Congress Cataloging-in-Publication Data

American foreign policy : opposing viewpoints / Carol Wekesser, book editor
   p. cm. — (Opposing viewpoints series)
  Includes bibliographical references and index.
  Summary: Presents opposing viewpoints on such aspects of American foreign policy as dealing with allies, intervention abroad, and foreign aid.
  ISBN 0-89908-199-1 (lib : acid-free) : — ISBN 0-89908-174-6
  (pap)
  1. United States—Foreign relations—1989-   [1. United States —Foreign relations.] I. Wekesser, Carol, 1963- . II. Series: Opposing viewpoints series (Unnumbered)
E881.A445 1993
327.73—dc20
                                     92-40707
                                          CIP
                                          AC

"Congress shall make no law . . .
abridging the freedom of speech,
or of the press."

First Amendment to the U.S. Constitution

The basic foundation of our democracy is the first amendment
guarantee of freedom of expression. The Opposing Viewpoints
Series is dedicated to the concept of this basic freedom and the
idea that it is more important to practice it than to enshrine it.

Contents

Why Consider Opposing Viewpoints?

"The only way in which a human being can make some approach to knowing the whole of a subject is by hearing what can be said about it by persons of every variety of opinion and studying all modes in which it can be looked at by every character of mind. No wise man ever acquired his wisdom in any mode but this."

John Stuart Mill

In our media-intensive culture it is not difficult to find differing opinions. Thousands of newspapers and magazines and dozens of radio and television talk shows resound with differing points of view. The difficulty lies in deciding which opinion to agree with and which "experts" seem the most credible. The more inundated we become with differing opinions and claims, the more essential it is to hone critical reading and thinking skills to evaluate these ideas. Opposing Viewpoints books address this problem directly by presenting stimulating debates that can be used to enhance and teach these skills. The varied opinions contained in each book examine many different aspects of a single issue. While examining these conveniently edited opposing views, readers can develop critical thinking skills such as the ability to compare and contrast authors' credibility, facts, argumentation styles, use of persuasive techniques, and other stylistic tools. In short, the Opposing Viewpoints Series is an ideal way to attain the higher-level thinking and reading skills so essential in a culture of diverse and contradictory opinions.

In addition to providing a tool for critical thinking, Opposing Viewpoints books challenge readers to question their own strongly held opinions and assumptions. Most people form their opinions on the basis of upbringing, peer pressure, and personal, cultural, or professional bias. By reading carefully balanced opposing views, readers must directly confront new ideas as well as the opinions of those with whom they disagree. This is not to simplistically argue that everyone who reads opposing views will—or should—change his or her opinion. Instead, the series enhances readers' depth of understanding of their own views by encouraging confrontation with opposing ideas. Careful examination of others' views can lead to the readers' understanding of the logical inconsistencies in their own opinions, perspective on why they hold an opinion, and the consideration of the possibility that their opinion requires further evaluation.

Evaluating Other Opinions

To ensure that this type of examination occurs, Opposing Viewpoints books present all types of opinions. Prominent spokespeople on different sides of each issue as well as well-known professionals from many disciplines challenge the reader. An additional goal of the series is to provide a forum for other, less known, or even unpopular viewpoints. The opinion of an ordinary person who has had to make the decision to cut off life support from a terminally ill relative, for example, may be just as valuable and provide just as much insight as a medical ethicist's professional opinion. The editors have two additional purposes in including these less known views. One, the editors encourage readers to respect others' opinions—even when not enhanced by professional credibility. It is only by reading or listening to and objectively evaluating others' ideas that one can determine whether they are worthy of consideration. Two, the inclusion of such viewpoints encourages the important critical thinking skill of objectively evaluating an author's credentials and bias. This evaluation will illuminate an author's reasons for taking a particular stance on an issue and will aid in readers' evaluation of the author's ideas.

As series editors of the Opposing Viewpoints Series, it is our hope that these books will give readers a deeper understanding of the issues debated and an appreciation of the complexity of even seemingly simple issues when good and honest people disagree. This awareness is particularly important in a democratic society such as ours in which people enter into public debate to determine the common good. Those with whom one disagrees should not be regarded as enemies but rather as people whose views deserve careful examination and may shed light on one's own.

Thomas Jefferson once said that "difference of opinion leads to inquiry, and inquiry to truth." Jefferson, a broadly educated man, argued that "if a nation expects to be ignorant and free . . . it expects what never was and never will be." As individuals and as a nation, it is imperative that we consider the opinions of others and examine them with skill and discernment. The Opposing Viewpoints Series is intended to help readers achieve this goal.

David L. Bender & Bruno Leone,
Series Editors

Introduction

"We are not the policeman of mankind. We are not able to run the world, and we shouldn't pretend that we can."

Walter Lippmann, February 22, 1965.

"We have learned that we cannot live alone, at peace; that our own well-being is dependent on the well-being of other nations, far away."

Franklin D. Roosevelt,
Fourth Inaugural Address, January 20, 1945.

Since its inception, the United States has struggled with the dilemma of how to relate to other nations. In U.S. foreign policy decisions, two conflicting ideologies have often dominated debate: isolationism and interventionism.

A nation practicing isolationism avoids alliances and other international political and economic relations. Early Americans were staunchly isolationist, mainly because they came to the New World seeking new lives and fleeing the problems, prejudices, and lack of opportunity that plagued the Old World. These pioneers sought lives geographically and philosophically separate from Europe. As historian Wayne S. Cole of the University of Maryland explains:

> Settlers came to escape religious persecution, economic hardship, wars, or personal problems in Europe. From the beginning there was the assumption (or the hope) that the New World would be better than the Old. The long and dangerous journey magnified the geographic (and moral) separateness of America. . . . The attitudes undergirding isolationism were well established long before independence.

This belief that America was different from the rest of the world and consequently should separate itself from the world's problems continued to be a factor in American foreign policy after America won its independence and into the twentieth century. For example, Americans strongly resisted the nation's involvement in both world wars, which were largely viewed as "European" problems. Only after America's security was threatened—by German submarines in World War I and by the

Japanese attack on Pearl Harbor in World War II—did the United States enter the wars.

The nation's isolationist instincts, however, have often been curbed by the desire to exercise another role, that of the world's chief advocate of democracy and champion of the underdog. Many writers and thinkers have seen this as a unique and predominant American motivation. Daniel Webster, for example, called America "the home of freedom, and the hope of the down-trodden and oppressed among the nations of the earth."

This twofold mission of democratizing the world and rescuing the oppressed has spurred Americans to noble actions, such as the 1948-1949 airlifts of food and fuel to West Berliners trapped by a Soviet blockade. These airlifts not only helped the suffering people of West Berlin, but also prevented the Soviets from taking over all of the city. During the years that followed, West Berlin became a lone outpost of democracy in a sea of communism. The selflessness shown in the Berlin airlift continues, especially in the area of U.S. humanitarian aid. The United States gives about five billion dollars in this type of aid annually.

These altruistic tendencies, however, have also been used as a pretext for interventions that were motivated primarily by self-interest. For example, in 1989 the Bush administration claimed that freeing Panamanians from Manuel Noriega's oppressive regime was the administration's primary motive for the U.S. invasion of Panama. In fact, ridding the United States of an uncooperative neighbor was most likely the primary motive. Throughout America's history, presidents from William McKinley to George Bush have claimed that interventions in Cuba, Korea, Vietnam, and Central America would promote freedom and democracy. Sometimes these claims were sincere, sometimes deceptive; American leaders have often cited altruistic motives to persuade the American public to support actions it might otherwise oppose. Whether the motivation was sincere or not, the mission of bringing democracy to the world and helping the downtrodden has played an important role in the nation's foreign policy.

Throughout the cold war, America adopted a primarily interventionist foreign policy, repressing traditional American isolationist tendencies. With the end of the cold war, however, the United States is once again experiencing a clash between its desire to pull away from the world and its need to engage in it. Without a Soviet threat, U.S. leaders can no longer use communism as a pretext to propel American involvement in world affairs. Consequently, the voices of those who urge that America play a more circumscribed role in foreign affairs are being heard once again. Columnist Stephen Chapman, for example, warns about the dangers of an interventionist foreign policy:

"The same liberal internationalist vision of America's global role that led us into Vietnam could lead us into new disasters." The voices of Chapman and others, however, continue to be challenged by those, such as *Wall Street Journal* foreign affairs columnist George Melloan, who advocate an expansion of America's interventionist foreign policy. As Melloan states: "Does the U. S. have any business playing policeman for the world? The answer, I think, is a qualified, 'yes, where possible.' Human compassion, an edifying component of modern democracy, demands it." Isolationism, in addition to being opposed by Melloan and others on ideological grounds, is also becoming more difficult to maintain in practice as the nations of the world become increasingly intertwined politically and economically.

This conflict between isolationism and interventionism is just one of the issues examined in *American Foreign Policy: Opposing Viewpoints*. The book, which replaces Greenhaven's 1987 book of the same name, debates foreign policy issues in the following chapters: What Should Be the Goals of U.S. Foreign Policy? How Should the U.S. Deal with Its Allies? Is U.S. Intervention in Other Countries Justified? What Are the Effects of U.S. Foreign Aid? How Should the U.S. Deal with the Former Soviet Republics? The issues in *American Foreign Policy* seem especially pressing in light of the new world political climate created by the fall of the Soviet Union and the end of communism. These changes offer new problems and possibilities for the United States and present new challenges to American foreign policy.

What Should Be the Goal of U.S. Foreign Policy?

AMERICAN
FOREIGN POLICY

Chapter Preface

Prior to the late 1980s and early 1990s, American foreign policy was largely driven by one primary concern: the communist threat. So-called hawks labeled the communists as America's greatest worry and cited communism as the reason to intervene in Southeast Asia, Central America, Europe, Africa, and Afghanistan, among other places. All Americans dreamed of a day when communism would no longer be perceived as a threat and the possibility of a nuclear war would be removed.

Yet, when that day arrived after the fall of the Berlin Wall in 1989 and of Soviet communism in 1991, Americans were not suddenly relieved of the burden of foreign policy. Instead, they were forced to reevaluate the world and their role in it. With a clear enemy, America's role had also seemed clear; without that enemy, no clear path appeared.

To fill this vacuum, foreign policy analysts have begun debating the pros and cons of various foreign policy goals. Some, like Richard Nixon, urge American leaders to "seize the moment" and take the reins of world leadership. Nixon's proposal, termed "internationalism," is espoused by many who believe that America is the only nation capable of leading the world morally, militarily, and economically. Still others, such as Ted Galen Carpenter of the Cato Institute, have called for a return home of American troops and money. The cold war is over, they argue—time to resist foreign entanglements and once again focus on America's domestic problems.

Whether leading the world can or should be a principal goal of America's foreign policy is one of the issues debated by the authors of the following chapter.

> *"The world needs U.S. leadership militarily, politically, and economically."*

The U.S. Must Lead the World

Richard Nixon

Richard Nixon was president of the United States from 1968 to 1974. Since leaving office, he has become an unofficial foreign policy advisor to several presidents and has written numerous books, including *Seize the Moment: America's Challenge in a One-Superpower World*, from which the following viewpoint is excerpted. In the viewpoint, Nixon maintains that the United States is the only nation capable of leading the world because it is the only nation with democratic ideals and the necessary military and economic power. He concludes that it is America's duty to guide the world into the twenty-first century.

As you read, consider the following questions:

1. What three values does America represent, in Nixon's opinion?
2. What evidence does the author give to show that the United States is the most successful nation in the world?
3. Why does Nixon believe most nations of the world respect the United States?

From Richard Nixon, *Seize the Moment: America's Challenge in a One-Superpower World*. New York: Simon and Schuster, 1992. Copyright 1992 by East-West Research, Inc. Reprinted with permission.

Today, we are witnessing one of the great watersheds in history. The cold war world order—based on two clashing ideologies, two opposing geopolitical blocs, and two competing superpowers—has been irrevocably shattered. We now have a cause even greater than the defeat of communism—the victory of freedom. If we meet the challenges of peace, our legacy will be not just that we saved the world from communism but that we helped make the world safe for freedom.

Yet those who have hailed the beginning of a new order in which peace and freedom are secure speak prematurely. The peaceful revolution in Eastern Europe did not prevent the violent conquest of Kuwait by Iraq. Those who in 1990 touted the conventional wisdom that economic power had replaced military power as the major instrument of foreign policy were exposed as false prophets when Japan and Germany proved impotent in responding to Saddam Hussein's aggression. Despite the great victories for freedom in 1989 and 1991, both the Persian Gulf crisis in 1990 and the coup attempt by Soviet hard-liners in 1991 demonstrated that the world remains a dangerous and unpredictable place.

The Appeal of American Ideals

America has an indispensable role to play in the world. No other nation can take our place. Some might eventually be able to replace us militarily. Others might be able to take our place economically. But only the United States has the military, economic, and political power to lead the way in defending and extending freedom and in deterring and resisting aggression. More important, our influence stems not only from our military and economic power but also from the enormous appeal of our ideals and our example. We are the only great power in history to have made its entrance onto the world stage not by the force of its arms but by the force of its ideas. . . .

Is the United States worthy to play a leadership role in the world? In a word, yes—and the world needs our example. . . .

America preeminently represents three values: freedom, opportunity, and respect for the individual human being. These values transcend borders. They rise from the human spirit, and they speak directly to that spirit. They are inextricably linked with the virtues of individual responsibility, competitiveness, self-reliance, and compassion grounded in an understanding of human nature. America's dedication to these values and its practice of these virtues are what, through the years, has given such power and reach to the American idea. They are the source of our strength and cohesion at home. They also give powerful moral sanction to our voice in the councils of nations abroad.

American progress, based on these values, has been spectacular. We are the richest nation in the world. The very poor in the United States would be rich in three-quarters of the world today. We are the strongest military power in the world. We have the world's best universities. Americans have won more Nobel Prizes in the sciences than any other people have. We have the best medical care in the world, with those abroad who can afford it coming here for treatment rather than using their own countries' nationalized health care programs. We have the most advanced programs for protecting the environment. We have less racial prejudice and more opportunity for all in our society than virtually any other multiethnic nation. That is why the traffic is all one way. Those who want to leave America and live in another country number in the hundreds. Those who want to leave their home countries and live in America number in the millions. . . .

U.S. Leadership Is Vital

The U.S. role in the world is likely to be the most important of any in determining whether international relations become increasingly well ordered or sink instead into increasing disorder. And in assessing the dangers ahead, it is important to recognize that the likelihood of increased conflict depends very much on what the United States does—or does not do—with respect to specific existing political problems. The "new world order" thus depends very much on the United States—on the choices it makes and the leadership it seeks to exercise.

Zbigniew Brzezinski, *The Washington Quarterly*, Spring 1992.

How should the United States exercise its leadership in today's world? The world needs U.S. leadership militarily, politically, and economically. Most of all, it needs our leadership in the critical arena of ideas.

Even within and among the countries of Western Europe, bitter conflicts have arisen over the extent to which markets should be controlled by the state and over the degree to which democratic choices of individual nations should be turned over to a new supranational bureaucracy. The danger that the united Europe after 1992 will become protectionist and socialist is real. This is one reason why a continued active American presence is essential to Europe, the United States, and the world. . . .

As I have traveled around the world during the past forty-five years, I have found that some hate us, some envy us, and some like us. But I have found that almost all respect us. All know that without the United States peace and freedom would not have survived in the world in the past and will not survive in the future. But the question that has arisen again and again has been whether the United States had the will to play a world role over the long haul.

The U.S. Must Play a World Role

We have demonstrated that will during the decades of the cold war, and we must sustain that will in the decades to come. We should commit ourselves to a world role not just to keep the world from becoming worse but to make it better. We need to restore our faith in our ideas, in our destiny, and in ourselves. We exist for more than hedonistic self-satisfaction. We are here to make history, neither to ignore the past nor to turn back to the past, but to move forward in a way that opens up new vistas for the future. . . .

Only 5 percent of the world's people live in the United States. But what we do can make the entire world a better place. We are not mere passengers on the voyage of history. We are its navigators. We have the opportunity to forge a second American century.

In his Iron Curtain speech in 1947, Winston Churchill said, "The United States stands at this time at the pinnacle of world power. It is a solemn moment for the American democracy. For with primacy in power is also joined an awe-inspiring account-ability for the future." Those words are as true today as when he spoke them forty-five years ago. We hold the future in our hands.

This is not a burden to be grimly borne. It is a high enterprise worthy of a great people. We are privileged to live at a moment of history like none most people have ever experienced or will ever experience again. We must seize the moment not just for ourselves but for others. Only if this becomes a better world for others will it be a better world for us, and only when we partici-pate in a cause greater than ourselves can we be fully true to ourselves.

"The age-old temptation—the imperial temptation—may prove compelling for the United States."

The U.S. Should Resist Becoming the World's Leader

Robert W. Tucker and David C. Hendrickson

The fall of the Soviet Union has left the United States as the only remaining world superpower. This position might tempt the United States to exert its influence, Robert W. Tucker and David C. Hendrickson contend in the following viewpoint. Tucker and Hendrickson believe the United States should resist this temptation. The authors argue that attempting to control world events through influence or force will only lead the United States into unwanted conflicts. Tucker and Hendrickson are fellows at the Council on Foreign Relations, a New York City-based foreign policy think tank. They are the authors of the book *The Imperial Temptation: The New World Order and America's Purpose*, from which this viewpoint is excerpted.

As you read, consider the following questions:

1. How would an American empire of today differ from traditional empires, according to the authors?
2. Why do Tucker and Hendrickson believe Americans might support an increased use of U.S. military force?
3. What is being threatened by America's increased willingness to use military force, in the authors' opinion?

From Robert W. Tucker and David C. Hendrickson, *The Imperial Temptation: The New World Order and America's Purpose*. New York: Foreign Relations Press, © 1992 by the Council on Foreign Relations, Inc. Reprinted with permission.

The United States is today the dominant military power in the world. In the reach and effectiveness of its military forces, America compares favorably with some of the greatest empires known to history. Rome reached barely beyond the compass of the Mediterranean, whereas Napoleon could not break out into the Atlantic and went to defeat in the vast Russian spaces. During the height of the so-called *Pax Britannica*, when the Royal Navy ruled the seas, Bismarck remarked that if the British army landed on the Prussian coast he would have it arrested by the local police. The United States has an altogether more formidable collection of forces than its predecessors among the world's great powers. It has global reach. It possesses the most technologically advanced arms, commanded by professionals skilled in the art of war. It can transport powerful continental armies over oceanic distances. Its historic adversaries are in retreat, broken by internal discord.

The Temptation of Imperialism

Under these circumstances, an age-old temptation—the imperial temptation—may prove compelling for the United States. That this temptation is pursued under the banner of a new world order, an order that promises to universalize both peace and the institutions of freedom, does not relieve its dangers. Nor are these dangers lessened by the consideration that the imperial temptation to which the nation succumbed in the gulf war—and to which it may yet fall victim again—involves not rule over others but the brief, massive use of military power in which the emphasis is placed on punishment and not rehabilitation. The nation is not likely to be attracted to the visions of empire that animated colonial powers of the past; it may well find attractive, however, a vision that enables the nation to assume an imperial role without fulfilling the classic duties of imperial rule.

The imperial temptation has arisen, in the first instance, because of the novel circumstances in international relations brought on by the end of the cold war. By virtue of the balance that existed in international politics during the cold war, which restrained both the Soviet Union and the United States, certain actions were foreclosed on both sides because they seemed altogether too dangerous. In the absence of a central balance, internal as opposed to external restraints on the use of force now have a greater importance than they formerly did. At the same time, however, these internal restraints have been weakened by the discovery of a way of war that enables the United States to throw the burdens of military conflict almost wholly onto the shoulders of the adversary. Moral and legal restraints on the use of force, which have always rested primarily on prudential considerations, have thus been considerably weakened. Under the right circumstances, this way of war enables us to go to war with greater precipitancy than we otherwise might while also allowing us to walk away from the ruin thus created without feeling a commensurate sense of responsibility.

Reprinted by permission from *People's Weekly World*.

Restraints, both internal and external, will doubtless continue to inhibit the use of American military power. How formidable these barriers will be, however, is questionable. A public resentful of foreign aid and increasingly nationalistic may still give its approval to uses of American force that do not require inordinate outlays of blood and treasure. Traditional allies and former adversaries, who have their own reasons for maintaining good relations with the United States, may do the same. A nation resentful of its declining economic performance, which finds that its status as the world's only superpower rests above all on its military strength, may find itself tempted to demonstrate that its own peculiar asset, built up in the course of a rivalry that is no more, still has a continuing relevance in world politics. A president who believes—not without reason—that his popularity rests upon the conduct of foreign policy, and who found himself most in his element when exercising decisive leadership in war, may also face temptations of a similar kind. No historical inevitability decrees that the nation must make this fateful choice; on the contrary, its vital interests and its deepest purposes would best be served by a far different course. But the temptation exists.

In the pursuit of a new world role, one required neither by security need nor by traditional conceptions of the nation's purpose, the Bush administration has given military force a position in our statecraft that is excessive and disproportionate. It has done so with the consent, and even enthusiasm, of the nation. That excess, and that disproportionality, are nowhere more apparent than in the readiness with which the United States went to war against Iraq, despite the availability of an alternative strategy that promised to secure American vital interests short of war. These traits are equally apparent in the readiness with which American leaders and the broader public are now prepared to consider measures of preventive war that the nation had previously deemed to be dangerous and wrong. They attest to the development in the United States of an attitude toward force that the nation embraces at its peril.

U.S. Must Value, Not Betray, Ideals

The peril is not preeminently to the nation's purse; it is to its soul. The danger is not so much that we will fail to protect our interests; it is that we will betray our historic ideals. By recalling those ideals in the course of this work, it is to be hoped that Americans will realize that the nation has assumed traits it once shunned and adopted habits it once excoriated. There is no assumption made here that the nation has always lived up to its ideals; it did, however, always look up to them. We believe that it needs to do so again.

===

"With the Cold War over, America must look homeward."

===

Domestic Affairs Must Take Precedence over Foreign Policy

Patrick J. Buchanan

In the following viewpoint, Patrick J. Buchanan argues that the United States should focus on its own domestic problems rather than wasting resources on the problems of other nations. Buchanan believes that for too long the United States has put the interests of its allies above its own interests. If America is to remain a world power, the author concludes, it must first be strong at home. A well-known conservative journalist and politician, Buchanan was a Republican candidate for president in 1992.

As you read, consider the following questions:

1. What does Buchanan dislike about America's current foreign policy?
2. How would a "New World Order" harm the United States, in the author's opinion?
3. Why does Buchanan believe it is wrong for American soldiers to fight under the direction of the United Nations?

Patrick J. Buchanan, "An America-First Foreign Policy," *Human Events*, May 2, 1992. Reprinted with permission.

My subject is one dear to the hearts of us all: the lady we all love, America the Beautiful. Where is she going?

In the decade just ended, with the grace of God, we Americans won the Cold War. We triumphed over the evil empire of Lenin and Stalin. Our enemy collapsed and came apart. But now that the Cold War is over, *quo vadis*? Where do we go from here?

No new foreign policy has been advanced to command the allegiance of our people.

Our leaders talk of a New World Order, yet they seem tied to the institutions and individuals of a Cold War past. Frozen in the old certitudes, our foreign policy establishment seems to have adopted as its operative slogan, "Read our lips: no new thinking."

The United States supported reunification of Germany. We now seem fearful Germany and France will build a new army to take over the defense of Europe. But why be afraid of this? Isn't this what we wanted all along? To bring our soldiers home, and let the Europeans defend themselves? Why fear the very democracies we nurtured and defended? Are we not behaving like fretful parents who, lacking confidence in their own children, are fearful of letting go?

Well, it is time we learned how to let go.

Freedom Replaced by Stability

Stability and order seem to have replaced liberty and freedom as the values most cherished by our statesmen; we seem to have adopted as our highest goal the preservation of the status quo.

Too often in recent years our country has found herself on the wrong side of America's ideals, on the wrong side of America's interests, and on the wrong side of history.

When Chinese students were run down by tanks in Tiananmen Square, our government sent two of its highest officials to Beijing to reassure the butchers who did it that we understood. Can anyone believe the future in China is represented by an 85-year-old, chain-smoking Communist ruler named Deng Xiaoping?

When Lithuania finally broke free of 50 years of Soviet bondage, America was 37th in line to recognize her. Thirty-seventh in line! When Croatia declared her independence and fought for freedom against Serbian Stalinists, our own State Department waited through nine months of massacre before heeding Croatia's cry for recognition.

Where is the principle? What do we stand for in the world?

Chinese rulers who crush freedom under tank treads and send missiles to Teheran are favored with World Bank loans. Yet, when Haiti's army ousted a leftist demagogue who admires Fidel Castro and speaks warmly of burning his enemies alive, we impose sanctions.

Hard on Haiti, but soft on Communist China. We mollify Deng, but condemn Peru's president who seized power to fight the Maoist guerrillas who are terrorizing his nation.

Where is the consistency? Where is the principle?

Foreign Policy Should Reflect Traditions

Today, the U.S. is imposing an embargo on Libya for refusing to surrender two suspects in the bombing of Pan American flight 103. And that is right and just. Yet, we are warming up to Hafez Assad of Syria who has provided sanctuary to terrorists for decades.

Danziger, for *The Christian Science Monitor*, © 1990 TCSPS.

As Churchill once said, "Take away this pudding; it has no theme."

But Lincoln said, "They have a right to criticize, who have a heart to help." So let me outline a foreign policy rooted in traditional principles that can command the respect and support of the American people.

It is time we looked back to the wisdom of our founding fathers:

"My ardent desire," wrote Washington, "is to keep the United States free from all political connections with every other country. . . . My policy has been to be on friendly terms with, but independent of, all nations of the earth. . . ."

27

Jefferson's policy was: "Peace, commerce and honest friendship with all nations, entangling alliances with none."

John Quincy Adams, son of a President, a secretary of state and a future President, wrote in 1821: "Wherever the standard of freedom and independence. . . shall be unfurled, there will [be America's] heart, her benedictions and her prayers. . . . She is the well-wisher to the freedom and independence of all. She is the champion and vindicator only of her own."

Today, we hear their counsel ridiculed, as we heed the siren's call for a global crusade to impose our democratic system on the less enlightened of the Earth. Friends, that has been the road to ruin for every empire from the Romans' to the Romanovs'.

The Pentagon has circulated a document outlining a new foreign policy where it will be America's duty to block the rise of any new regional power, and to go to war to protect the interests of our allies, all over the world, indefinitely.

U.S. to Be Planet's First "Globocop"?

America is to be the planet's permanent policeman, the world's first Globocop. We are to expand NATO's reach to cover Eastern Europe, even as we reduce the U.S. defense budget to a level lower than before Pearl Harbor. And some of the more fevered brains on our op-ed pages hail this blueprint for a Pax Americana as a "bargain."

Friends, this Pentagon document is a product of hubris, a formula for endless intervention in quarrels that are none of our business; it is a prescription for permanent war for permanent peace. In the deepest historic sense, it is un-American.

With the Cold War over, America must look homeward.

We must repair the damage done our society and nation. With 500 homicide victims every year in our own capital, with the mayor of New York talking about cutting off every fourth street light to save money, America cannot afford to be bailing out every bankrupt regime on Earth and pulling everybody's bacon out of the fire.

Our foreign policy elite is succumbing to a new temptation, the "Democratist Temptation," the belief that America's experiment in freedom and self-government can be replicated from the steppes of Asia to sub-Sahara Africa, from Afghanistan to the Andes, if only we put enough men, money and muscle into the great crusade.

But to put all the might of this republic at the service of a Utopian New World Order is the March of Folly, the antithesis of what our founding fathers wanted for this land of ours across the sea.

The architects and acolytes of this New World Order envision a world in which America's sovereignty is gradually diminished,

America's independence is gradually restricted and, ultimately, America evolves into some Western hemispheric province of a new world government.

Look at Europe. There, one after another, nations are yielding their sovereignty for a cushioned seat at the head table of a new Socialist superstate called the European Community. Only Margaret Thatcher, among the statesmen of Europe, seems to be fighting against the tide.

So the battle for the future is on. Between New Age globalists and old-fashioned patriots, between those who believe America must yield up her sovereignty to a New World Order and those who believe we must preserve the Old Republic.

If we are to remain true to the legacy of the founding fathers, and of the Daughters of the American Revolution, we must battle this New World Order as resolutely as they battled the old British Empire.

It is time Americans took their country back. Before we lose her forever, let us take America back from the global parasites of the World Bank and the International Monetary Fund, who siphon off America's wealth for Third World Socialists and incompetents. And let us take her back from agents of influence who occupy this city and do the bidding of foreign powers.

The Definition of "America First"

So let me tell you what I mean by "America First."

America must remain the first military power on Earth: first in the air, first at sea, first in space. The genius of American scientists and engineers, and the craftsmanship of our defense workers, has produced weapons that allow us to target the enemies who attack us—while sparing the lives of innocent civilians. Maintaining this technological edge is a strategic and moral imperative. So, instead of *talking* about a missile defense for the United States, isn't it time we *built* a missile defense for the United States?

It is also time for a reappraisal of all the institutions of the Cold War. From the United Nations to foreign aid, from the International Monetary Fund to the World Bank, all should be measured by a new yardstick: do they any longer advance the national interests of the U.S.A.? If not, if we are only paying the bill for anti-Western diatribes, let's pack up and get out—and let the inmates run the asylum.

In 1950, Dwight Eisenhower said that U.S. troops should go into Europe for 10 years, until Europe could provide for her own defense. That was 42 years ago. Now the Soviet Union is dead, the Red Army is leaving Germany, Hungary, Poland, Czechoslovakia and Ukraine. Why do we still need 150,000 troops in Bavaria?

Like the French, who thought they had found security behind the Maginot line, we Americans seem to be preparing for the last war. But the world has changed. America's new challenges are not from Japan's imperial fleet or the German Wehrmacht but from dynamic Asian capitalism and the Socialist superstate in Europe.

If Germany and Japan are rich enough and powerful enough to steal our markets and buy up our greatest corporations, they are rich enough and powerful enough to start paying the full cost of their own defense.

Under the Nixon Doctrine enunciated at Guam 23 years ago, our allies were to provide the troops for their defense; we would send the arms. That is the formula America should pursue.

We should pull up these tripwires laid down all over the world, from the 38th parallel to the Sinai Desert to Central Europe, and provide our allies access to the Great Arsenal of Democracy—so they can provide for, and pay for, their own national defense.

Obsolete Alliances

Instead of seeking to preserve an expensive system of American-dominated alliances, the U.S. should view the eclipse of Soviet power as an opportunity to adopt a less pretentious and more cost-effective policy. For the first time in 50 years, there is no powerful challenger, such as Nazi Germany or the Soviet Union, that could pose a grave threat to America's security, nor is there a potential new threat visible on the horizon. That is a watershed development that fundamentally should alter U.S. defense policy in these changing times.

The post-Cold War world is likely to be a disorderly place, but, without a powerful rival to exploit the turmoil, most of the conflicts and quarrels will be largely irrelevant to America's security interests. The U.S., therefore, can afford to view them with detachment, intervening only as a balance of last resort if a conflict cannot be contained by powers in the affected region and is expanding to the point where America's security is threatened.

Ted Galen Carpenter, *USA Today*, September 1992.

Because our critics cannot answer our questions, they call us names. The very people who seek to resurrect the Utopian policies of Woodrow Wilson, who 75 years ago thought he had fought and won "the war to end war" and to make the world safe for democracy, now accuse us of illusion and delusion. They say we are "isolationists."

But we will never turn our backs on the world. Because we Americans come from every continent, we want to travel the world. Because we are the greatest trading nation in history, we want peaceful commerce with all nations, and we want contact and communications, both cultural and diplomatic, with all the peoples of the planet.

We simply do not want to fight other peoples' wars, or use the tax dollars of our citizens to pay other nations' debts. Those who would have us spill the blood of American soldiers in a quest for global empire, or empty our treasury to buy the transitory friendship of distant emirs and despots—these are the true isolationists. They would isolate Americans from their dreams, their traditions and their national interest.

The next time America takes up arms, it should not be under the banner of the U.N. but under the flag of the U.S. If our armed forces have to settle accounts with Col. Qaddafi for the air massacre of Pan Am 103, we must never again be told by the U.N. Security Council how far our army may go, and when it must stop—as happened in Iraq.

Let us turn to this issue of foreign aid. Every single week America sends $300 million in foreign aid to Socialist and Third World regimes, not one of which has gotten off Uncle Sam's welfare rolls in 20 years.

An End to Foreign Aid

Enough is enough. We have become the greatest debtor nation on Earth. We can no longer afford these mindless handouts. We must begin phasing out foreign aid and begin thinking about the forgotten Americans here in the United States.

If we don't believe government has the answers here at home, why do we think government has the answer in Russia? Yet our leaders are now seeking another $12 billion for the IMF, part of a $24-billion aid package for Russia. But how do you help a bankrupt Russia, $80 billion in debt, by plunging her $24 billion deeper into debt?

This Moscow bailout was not thought through. It pours billions of tax dollars down the sinkhole of a Socialist bureaucracy even less capable of managing a modern economy than our own.

We will never see the money again. Much of it will be siphoned off by international bankers. Of all the aid sent to Moscow in 1991, 84 per cent went to service old debts to governments and big banks.

What Russia, Ukraine and the Baltic republics need is not new debts, but forgiveness from old debt. The U.S. should take the lead in providing these free people a clean slate, forgiveness for the foolish Western loans made to their Communist rulers. But that would entail huge write-offs for Europe's bankers, and no IMF role running Russia's economy. Which is why it will be bitterly resisted.

The hidden agenda here—and Russian patriots already see it—is to get these countries hooked on the narcotic of foreign aid, so they will never escape the cloying embrace of the New World Order. We must not let that happen.

Meanwhile, our own country is undergoing the greatest invasion in history, a mass immigration of millions of illegal aliens yearly from Mexico. This invasion is eroding our tax base, swamping social services and undermining the social cohesion of the Republic.

Time to Secure Our Borders

Our government seems paralyzed. We can send a mighty army around the world to secure the border of Kuwait, but cannot secure the borders of our own country. Why? It is time to enforce America's laws, and defend America's borders against this invasion, if necessary, using the armed forces of the United States.

Like Gulliver, America is being tied down by the myriad tiny strands of this New World Order. . . .

Now that the Cold War is over, we need a new foreign policy, of Americans, by Americans, and for Americans. Time to set aside all this geo-babble about a New World Order and begin restoring the Old American Republic. Time to set aside the temptation to empire, time to put America first. And all else will follow.

"No president of the United States would be able to carry out an isolationist policy without doing great damage to the American people."

Foreign Policy Must Remain a U.S. Priority

Richard J. Barnet and John Cavanagh

The nations of the world are increasingly tied economically and politically. The authors of the following viewpoint contend that these ties make it impossible for the United States to withdraw from world affairs. Richard J. Barnet and John Cavanagh assert that attempting to do so would threaten the U.S. economy and would make it difficult for the world to solve global political, economic, and environmental problems. Barnet and Cavanagh are fellows at the Institute for Policy Studies, an independent center for policy research and education in Washington, D.C.

As you read, consider the following questions:

1. The authors give several examples to show that America is inextricably tied to the rest of the world. Name three of these examples.
2. How would isolationism affect America's national debt, in the opinion of Barnet and Cavanagh?
3. How are many wealthy Americans dealing with the nation's economic and social problems, according to the authors?

From Richard J. Barnet and John Cavanagh, "National Interest and Global Realities," *Institute for Policy Studies Briefing Paper*, Security Series, no. 2, January 1992. Reprinted with permission.

The Cold War defined almost fifty years of history. The collapse of the old order, which has come with such suddenness, has left the world in the grip of a continuing process of astounding change and has left the people of the United States in need of leaders with new visions of the national interest based on the new global realities.

Without a clear and widely supported understanding of what we are to be and what we want our society to stand for in the new century, no president of the United States can successfully address either foreign dangers or domestic needs. Without some working assumptions about the most plausible dangers from abroad as well as an understanding of the nature of the world economy and how it affects the people of the United States, the next president will be unable to develop either an affordable national security strategy or constructive policies to strengthen the economy.

Unfortunately, most participants in the current national debate so far have fallen into the trap of a false polarization between an isolationist vision of "America First" and a neo-Cold War vision based on the old Cold War slogan of "global responsibility." Some of the "America Firsters" employ just a dollop of jingoism, while others flaunt their isolationism, but none show much awareness of the impact of global changes on the lives of the voters whom they are courting. The neo-globalists try to adapt the Cold War vision to the post-Cold War world by proposing modest "downsizing" to a "lean, mobile" military force on guard against all sorts of new, unpredictable dangers. They call upon the United States to take on an even greater "world leadership" role now that the archenemy is gone.

The U.S. Has Neglected Itself

The "America Firsters" argue that we are neglecting our own society by taking on the defense of the world and spending money on other nations. They say it is time to spend more money here, a prescription that even the neo-globalists now share and which has merit. Any plausible threat posed by the Soviet Union has collapsed, and the military hardware, doctrines, and threat assessments developed during the Cold War world are largely obsolete. The consequences of years of neglecting our domestic society are apparent as the recession drags on and the employment, education, housing, and health crises deepen.

For the United States to forget the rest of the world or to relate to it selectively is as sensible as rejecting the law of gravity. Just as national security based on nuclear deterrence was the central idea of the Cold War period, the dominant reality of the new era in world politics is the rapid globalization of much of the world's economic activity. The U.S. economy is now so thoroughly integrated into the global economy that the isolationist option no longer exists. No president of the United States would be able to carry out an isolationist policy without doing great damage to the American people, no matter how overwhelming the mandate to try.

Why Isolationism Will Not Work

The isolationist option is outmoded for several reasons.

• The great engines of the U.S. economy—banks, industrial corporations, and service providers such as worldwide insurance companies, accounting firms, law firms, and advertising agencies—are all global actors with loyalties and interests that extend far beyond the shores of this country. No national government can control them, much less force them to serve a nationalistic policy that is clearly not in their interest. At best, our government can influence their behavior in ways that benefit the people and territory of the United States by creating incentives and disincentives.

The Failure of Isolationism

Most of the purer strains of isolationism have failed to take root. Patrick J. Buchanan, in his campaign for the Republican presidential nomination, promised to "put America first" by cutting trade, immigration, aid, and the U.S. political/military presence abroad. But Republican primary voters seem to have recognized that America already was "first," and that Buchanan's platform would only squander that position.

Joshua Muravchik, *Commentary*, July 1992.

• Every American worker is part of a global labor pool. Even top executives are now competing with non-Americans for management jobs. (A number of major corporations flying the U.S. flag have CEOs who are foreign nationals.) American factory workers in virtually every industry have been challenged over the past twenty years by increasingly efficient, lower-wage workers across the world. The consequence of the global shift in production is the loss of American jobs and the decline in living standards and expectations for all except the very rich. Protectionism and the economic warfare that such policies inevitably trigger only accelerate the loss of jobs.

• Environmental problems, from greenhouse gas emissions to acid rain, now threaten everyone. To offer but one prominent example, waste disposal is now a global operation. Rich countries are exporting toxic industrial by-products to poor countries around the world, after decades of burying such materials in their own poorer communities. The global traffic in waste actually complicates the task of governments everywhere. As poorer countries compete with one another to house the industrial waste products of the richer countries and to attract pollution-producing industry, the result is not only a lowering of environmental standards but the frustration of environmental policy. Toxic waste does not respect borders. One consequence of environmental deterioration is more refugees and immigrants.

• No national government, including the U.S. government, can control the huge movements of capital that travel across the world via computer at a speed five hundred times the snap of a finger; twenty-four hours a day every day more than $500 billion flows through the world's major foreign exchange markets, beyond the reach of any effective regulation. Because money can be borrowed and invested anywhere in the world, national governments can no longer manage their economies effectively by simply adjusting interest rates. In times of inflation or recession, the medicine—raising or lowering the rate—must be administered in such strong doses that dangerous side effects are virtually inescapable.

• The United States is the world's largest debtor nation. Our national government would be unable to meet its payroll unless it received the $100 billion or more a year from the non-American financiers on whom it has come to depend. This dependence necessarily restricts the United States in dealing with its creditors on political matters. The nations that finance the U.S. deficit also happen to be our major commercial rivals. But the isolationist alternatives are either to print more money or slash essential services even further. Neither is a basis for building national strength.

Redefine National Interest

The crisis facing the United States and every other nation-state demands new understandings of what a nation is. National interest is an old-fashioned term. It is most frequently invoked by presidents to describe or to defend whatever they have decided to do. For that reason many people reject the term as vacuous or meaningless. But the term is as good as any to describe a set of principles and understandings that bind a people into a political community. Without at least an intuitive sense of a common commitment to a common destiny, people are unwilling and even unable to sacrifice short-term advantage for the common good.

The rich have abundant opportunities to break their covenant with the nation, and we have seen many examples in the last decades: Multibillion-dollar scams on Wall Street, the great savings-and-loan larceny, and tax avoidance and evasion on a monumental scale. The consequences of these great treasury raids are felt by millions of taxpayers, depositors, and investors. The growing economic inequities in the nation, compounded by racial and gender tensions, are becoming more apparent. In the 1980s the average after-tax income of the top 1 percent of households increased 122 percent, while that of the bottom fifth of households fell 10 percent. Those with money and marketable professional skills can transcend the economic and social problems that beset their fellow citizens. They are mobile. They can invest abroad. They can work abroad. They have the money to buy private education for their children, health care for their families, and to insulate themselves from the crime and squalor all around them. Many enthusiastic flag-wavers with the money and intellectual resources to opt out of a troubled society are disengaging from the nation psychologically, economically, and even physically.

Expensive Isolationism

We must learn—and this time avoid—the dangers of today's isolationism and its economic accomplice, protectionism. To do otherwise—to believe that turning our backs on the world would improve our lot here at home—is to ignore the tragic lessons of the 20th century.

The fact is, this country has enjoyed its most lasting growth and security when we rejected isolationism—both political and economic—in favor of engagement and leadership.

George Bush, speech before World War II veterans, December 7, 1991.

Most Americans cannot follow that course. They are rooted in a place. They are dependent on jobs on American soil. They have little to invest in stock markets that are opening to foreign shareholders all over the world. As the nation becomes more dependent on the global economy, the gulf widens between those who are able to benefit from the age of globalization and those who cannot. The victims of the extraordinary changes in the position and condition of our nation are also withdrawing from the political community that we call the United States of America. In increasing numbers they are turning their backs on politics, giving up on school, trafficking in drugs. Having witnessed the breakup of the Soviet Union, we would do well to realize that nations can collapse in many different ways.

The United States was founded on a highly individualistic

ethic, but that ethic existed within a strong framework that defined a common destiny and a common good. That framework has broken down. The essential task of the next president is to lead the effort to build a new framework for an American Community in the twenty-first century. . . .

Redefining U.S. Leadership

In recent years discussions about U.S. leadership have ranged from President Bush's grandstanding proclamation of a new "American Century" to self-pitying hand-wringing about the "American decline" to indignant denials that such a fate could ever overtake this nation. With such divergent views, what should American leadership mean today?

What it should *not* mean has become more evident in the months since the Cold War ended. The world's single remaining global military power cannot organize a new world order. The United States has been largely a bystander, watching with amazement the phenomenal changes that have transformed the map of Europe, east and west. There has been little gratitude for military services rendered the oil-consuming nations in the Gulf War, and no encouragement for the United States to play the sheriff's role anywhere else.

The United States can and should exercise leadership in those areas where it has unique expertise and resources to contribute and where, by force of circumstance rather than self-proclamation, it bears special responsibility. Effective leadership requires identifying and addressing the key new problems of the increasingly globalized post-Cold War world:

• As the world's greatest military power, the United States should take the lead in developing international police forces and arrangements for the verification and control of global arms reduction.

• As the world's most developed market, the United States should take the lead in establishing a new world trade system based on fairness and the protection of workers, consumers, and the environment.

• As one of the world's oldest and most admired democracies, the United States should take the lead in seeking to establish the global economic conditions in which democracy can flourish and in providing technical assistance based on our experience—both our successes and our failures.

• As a nation with much to lose in a world of instability and disorder, the United States should take the lead in promoting a system of international law that will encourage desperately needed international cooperation to address the global problems that now define what a nation is and what it can and cannot be.

===

*"Advancing the democratic cause can be
America's most effective foreign policy."*

===

The U.S. Should Promote Democracy Throughout the World

Joshua Muravchik

Promoting democracy in other nations has always been and
should continue to be a primary foreign policy goal of the
United States, asserts Joshua Muravchik, the author of the following viewpoint. Muravchik maintains that promoting democracy would promote world peace because democratic governments are less likely to wage war. Muravchik, a resident scholar
at the American Enterprise Institute, is the author of the book
Exporting Democracy: Fulfilling America's Destiny, from which
this viewpoint is excerpted.

As you read, consider the following questions:

1. What does Muravchik mean when he says that democracy is
   natural?
2. Give three reasons why the author believes America should
   spread democracy.
3. How could the triumph of democracy lead to America's
   decline, according to the author?

From Joshua Muravchik, *Exporting Democracy: Fulfilling America's Destiny*, AEI Press, 1991.
Reprinted by permission of The American Enterprise Institute for Public Policy Research,
Washington, D.C.

America has won the cold war—almost without trying. America's aim, at least since 1956 when the stark exigencies of the Hungarian uprising disabused Americans of the illusions of a Communist rollback, has been not to win this conflict but to negotiate a truce. It won nonetheless, not on the strength of its arms or the skill of its diplomats, but by virtue of the power of the democratic ideas on which the American system is based and the failure of the Communist idea.

America's founders began with the premise that man had been created in the image of God and that all were of equal worth and endowed with unalienable rights. In founding the modern world's first democracy, they set out to create a system that would follow this premise and that would suit human nature as they understood it. Their vision has been profoundly vindicated.

The system they created has proved enduring, in large measure because its flexibility enables it to repair its own flaws, even the most grievous flaws of slavery and racial discrimination. The system has also proved successful, the most successful of any in history, in providing the good life for the vast majority of its citizens, including numberless refugees who arrived empty-handed. And it has proved that it is indeed natural.

Democracy Is Natural

Natural does not mean that democracy is the state in which man is ordinarily found. On the contrary the founders were well aware that they were creating institutional arrangements that were quite new, bearing little resemblance even to the democracies of classical antiquity. But democracy has proved itself natural in the sense that it answers something innate in human nature: a longing to be treated with dignity and not to be subjected to the arbitrary rule of others. Its naturalness has been proved by America's polyglot history. Immigrants of every conceivable stock have melded into American life, enriched it, and died defending it. And it has been proved too by the fact that where democracy has been transplanted, even by force, to extremely distant and diverse lands, such as Japan, Germany, or India, it has often sunk roots and flourished.

Communism in contrast began less with a theory of human nature than with a theory of history, one that has long ago shown itself to be erroneous. The system it spawned proved as unnatural as democracy is natural. Where communism was transplanted, it rarely outlasted the coercive force that brought it. When the Soviet Union decided to give up its empire in Eastern Europe after forty years, those polities sloughed off communism like a body rejecting a foreign organ to which it is violently immune.

40

The impending final collapse of communism . . . will free America from the threat that has disturbed peace for forty-odd years. It will be America's greatest victory, greater even than the victory over Hitler and the Axis in the sense that the victory in World War II came at the expense of nearly a million American casualties and millions among the Allies. In contrast victory over communism has come at much smaller human cost. Like nazism, communism has devoured scores of millions of lives, including thousands of Americans in Vietnam and Korea. Until 1989 there was every reason to suppose defeating communism would require horrendous sacrifice. But this final struggle has been almost bloodless so far, save for a few thousand martyrs in Tiananmen Square, a few score in Timisoara, a few dozen in Tbilisi. It is too much to hope that these will be the last martyrs of this cause, but there is every reason to hope that their numbers will in no way approach those lost in defeating fascism. This new victory has largely been sealed in the minds of men and women. . . .

Democracies Promote Peace

The United States has a vital interest in promoting and maintaining democracy abroad, especially in geopolitically crucial states. Actually, American ideals and self-interest will remain largely complementary in the post-Cold War era. One does not have to accept the argument that the spread of democracy will inevitably end war to recognize that Michael Doyle has given powerful if not conclusive empirical confirmation of Immanuel Kant's prediction offered more than 200 years ago: Constitutionally secure democratic regimes not only tend not to fight one another, but are more likely to cooperate and manage conflicts of interests harmoniously.

Robert G. Kaufman, *The Heritage Lectures*, June 12, 1991.

As Communist regimes tumbled in Eastern Europe, we Americans were surprised to see the depth of yearning for democracy and the degree to which people understood at least the essential outlines of the democratic idea. When East Germans took to the streets of Leipzig, Czechs to the streets of Prague, or even Romanians to the streets of Bucharest, they were strikingly clear in their demands. They asked not for a true press but a free press, not for enlightened rulers but for free elections, not for a reformed party but a multiparty system. They homed-in on the essence of democracy despite the confusion that their rulers attempted to sow about the meaning of "democracy," an effort that seems to have borne more fruit among Western academics and publicists than among East European subjects. And now that we have seen how firmly East Europeans grasped the concept of democracy, we often hear that the Chinese students who gathered in Tiananmen Square to demand democracy did not really understand the meaning of the term. Perhaps not. But it is striking that they chose to model their goddess of democracy in the shape of the Statue of Liberty.

The lesson in all of this is that advancing the democratic cause can be America's most effective foreign policy in terms not merely of good deeds but of self-interest as well. The immediate goal of U.S. foreign policy must be to complete the dissolution of communism. . . . The end of communism in China and the USSR means the end of communism per se. This will be not only a blessed deliverance for all of its unhappy subjects but also the greatest possible boon to America's security. . . .

U.S. policy should make the promotion of democracy its main objective. Voices are already being raised to say that if the Communist threat disappears, America should withdraw into itself. But withdrawal would be foolhardy as well as selfish. Once before, in 1919, we withdrew to isolation as soon as we had won the war and "made the world safe for democracy." The result was the rise of forces more terrible and destructive than those that we had put to rest. In the wake of communism, we are unlikely to see forces more terrible and more destructive, but we would be foolish to assume that all troubles will cease or to risk turning our back on the world. That we cannot foresee the shape of any possible new threat does not mean that none exists; it may show only the limits of our imagination.

The Post-Communist World

We should concentrate on continuing to spread democracy in a post-Communist world for three good reasons. The first is empathy with our fellow humans. Democracy does not make everyone happy, but it does deliver on its promise to allow, in our forefathers' brilliant phrase, the pursuit of happiness. Some people will never find their own happiness no matter how free they are to pursue it, but more people find happiness through their own pursuit than when it is defined for them by others.

Second, the more democratic the world, the friendlier America's environment will be. True, some democratic governments have been nuisances for the United States. Those of Sweden, India, France, and Costa Rica have at times played that part. But none has ever been our enemy. We could live comfortably indeed in a world where our worst antagonists were an Olof Palme, a Charles de Gaulle, an Indira Gandhi, or an Oscar Arias.

Third, the more democratic the world, the more peaceful it is likely to be. Various researchers have shown that war between democracies has almost never occurred in the modern world. . . .

A world in which the proliferation of democracies leads to a diminution of armed conflict would be a real Pax Americana. Is this vision utopian? Some would say that fostering a world of democracies and of peace is more ambitious an undertaking than the conquests that made the Pax Romana. To be sure, the evolution of other states is difficult to influence, but this truism can be overemphasized. Today roughly 40 percent of the world, measured either in numbers of countries or in population, lives under democratic government. Most of those democracies arose in large part as a result of the influence of America or of England (many were once British colonies).

America's National Purpose

The ultimate goal of American foreign policy is not just the prevention of war but the extension of freedom—to see that every nation, every person someday enjoys the blessings of liberty.

Ronald Reagan, *The New York Times*, October 7, 1986.

Although exporting democracy is never easy, it will grow easier with the demise of communism. With the collapse of its ideological rival, democracy gains new normative force in the global Zeitgeist. Rulers and subjects alike will find it harder to escape the idea that democratic behavior is right behavior. For decades, communism blurred that recognition. It vitiated the international consensus that had been growing since the Enlightenment that popular sovereignty is the sole basis on which states can claim legitimacy. Paying lip service to that principle, communism claimed that through the vanguard party the people could somehow be sovereign even without being consulted. Now, however, the Soviet president himself has acknowledged the preposterousness of this claim: in the name of democratizing his country he called for rule of law, competitive elections, free expression, multiple parties—in short the very institutions that Communists once dismissed as bourgeois democracy. Is it too much to expect the world to resist another such egregious imposture?

America's Triumph, America's Decline

The death throes of communism mark the beginning of the twenty-first century. It may be the American century. Henry Luce once said that the twentieth century would be the American century. But in fact it is better recognized as the totalitarian century. The various totalitarian systems now all seem to be ending in failure, but while they lived, they called the action. America emerged victorious over them all, but each of those victories came in defense. If, however, we can advance the spread of democracy, perhaps not everywhere but at least to the majority of mankind, then the twenty-first will be the true American century. This will come about not by the spread of American power or by the exact imitation of American institutions but by the spread of those profound and humane ideals on which America was founded.

Ironically such a triumph is bound to lead to the relative decline of America's power, the very decline that those who view the American experiment through jaundiced eyes have been yearning for or proclaiming. As other nations become democratic, they will discover the key to our success and come to rival it, as Japan and the democracies of Europe are already doing. Our preeminence will diminish. Just witness how Asian immigrants have flourished in recent decades with the opportunities they have found in a democratic America, and imagine the prowess of a democratic Asia. As more countries become democratic, America will for a time retain the advantage of our heterogeneity. The invigorating transfusion of immigrant talent that flows into our economy is matched by no other country. But even that advantage will eventually fade: as more countries become democratic, fewer of their citizens will flee, more will find their happiness at home. Deprived of that tonic, America will find that its stature will continue to sink to that of one country among countries, one democracy among democracies. It will be our greatest triumph.

> *"An imposed abstract 'democracy' thrust upon peoples unprepared for it would produce at first anarchy, then rule by force and a master."*

The U.S. Should Not Force Democracy upon Other Nations

Russell Kirk

Other nations have histories and cultures that differ greatly from America's, Russell Kirk states in the following viewpoint. These differences make it difficult for these nations to accept democracy, Kirk believes. He proposes that the United States try to influence other nations by example, not by actively working to promote democracy. Kirk is a lecturer and author of numerous books, including *The Conservative Mind*.

As you read, consider the following questions:

1. What three qualities does the United States possess, according to Kirk?
2. The author states that attempts at democratizing Africa have failed. Why do you think this is so?
3. In what areas can the United States set an example for the rest of the world, in the author's opinion?

From Russell Kirk, "Pax Americana—Can America Impose Peace?" *St. Croix Review*, January 1992. Reprinted with permission.

Ever since the First World War, certain Americans of an "interventionist" appetite have looked forward eagerly to an American domination of the world. George Santayana described such a zealot in his novel, *The Last Puritan* (1935), in the person of his character Cyrus P. Whittle, a sour New England schoolmaster. Whittle's joy was to vilify all distinguished Americans of the past (in this very like one of today's "deconstructionists"); but he had his secret devotion. "Not only was America the biggest thing on earth, but it was soon going to wipe out everything else; and in the delirious dazzling joy of that consummation, he forgot to ask what would happen afterward."

Military Might

We Americans urgently need to ask ourselves what would happen afterward—that is, supposing we push forward some New World Order imposed by American military strength and American economic resources, what would happen to the American Republic and to the other cultures of the world? President Bush's perplexity as to what can be done about Kurds and Shia Muslims in Iraq is merely the first of the troubles that must arise if the government of the United States presumes to issue decrees to distant nations and to assume that a design of "democratic capitalism" planned in Washington and New York may be readily imposed upon ancient cultures of origins altogether different from American civilization. . . .

The United States of America has enjoyed blessings, but those blessings are of a nature difficult to export. Three characteristics in particular must evoke the admiration of any acute observer: a constitutional system more friendly to order and liberty than any other in this century; an amenity of conduct and disposition which pervades, despite exception, most of the American people; and a spirit of responsibility not yet enfeebled. But these qualities cannot be canned and shipped, standardized, to Chad or Timor, China or Brazil. As Dr. Daniel Boorstin, one of our wiser living historians, puts the matter, "The American Constitution is not for export." Our American advantages are the product of peculiar historical circumstances in large part.

Some thirty-five years ago, the American Department of State and various public men were well into a program for liberating Africa from "colonialism" and substituting an Americanization of the Dark Continent; such had been the dream of Woodrow Wilson and of Franklin Roosevelt; such designs still are at work against South Africa, the only African state where constitutional government and some prosperity have survived.

That intended translation of American institutions to Africa has been a dismal failure: Africa has obdurately insisted upon remaining African. Not one liberal democracy exists in "emergent" Africa, nor is there any prospect of such development. The one country that was founded in emulation of American ways, Liberia, has collapsed into a ghastly anarchy. The United States is denounced in many African countries as the menacing new imperialist power. No large-scale industrialization has come to pass in "emergent" Africa; on the contrary, in most of that continent agriculture and mining have sadly declined since independence. Constitutionalism is a sham in nearly all African states; squalid new oligarchs supplant tribal chiefs; the military junta and the monolithic repressive party stand triumphant.

This is not a heartening record for the New World Order being concocted in Washington. And if now, under American pressure, order in the Republic of South Africa is undone and civil war erupts there, what course is Washington to follow—to establish American garrisons at Cape Town, Johannesburg, and Pretoria? Already such measures are being discussed in American periodicals.

No Crusade for Democracy

The United States must exercise leadership without imposing its political and cultural values on others. This is a fine line to walk. But we can advance our values and ideals with restraint dictated by realism. We should cultivate the growth of democratic principles where a reasonable prospect exists for their success and where they would be supported by national traditions, customs, and institutions. We should not, however, engage in an indiscriminate global ideological crusade.

Richard Nixon, *Seize the Moment: America's Challenge in a One-Superpower World,* 1992.

Consider yet another instance of the fallibility of Washington's makers of foreign policy in the abrupt announcement by Secretary of State James Baker that the United States would not recognize or assist Croatia and Slovenia; the United States instead would support the territorial integrity of Yugoslavia, as represented by the Marxist government at Belgrade—this early in June, 1991. A few days later, the State Department shame-facedly abandoned this stand, declaring instead that America would support whatever the Yugoslav people might desire. The historical fact that no true "Yugoslav people" exists—that Serbs, Croats, Slovenes, Albanians, and other peoples within the Yugoslav frontiers differ in language and culture widely—seems to have been ignored by Washington's Department of State. How intelligent would Washington's bureaucracy be in estab-

lishing some New World Order, or in maintaining the peace
once some such artificial order had been decreed and financed
by the United States?

The Consequences of Imposed Democracy

I venture to suggest that it would be highly imprudent for the
government of the United States, in the name of some New
World Order of Democratic Capitalism, to set about undermining régimes that do not seem perfectly democratic to the editors
of the *New York Times*, say—whether that undermining be
worked through the suasion and the money of the Endowment
for Democracy, or through the CIA and military operations.

"Four legs good, two legs bad"—such is the ideology of the
pigs in *Animal Farm*. "Democracy good, all else bad"—such is
the democratist ideology. A politicized American army operating
abroad would be no more popular than the Red Army has been.
An imposed abstract "democracy" thrust upon peoples unprepared for it would produce at first anarchy, then rule by force
and a master. The differing nations of our time must find their
own several ways to order and justice and freedom. The
Americans have not been appointed their keepers. It is not the
American *government* that could bring into being a Pax
Americana: only the American people, who, working in ways
nonpolitical, might persuade other peoples to benefit from emulation.

The Costliness of Empire

By meddling, with good intentions, in the affairs of distant
lands, empires have been created in a fit of absence of mind. So
it was that the Roman Republic became the Roman Empire.
Roman peace-keeping garrisons were stationed in remote regions; presently the cultures of those remote regions decayed
sadly, under Roman dominion. Increasingly the resources of the
Empire were dissipated by the enormous expense of policing
the known civilized world; and the economy virtually collapsed
under the burden of taxation.

That ruinous process seems to have begun for America already. American troops remain in the region of the Persian Gulf
months after American victory there, and American officials negotiate for permanent bases. "Desert Shield" and "Desert Storm"
cost the federal treasury a billion dollars *per day*, at the lowest
estimate: that is, for the two months of Shield and Storm, a total
of at least *sixty billion dollars* ($60,000,000,000). Is that merely
the beginning of the expansion of American hegemony to get
other countries? In empires, over-expansion of military commitments and political administration soon becomes a running
sore: the homelands may be drained dry by taxation. So it was
with the Pax Romana.

Should a Pax Americana ever take form—in the twenty-first century, say—it would have to be something other than the sort of hegemony attempted in varying degrees by Presidents Truman and Eisenhower and Kennedy and Bush. Nor could it be a patronizing endeavor, through gifts of arms and money, to cajole or intimidate the peoples of the earth into submitting themselves to a vast overwhelming Americanization. Nor could such adventures as President Bush's carpet-bombing of Mesopotamia, the cradle of civilization, bring about an enduring peace or a New World Order.

No, a Pax Americana is conceivable only so far as the United States, without aspiring to dominate the world, instead offers the world an example, a model of ordered freedom for possible emulation. Setting an example is very different from bullying one's neighbors or from bribing them. In an age of ferocious ideologies and fantastic political schemes, the United States may offer a model of the just society, reconciling the claims of order and the claims of freedom and settling for politics as the art of the possible.

Democracy Ineffective for Some Nations

Democracy presupposes a framework characterized by a broad consensus on the fundamental principles of nationhood, the structure of government, and the shaping and sharing of power, wealth, and other natural resources. Where consensus on these fundamentals is lacking, the people lack even a shared sense of belonging to the nation, even the concepts of majority and minority cannot apply. Parliamentarian democracy under those circumstances becomes the rule of a numerical majority imposed on an alienated minority.

Francis Deng, quoted in *Center Focus*, May 1990.

The United States should be able to show a pattern of domestic tranquility, in which people may safely walk cities' streets. We have lost ground in this during recent decades.

The United States should be able to exhibit a plan of fiscal responsibility, in which governments balance budgets, diminish national debts, and prevent inflation of the currency. We have not been moving that way.

The United States should be able to point to an educational system designed to impart wisdom and virtue, reaching an ethical end through an intellectual means. But everybody knows we have developed nothing of the sort.

The United States should emphasize the high success of its

plan of representative government. Yet nowadays it is painfully clear that American representative bodies are intimidated or cajoled by special interests and "minority" lobbies, with disastrous consequences.

Prospects Could Be Bright

If Americans can remedy the afflictions mentioned above, and other such national afflictions, the United States will be admired and emulated by intelligent people in every country. Prospects in the world of the twenty-first century will be bright—supposing that we Americans will not swagger about the globe, proclaiming our omniscience and our omnipotence. But if the United States can work no reform, we shall hear mockery: "Physician, heal thyself!" Have we Americans sufficient fortitude and imagination to commence this task?

a critical thinking activity

Ranking Foreign Policy Concerns

This activity will allow you to explore which values you consider important in making foreign policy decisions. In studying world politics you will discover that countries have different foreign policy priorities. These priorities are affected by each country's location, military strength, economic power, and other factors. Consider the difference in foreign policy concerns between Canada, which is bounded by its ally the United States, and three oceans, and Israel, which is bounded by hostile nations. Since Canada is relatively isolated, the likelihood of surprise external attack is fairly small, allowing national security to be a lower priority than trade, for example. Israel, on the other hand, must continually be on guard against its aggressive neighbors. For Israel, protecting national security is a main priority.

From 1945 to 1989, America largely determined its foreign policy priorities by strategic and ideological interests. Because

Mike Keefe, for *USA Today*. Reprinted with permission.

51

the United States perceived itself as the world's foremost advocate of democracy and believed communism to be a threat to democracy, U.S. foreign policy was largely directed at preventing the spread of communism. U.S. policies were especially directed at counterbalancing the actions of the Soviet Union.

After the 1989 demise of communism in Eastern Europe and the 1991 disintegration of the Soviet Union, however, the United States found itself without a clear foreign policy goal. Although America led the world as the only remaining superpower, as the cartoon shows, its leaders were unsure about which foreign policy goals should be a priority now that the cold war was over.

The authors in this chapter offer several suggestions on what foreign policy goals should take priority now that the cold war is over. To some, the end of the cold war should be treated the same as the end of any other war: The war is over, bring home the troops. In other words, now that the United States is no longer threatened strategically or ideologically by the Soviet Union, American troops no longer need to be stationed abroad, nor does America need to involve itself deeply in the affairs of other nations.

Not all Americans agree with this analysis, however. Some argue that America has spent more than four decades establishing itself as the world's leading power and it should continue to use this power to influence world events. These are just a couple of viewpoints on the issue. Additional foreign policy concerns are listed in Part I below.

Part I

Working individually, rank the foreign policy concerns listed below. Decide what you believe to be the most important priorities for America's foreign policy and be ready to defend your answers. Use number 1 to designate the most important concern, number 2 for the second most important concern, and so on.

_____ promoting peace in the Middle East

_____ providing economic aid to the former Soviet republics

_____ protecting America's trade interests

_____ encouraging Americans to travel to other nations

_____ providing military aid to Israel

_____ promoting human rights

_____ ensuring that the United States has a strong defense

_____ fostering democracy in other nations

_____ decreasing America's economic and political ties to its cold war allies

_____ using America's military to quell unrest in other nations

_____ using America's military for humanitarian purposes throughout the world

_____ creating exchange programs between U.S. students and those of other nations

_____ strengthening America's ties to its NATO allies

Part II

Step 1. Break into groups of four to six students. Participants should compare their rankings with others in the group, giving reasons for their choices. Then the group should make a new list that reflects the concerns of the entire group.

Step 2. In a discussion with the entire class, compare your answers. Then discuss the following questions:

1. Did your individual rankings change after comparing your answers with the answers of others in the group?
2. Why did your reasons differ from those of others in the group?
3. Consider and explain how your opinions concerning America's foreign policy concerns might change if you were:
   a. the Israeli prime minister
   b. the president of Russia

Periodical Bibliography

The following articles have been selected to supplement the diverse views presented in this chapter.

Elliott Abrams — "Why America Must Lead," *The National Interest*, Summer 1992. Available from Dept. NI, PO Box 3000, Denville, NJ 07834.

James A. Baker III — "Securing a Democratic Peace," *U.S. Department of State Dispatch*, April 13, 1992.

Patrick Barnard — "The Burdensome Costs of 'Victory,'" *Commonweal*, January 17, 1992.

The Brookings Review — "Foreign Policy for a Post-Cold War World," Fall 1992. Available from 1775 Massachusetts Ave. NW, Washington, DC 20036.

Zbigniew Brzezinski — "Order, Disorder, and U.S. Leadership," *The Washington Quarterly*, Spring 1992. Available from MIT Press Journals, 55 Hayward St., Cambridge, MA 02142.

McGeorge Bundy — "Our Country's New Role in the World," *Time*, special advertisement section, July 20, 1992.

Holly J. Burkhalter — "America's Post-Cold War Human Rights Policy," *Peace & Democracy News*, Winter 1992.

George Bush — "The Need for an Active Foreign Policy," *U.S. Department of State Dispatch*, March 16, 1992.

Noam Chomsky — "Force and Opinion," *Z Magazine*, July/August 1991.

Larry Diamond — "A World of Opportunity: Promoting Democracy," *Foreign Policy*, Summer 1992.

David C. Hendrickson — "The Renovation of American Foreign Policy," *Foreign Affairs*, Spring 1992.

Joanne Landy — "We Must Redirect U.S. Policy," *The Progressive*, April 1992.

Joshua Muravchik — "Losing the Peace," *Commentary*, July 1992.

How Should the U.S. Deal with Its Allies?

AMERICAN
FOREIGN POLICY

Chapter Preface

In Thomas Jefferson's first inaugural address, he stated that his administration would seek to establish "peace, commerce, and honest friendship with all nations, entangling alliances with none." This would seem to be wise foreign policy. Yet, as many U.S. presidents have found, seeking such friendships with other nations is not always easy. As in a relationship between two people, a relationship between two nations is often an evolving, complex combination of give-and-take. Whether any specific U.S. alliance is worth while depends upon whether one believes the United States benefits from the relationship in the long run.

America's relationship with Israel is an example of the complex nature of international alliances. The United States originally established this alliance for humanitarian reasons: Following the Holocaust of World War II, Americans believed the Jews deserved to have their own homeland. In addition, the United States has the world's largest Jewish population and consequently shares many religious and cultural ties with Israel.

After 1945, however, the nature of the alliance between the United States and Israel became more strategic than humanitarian: Because Israel was the only democracy in the Middle East, the United States relied on it to thwart Soviet intrusions into the region during the cold war. Israel, in turn, benefited politically, economically, and strategically from having one of the most powerful nations in the world as its friend.

As with many alliances, the U.S.-Israeli alliance has become more controversial as it has become more complex. While the Jews were originally viewed as an oppressed people seeking a homeland, today they are viewed by some as oppressors of the Palestinians they displaced. Disapproval of Israeli policies from those in the United States and throughout the world strains America's alliance with Israel. Now that the United States no longer needs to thwart Soviet ambitions, many Americans are reevaluating the U.S.-Israeli alliance and weighing its costs (animosity from the Arab world, a large amount of foreign aid to Israel) against its benefits (continuation of a strong cultural, religious, and political alliance).

Clearly, maintaining "honest friendships" with nations such as Israel while avoiding "entangling alliances" is difficult to do. In reality, most of America's alliances are both. The following chapter examines the nature of three of America's alliances.

"NATO . . . looms more important than ever in the new world of the 1990s."

The U.S. Should Continue to Support NATO

Gary L. Geipel

Gary L. Geipel is a research fellow at the Indianapolis-based Hudson Institute's Center for Soviet and Central European Studies. The institute is a foreign policy think tank. In the following viewpoint, Geipel maintains that it is in America's interest to continue its membership in NATO. NATO protects America's security by providing a stabilizing force in Europe and giving the United States a launching site for quick action in case of conflicts in Northern Africa or the Middle East. In addition, Geipel argues that membership in NATO helps America strengthen its relationship with its European neighbors and share the expense of defense.

As you read, consider the following questions:

1. What three reasons does Geipel give for the continued importance of NATO to Europe and the United States?
2. What risks warrant the continued existence of NATO, in the author's opinion?
3. How might NATO change in the future, according to Geipel?

Gary L. Geipel, "Why We Still Need NATO," *The American Legion*, July 1992. Reprinted with permission.

M any of Europe's leaders, institutions and countries have ended up in the trash can of history in recent years. In fact, we might even be tempted to believe that nothing from the Cold War was worth saving. That is not true in at least one case.

The Cold War brought the United States and 16 European countries together in the North Atlantic Treaty Organization (NATO), which looms more important than ever in the new world of the 1990s.

The United States and Europe still need NATO for at least three important reasons:

• First, Europe remains a dangerous neighborhood, especially on its fringes. Thus, military forces cannot be neglected.

• Second, if the United States stays in Europe to help keep the peace, chances are it will not have to fight any more wars there.

• Third, a good way to get a peace dividend and still maintain strong armed forces is to divide the burden of defense among several countries.

NATO delivers on all three counts.

The history of NATO is like the story of an arranged marriage in which the partners grow on each other. The NATO wedding took place in 1949, when western European countries still distrusted each other. But, since the threat of Soviet invasion loomed large, they realized that cooperation made more sense than going it alone.

The United States played the role of an honest broker—one who could provide the ultimate guarantee of protection.

"NATO used to get criticized for doing a lot of sitting around and talking," said an official of NATO's Atlantic naval command in Norfolk, Va. "You bet the NATO countries talk. It sure beats fighting like they used to do."

All that talking in NATO helped develop the trust found in today's European Community, a group of countries that share a dream called the United States of Europe. NATO also kept the Soviet threat from turning into a commanding influence over western Europe, or worse, into all-out war.

"Routine" Activities

Along the way, NATO accomplished something that no other military alliance had ever achieved: It became more than the sum of its parts.

Two admirals, an Italian and an American, commanded an exercise in March 1992 called Dog Fish. Under the Mediterranean Sea, 11 submarines from France, Greece, Italy, Spain, Turkey and the United States tried to escape detection by multi-nation aircraft such as British Nimrods, French Atlantiques, and U.S. and Dutch P-3C Orions.

If any military activities on that scale can be called "routine,"

NATO has made them so in Dog Fish and many other international exercises—on the ground, in the air, and especially at sea—with intriguing names such as Northern Wedding, Reforger and Teamwork.

NATO also boasts a standing naval force in the Atlantic. The 27-year-old force still turns heads during port visits, as warships with names like *Saguenay* (Canada), *Commandante Roberto Ivens* (Portugal) and *Bloys van Treslong* (Netherlands) steam in together. Ships and commanders of the naval force rotate frequently, so that in any five-year period, as many as 70 captains and their crews gain experience operating under common rules and obeying foreign commanders.

In peacetime, NATO nations keep ultimate control over their own forces; a captain can pull his vessel out on a moment's notice if his country needs it elsewhere.

NATO also guarantees civilian control. Political leaders from member countries, not admirals or generals, make the big decisions. NATO ensures that its naval commanders talk, plan, train and even develop some of their equipment together—so that if one or more of NATO's members are threatened, all can respond. Such preparation involves thousands of officers at dozens of NATO command posts in places as far-flung as Brussels, Heidelberg, Naples and Oslo.

NATO cooperation is not without its squabbles. Countries have different ideas about military threats and about how much to spend on armed forces. And the desire to keep their own industries strong causes many countries to back home-grown technologies over joint-development plans.

Still, the animosities of World War II are a distant memory. A newcomer to the noise and laughter of the officers' mess at NATO's naval command in Norfolk has to tell uniforms apart or scan for small lapel flags to detect the national origins of men and women whose camaraderie and common purpose took decades to evolve.

Risks to U.S. Security

But the need to preserve NATO goes well beyond international camaraderie and past achievements. The monolith of Soviet power is gone, but in its place are smaller risks to the security of the United States and its allies.

A long list of unanswered questions justifies military vigilance: Will Russia stabilize as a democracy or return to authoritarianism and empire-building?

Will the successor states to the Soviet Union sort out their territorial disputes peacefully? Will the nuclear weapons of the Soviet Union fall under reliable control and eventually be destroyed?

At the same time, events in the Middle East and the Persian Gulf remind Americans and Europeans of just how vulnerable our economies are to cutoffs in the flow of oil and trade from other parts of the globe.

Religious fanaticism and serious economic problems in North Africa and the Middle East grow as well, bringing with them the possibility of small, low-intensity conflicts near Europe's southern borders.

At least 40 non-NATO submarines ply the waters of the Mediterranean these days—some of them from unstable or hostile countries such as Algeria, Libya and Syria. These denizens of the deep have the capacity to disrupt shipping and attack civilian targets.

"[Southern Europe] is not a risk-free region, and during times of rapid changes in the world such as we are seeing now, nations and militaries need to cooperate," Adm. Jeremy Boorda, Commander of Allied Forces Southern Europe, recently told an Italian audience.

A Necessary Alliance

The dissolution of the Soviet Union has eliminated the adhesive that helped bind the Western alliance together for so many years. It has not negated NATO's value. There are other reasons for the alliance to stay united and also to expand. Future members could include the new democracies of Eastern Europe and perhaps Russia and other new nations rising from the ruins of the Soviet state.

The alliance has intrinsic worth if for no other reason than that nations sharing defense policies are less likely to meet as enemies in battle. . . .

For their mutual benefit, America needs Europe as much as Europe needs America. . . . Going it alone in trade or security is a certain road to disaster as the events that led to World War II proved. Today, commerce and defense are more intertwined than ever.

Stephen Green, *The Washington Times*, February 15, 1992.

Individually or without the involvement of the United States, European countries may not be able to defuse military crises. The weak European response to the breakup of Yugoslavia is an example of this problem.

An American military presence in Europe still adds stability on a continent known for its intrigues. Even among western European countries, for example, the existence of NATO and the influence of the United States helps to reduce tensions between Greece and Turkey, the spread of nuclear weapons in Europe, and concerns about German unification and Germany's growing influence in eastern Europe.

A Two-Way Street

Why is it so important for American taxpayers to pay for a continued military presence in Europe? History tells us that returning to Europe in the face of a crisis would be much more dangerous and more expensive than remaining in Europe with greatly reduced troop levels.

For the United States, cooperation in NATO is not just a one-way street. The war against Iraq was not a NATO effort—since the organization is prohibited from operating outside the defense of Europe—but 12 NATO members sent ships to the Persian Gulf.

For months, they imposed the blockade on Iraq and swept for mines in the gulf. Other allies sent ground troops and aircraft to assist in ousting Saddam Hussein from Kuwait.

The success of the campaign had much to do with the international training, common procedures and compatible technology that NATO imposes on its members.

The United States cannot afford the forces and equipment needed to respond to every military contingency in today's world.

In NATO, however, even small countries add value to certain missions. Belgium and the Netherlands, for example, contribute minesweeping expertise that fills a crucial gap in U.S. naval capabilities.

Some American military officials doubt the wisdom of relying on foreign capabilities. Soon, however, cuts of 25 percent or more in the U.S. military budget may give them no choice.

International military divisions-of-labor should be encouraged and expanded in the 1990s, not done away with.

Changes in NATO

Backing NATO does not mean backing an unchanged NATO. For one thing, the United States has the right to expect that rich European countries will pay for a greater share of NATO's costs.

The value of U.S. contributions to NATO is hard to calculate, but may be as high as $150 billion each year. That bill will get smaller as the U.S. troop presence in Europe declines from more than 300,000 to about 150,000 by the mid-1990s.

Just as important, NATO must focus its remaining resources on real military risks and accommodate countries that broke away from communism.

The early signs are good. To confront risks to southern

Europe, the NATO standing naval force was activated in the Mediterranean in April 1992. It is composed of U.S., British, Dutch and German ships on a full-time basis and ships from other NATO countries for shorter periods. And NATO land forces will be more mobile, away from the central front in Germany that no longer exists.

In December 1991, NATO formed the North Atlantic Cooperation Council as its communications link with the republics of the old Soviet empire.

For starters, the council aims to cut the number of troops in Europe, ensure that tactical nuclear weapons in the ex-Soviet Union are destroyed, get new democracies to sign the nuclear non-proliferation treaty, and find civilian work for Russia's nuclear scientists. That will take a lot of talking and a lot of time.

The sight of visiting Russian politicians and generals at NATO headquarters still seems strange, but something even stranger may find its way on the agenda soon: Russian membership in NATO. Why not?

Recruiting New Members

The United States and its NATO allies believe that military cooperation among the world's strongest countries is a good thing. NATO helps Europeans overcome their military rivalries and work toward economic and political unity. NATO brings together the "nuclear club" and helps them plan reductions in nuclear weapons.

Looking at it that way, a democratic Russia is just the kind of new member that NATO should recruit.

Finally, NATO should consider changing its charter to allow it to organize military responses outside Europe—which is, after all, where most crises probably will originate. One day, NATO might even serve as the agent of the United Nations to enforce major Security Council resolutions.

Critics of such a change should remember that expanding NATO's mandate would not force it to respond to every international crisis, or force all of its members to take part in any given operation.

It would, however, ensure that U.S. and European military strength looks formidable, that countries do not go off on private military adventures, and that the costs of responding to serious crises are shared. Those, after all, are the goals that NATO was built on.

"America . . . can hardly continue to spend half
of its defense budget protecting nations that
ought to protect themselves. "

The U.S. Should Withdraw from NATO

John F. McManus

Membership in NATO has harmed the United States, John F.
McManus asserts in the following viewpoint. McManus contends that America's role in NATO has been expensive both economically and politically. Its leadership of NATO has turned the
United States into the world's policeman, the author argues,
forcing America into costly alliances and world conflicts. The
United States must withdraw from NATO and force its European allies to pay for their own defense. McManus is the pub-
lisher of the *New American*, a biweekly magazine of conservative political and social opinion.

As you read, consider the following questions:

1. Why does McManus doubt the intentions of the politicians
   who created NATO?
2. Why does the author believe it is absurd for U.S. forces to be
   deployed in Germany?
3. What kind of defense force should the United States support,
   in the author's opinion?

John F. McManus, "Give Our Seat to Yeltsin," *The New American*, January 27, 1992.
Reprinted with permission.

NATO was formed in 1949 under UN auspices for the ostensible purpose of military opposition to the Soviet Union's takeover of Eastern Europe. The same U.S. officials who engineered the betrayal of Poland and other nations of Eastern Europe into communist hands worked to establish the alliance.

Then, American aid to the communist nations under one pretext after another kept feeding and equipping the supposed communist enemy, and kept justifying the stationing of hundreds of thousands of American troops in Western Europe. We have actually spent about $4 trillion defending ourselves and Europe from an enemy our own leaders created and armed.

Looking at the alliance with the benefit of years of hindsight, NATO introduced the notion that our nation is the policeman of the world, something totally unauthorized by the Constitution. It entangled us deeply in European affairs, compromised our independence, and gave U.S. leaders an excuse to favor "world opinion" rather than do what was best for the U.S.

Warsaw Pact Meets NATO

On December 20, 1991 foreign ministers from several of the nations once entwined in the Soviet-led Warsaw Pact (Poland, Romania, Czechoslovakia, Hungary, and the USSR) met for the first time with representatives of the 16 NATO nations at the alliance's headquarters in Brussels. During the meeting, Soviet Ambassador to Belgium Nikolai Afanasyevsky announced that his country no longer existed and that all references to the Soviet Union should be stricken from the written proceedings.

That shocker was followed by the delivery to NATO of a letter from the President of newly independent Russia, Boris Yeltsin, expressing hope that his nation might join the alliance. NATO's Secretary General, Manfred Wörner of Germany, downplayed the importance of the request and called it "a long-term political aim." Aware that Yeltsin's wish dramatically called into question the organization's supposed reason for existence—military opposition to the Soviet bloc—Wörner obviously realized the need for a fundamental redefinition of the alliance.

U.S. Troops Still in Europe

At great cost to the American taxpayers, approximately 300,000 U.S. troops remain stationed in Germany. Are they supposed to be protecting West Germany from East Germany? Even after the two Germanys became united as one nation? Now that the dissolution of the Warsaw Pact has removed the pretense for maintaining U.S. troops in Europe, why not bring them home?

They are still there partly because it is the intention of the Bush Administration to continue offering U.S. troops to the world. And they remain in Europe to undergird the conversion of NATO from a military alliance to a political grouping as called for by Secretary of State James Baker in a speech he gave in West Berlin in December 1989. The Baker proposal fits neatly into a scenario where regional groupings grease the skids for the creation of a world government that will be part of Mr. Bush's "new world order."

© 1971 *Chicago Daily News.*

In addition to extending a policeman role into Eastern Europe, NATO is also being touted for a similar presence in the Middle East. A July 1991 article in *American Legion Magazine* by Council on Foreign Relations member Timothy W. Stanley, a former U.S. representative at NATO, gushes with enthusiasm for NATO's expanding role, "provided that it would act only as an agent for the United Nations."

Troops Must Come Home

An America mired in a deep recession can hardly continue to spend half of its defense budget protecting nations that ought to protect themselves. This goes for so-called allies in the Far East as well as for the nations of Europe that have delighted for decades in having the American taxpayers pay their defense costs.

Bring the troops home—from Europe, from Japan, from South Korea, from anywhere! Keep an elite force ready for rapid deployment, but keep it here. If American troops are truly needed to defend American lives and property—the only purpose for their existence—modern technology and equipment exist to get them virtually anywhere on short notice.

As for NATO, let Yeltsin's Russia have a seat—ours. Let Europeans entangle themselves with each other's affairs if they choose to do so. It's time for the United States to worry about the United States—where there are plenty of worries, many of which were brought on by involving ourselves in and paying for everyone else's problems.

"The U.S. relationship with Israel produces the very adversaries that are pointed to as justifying the close relationship."

The U.S. Should Decrease Its Ties to Israel

Sheldon L. Richman

America's long-standing political and economic ties to Israel have harmed the United States and its relationships with other countries in the Middle East, Sheldon L. Richman writes in the following viewpoint. Richman states that by providing huge amounts of aid to Israel and by emphasizing its alliance with Israel above other alliances, the United States has lowered its standard of living and put its security at risk. America must decrease its ties to Israel and focus instead on its domestic problems and on its relationships to other nations, the author concludes. Richman is a senior editor at the Cato Institute, a libertarian public-policy think tank in Washington, D.C.

As you read, consider the following questions:

1. Why did the United States begin a strategic alliance with Israel, according to Richman?
2. How has U.S. military aid to Israel changed since 1959, according to the author?
3. In Richman's opinion, how do George Washington's words of advice concerning alliances relate to America's alliance with Israel?

From Sheldon L. Richman, "Ancient History: U.S. Conduct in the Middle East Since World War II and the Folly of Intervention," *Cato Institute Policy Analysis*, August 16, 1991. Reprinted with permission.

The idea of a strategic relationship between the United States and Israel emerged after the 1956 Suez crisis, when the Eisenhower administration realized that both countries had an interest in containing Gamal Abdel Nasser's influence. Because the Eisenhower administration feared that the Soviets were gaining clout in some Arab countries, such a relationship was seen as useful in containing the Soviet Union as well. When John F. Kennedy became president, he abandoned an initial preference for a balance of power between Israel and the Arabs in favor of a strategic relationship. He was the first to provide Israel with sophisticated weapons and to commit the United States to a policy of maintaining Israel's regional military superiority. In 1962 Kennedy privately told Israeli foreign minister Golda Meir that their countries were de facto allies, and shortly before his assassination, Kennedy reportedly guaranteed Israel's territorial integrity in a letter to Prime Minister Eshkol.

U.S. Aid to Israel

As the U.S.-Israeli strategic relationship matured, military and economic aid increased. But that increase does not mean the earlier aid had been insignificant. According to historian Nadav Safran:

> During Israel's first nineteen years of existence, the United States awarded it nearly $1.5 billion of aid in various forms, mostly outright grants of one kind or another. *On a per capita basis of recipient country, this was the highest rate of American aid given to any country.*

According to a recent Congressional Research Service report, between 1949 and 1965 U.S. aid to Israel averaged $63 million annually, and over 95 percent of that assistance was for economic development and food aid. The first formal military lending, which was very modest, occurred in 1959. However, from 1966 through 1970 average annual aid jumped to $102 million, and the share of military loans climbed to 47 percent. In 1964 the U.S. government lent no money to Israel for military purposes. In 1965 it lent almost $13 million. In 1966, the year before the Six-Day War, it lent $90 million. In the year of the war such loans fell to $7 million, but in succeeding years the total rose, reaching $85 million in 1969 and hitting a high of $2.7 billion in 1979. More significant, military *grants* began in 1974; they ranged from $100 million in 1975 to $2.7 billion in 1979. In the first half of the 1980s, loans and grants ranged between $500 million and nearly $1 billion. Then, beginning in 1985, the loans stopped and all U.S. military aid was made as grants, ranging from $1.4 billion in 1985 to $1.8 billion each year from 1987 through 1989. Economic grants hit a high of nearly $2 billion in 1985, before falling to $1.2 billion in 1989.

Although U.S. aid has been given to Israel with the stipulation that it not be used in the territories occupied in 1967, the Congressional Research Service reported that "because the U.S. aid is given as budgetary support without any specific project accounting, there is no way to tell how Israel uses U.S. aid." Moreover, the service wrote that, according to the executive branch, in 1978, 1979, and 1981, Israel "may have violated" its agreement not to use U.S. weapons for nondefensive purposes. In 1982 the United States suspended shipments of cluster bombs after Israel allegedly violated an agreement on the use of those weapons. In 1990 Israel accepted $400 million in loan guarantees for housing on the condition that the money not be used in the occupied territories, but the promise was soon repudiated.

Reprinted with special permission of King Features Syndicate.

Reporter Tom Bethell has written that of $1.8 billion in annual U.S. military aid to Israel, only about $350 million is sent by check. The rest never leaves the United States; it is spent on U.S.-made planes and weapons. Bethell also has reported that, according to the State Department, Israel returns $1.1 billion of $1.2 billion in economic aid as payment of principal and interest on old loans. It keeps the interest accrued from the time the money is received at the beginning of the year to the time it is sent back at the end of the year. . . .

The American people have not been well served by U.S. foreign policy in the Middle East. They have been forced to pay billions of dollars to foreign governments, and that has cost them untold opportunities for better lives afforded by an undistorted consumer economy. Even when the foreign "aid" was used to buy American-made products, it was merely a politically contrived transfer from the taxpayers to politically connected corporate interests. U.S. policy has put the American people at risk of war several times, including the risk of nuclear war with the Soviet Union. American lives have been lost—in Israel's attack on the USS *Liberty* during the 1967 war, in Beirut, and through desperate acts of terrorism. . . .

Washington's Words of Warning

In 1796 George Washington, in his farewell address, offered advice that now seems aimed directly at those who constructed the foreign policy we have suffered with for the past 45 years:

> Excessive partiality for one foreign nation and excessive dislike of another, cause those whom they actuate to see danger only on one side, and serve to veil and even second the arts of influence on the other. Real Patriots, who may resist the intrieues [sic] of the favorite, are liable to become suspected and odious; while its tools and dupes usurp the applause and confidence of the people, to surrender their interests.

By any standard, the relationship between the United States and Israel has been extraordinary. Criticism of any other American ally does not cost a person an elective or appointed position in government. Criticism of any other American ally does not bring accusations of being a hater of the dominant religious group in the allied nation. Both of those things happen, almost routinely, to anyone who criticizes Israel. Elected U.S. officials who have cast a single vote against an Israeli position have seen major opposition mounted by Israel's American supporters. The rare journalist who points out unattractive facts about Israeli conduct is likely to be smeared as an anti-Semite. The chilling effect that has had on public debate is too obvious to need elaboration.

As for the standard rejoinder that Israel has been the staunchest U.S. ally in the Middle East, one is reminded of the one-liner about lawyers: if we didn't have them, we wouldn't need them. The U.S. relationship with Israel produces the very adversaries that are pointed to as justifying the close relationship.

We have allowed our leaders to violate George Washington's sage advice, and it has cost us dearly. For Washington, "the Great rule of conduct for us, in regard to foreign Nations is in extending our commercial relations to have with them as little *political* connection as possible." We must rediscover the wisdom of our first president.

"The strategic cooperation between the U.S. and Israel is fundamental to both democracies and should be broadened and deepened."

The U.S. Should Strengthen Its Ties to Israel

William R. Van Cleave

William R. Van Cleave is director of strategic studies at Southwest Missouri State University in Springfield and senior fellow of the Stanford University's Hoover Institution in Stanford, California. In the following viewpoint, Van Cleave supports America's strong alliance with Israel. This alliance, the author asserts, protects the security interests of both the United States and Israel. In addition, he believes that America has a moral responsibility to help Israel, which historically has been the target of Arab threats and oppression.

As you read, consider the following questions:

1. Why is the author concerned about the future of the U.S.-Israeli alliance?
2. Why did the United States increase its ties to Israel during the Cold War, according to Van Cleave?
3. Why does the author believe that an end to the Arab-Israeli conflict alone would not bring peace to the Middle East?

From William R. Van Cleave, "U.S.-Israeli Relations: A New Crisis," *Global Affairs*, Spring 1992. Reprinted with permission of the International Security Council, Washington, D.C.

Early in 1989, at the outset of the Bush administration, I participated in a conference in Jerusalem, sponsored by the International Security Council, an independent American center of policy analysis. . . . A Consensus Statement issued by the participants, American and Israeli together, which was then published in the *New York Times* (February 28, 1989), read in part:

> The strategic cooperation between the U.S. and Israel is fundamental to both democracies and should be broadened and deepened. . . . Only a strong and secure Israel can achieve peace and serve the interests of the democracies. It is important for Israel and the U.S. to work in concert on political steps which will help make progress toward the mutual objective of peace in the area.

Nonetheless, throughout the conference, deep concern was expressed by the participants that the prospect of such cooperation was not good, that the special relationship between the two allies had already begun to fray. While participants from both countries had complaints about the policies of both countries, I believe it is fair to say that the American participants did not resist the ultimate conclusion that it was the behavior of the U.S. government that most threatened to dilute the special relationship.

The situation is now considerably worse than it was then. *Israel is in the political fight of its life without the firm base of political support it should have from the United States.* In this fight, Israel is not being helped, but is in fact being hindered, not only by the U.S. government, but also by the media (which goes almost without saying), the American Jewish community, Jewish Israeli support groups in the United States, and Israel's own internal political divisions.

It is up to Israel to defend itself—politically, as it has always done militarily. . . .

U.S.-Israeli Relations: Background

From the beginning (in the eyes of most relatively informed Americans, except for Biblical Christians, the beginning was the establishment of the State of Israel), U.S. policy toward Israel was based not so much on deep strategic or geopolitical thinking, and not even on cold war considerations, but on a strong grass-roots affinity for both the Jewish people and the State of Israel. This was a combination of affinities, and sympathies, and feelings of guilt—and of admiration. Americans identified themselves with the determination of the Jewish people to become a nation-state, to gain its rightful homeland, especially after the Holocaust, which America had done nothing to prevent and precious little to alleviate, save finally defeating Nazi Germany in war.

The United States, instinctually even, owed an enormous moral debt to those who founded and would protect Israel. And the United States would stand by it regardless of political, strategic, or economic considerations.

Israel: A New America

This was less a feeling of empathy, I hasten to reiterate, than one of admiration, and of a sense of right and wrong. The Jews—the new Israelis—were the underdogs struggling with great courage and determination for what was right and fair against overwhelming opposition and odds, against implacable enemies who themselves were alien to, and even inimical to, our own political and cultural values. Israel was a microcosm, a new rebirth, of America and of American values.

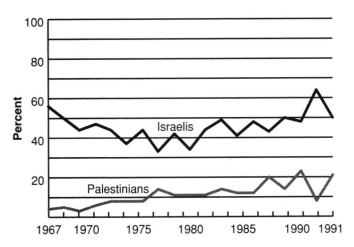

America's Sympathies Are with Israel

Response to the question: Are your sympathies more with the Israelis or more with the Arab nations/Palestinian Arabs?

Source: Gallup Organization

As Stuart Eizenstat, formerly chief domestic policy advisor in the Carter administration, correctly put it:

> The foundation for the generally positive U.S. policy toward the Jewish state for more than four decades is not the "Israel lobby." It is, rather, the consistent support for Israel by the general American public, based on shared democratic and Judeo-Christian values, a sentimental affection for the Holy

Land, and a sense of responsibility for the security of a Jewish state after the Holocaust.

That is what President Truman reflected—despite his subsequent embargo on arms to Israel—when he rejected the position of his State Department and the advice of his trusted friend, Secretary of State George Marshall, on the recognition of the State of Israel. As his recently published private memoirs recounted it:

> I'd recognized Israel immediately as a sovereign nation when the British left Palestine in 1948, and I did so against the advice of my own secretary of state, George Marshall, who was afraid that the Arabs wouldn't like it. This was one of the few errors of judgment made by that great and wonderful man, but I felt that Israel deserved to be recognized and didn't give a damn whether the Arabs liked it or not. . . .

Later, after Israel's birth, in the context of the cold war, U.S. policy *also* (I emphasize "also" to make it clear that this has been an *additional* reason for American support of Israel) regarded Israel as a partner, an ally, a geopolitical asset, in the larger context of Soviet-American conflict. Israel was a stronghold against Soviet hegemony—through the Arab states—over the Middle East.

A Counter to the Soviets

Israel was seen not only as a democratic oasis in the Middle East, but also as an important counter to Soviet military power and imperial ambitions. With the capability to project military power in the Middle East, as well as to defend itself, Israel not only helped the U.S. safeguard against the Soviet Union outflanking NATO from the south, it also helped secure the eastern Mediterranean, counterbalanced Arab radicalism, and served as an emergency multipurpose access point. It was a stabilizing factor. Its innovative military technology, its combat experience, and its renowned intelligence capabilities all served American interests.

As the 1980 Platform of the Republican Party formally stated:

> The sovereignty, security, and integrity of the State of Israel is a moral imperative and serves the strategic interests of the United States. Republicans reaffirm our fundamental and enduring commitment to this principle. We will continue to honor our nation's commitment through political, economic, diplomatic, and military aid. We fully recognize the strategic importance of Israel and the deterrent role of its armed forces in the Middle East and East-West military equations.

Now, with the internal problems of the former U.S.S.R. and the apparent collapse of Soviet influence in Eastern Europe, a body of opinion has emerged to argue that with the decline of the Soviet threat, the U.S. special relationship with Israel ought to be a relic of the past.

There *is* some evidence that Israel is no longer perceived as a strategic asset by the U.S. government. Indeed, the devaluation of Israel has become the hallmark of the Bush administration's Middle East policy. In its view, the preferred U.S. alliance is apparently with Arab states possessing the conventional indices of power in spite of the fact that the lack of social cohesion and of political stability within and among them has long nullified the promises of such alliances. In any event, U.S. policy in the Middle East, since before the Gulf war, has been increasingly Arab-oriented.

Arab Conflicts Are Numerous

For the privilege of protecting Arab interests from Iraqi aggression, the U.S. it seems is obligated also to reward them with payment in Israeli coin—that is to say, by pressuring Israel to relinquish land for the promise of peace, even perhaps to return to the lines of 1967.

Bush and Baker seem not to grasp that the sources of tension and conflict in the Middle East are Arab in origin, are multiple, complex, and generously distributed throughout the region. Territorial disputes among Arab states are persistent; ethnic and religious rivalries are rife.

Necessary Allies

Israel and the United States need each other. We benefit from each other. Our alliance is unshakable because it rests on two firm pillars: strategic interests and common values. Difficulties aside, Israel and the United States remain friends and allies today, and we shall be friends and allies forever.

Dan Quayle, address before the American Israel Public Affairs Committee, April 7, 1992.

Absent the Arab-Israel conflict, the Arab states themselves would sharply divide into at least two major hostile camps. The conservative monarchies would seek direct U.S. protection against expansionist states. No longer shielded by Israel, which bears the brunt of any attack by the radicals, the conservative camp would require ongoing U.S. military support to survive. Ever since its establishment, Israel has served as a "lightning rod" for the oil-rich Arab countries: it diverts the attention and energies of the Arab radicals away from them. Simply by being there, Israel is a factor for stability.

The Bush administration does not seem to understand that tilting the balance against Israel would result, not surprisingly, in regional instability, and erosion of U.S. credibility and influence. A PLO stronghold on the West Bank would turn it into a marshalling-yard far more dangerous than Lebanon. Its very existence would be a prescription for regional war. And this could not be any more in the interests of the United States than of Israel. These are the strategic realities that will ultimately undercut the Middle East policies of Bush and Baker.

In the final analysis, Israel is a priceless strategic stronghold, a reliable bastion, and a crucial link in what remains of America's defense structure. While its geostrategic importance transcends Soviet-American rivalry, its enduring function as a factor in regional stability underlines its true potential—if only we would learn to nurture it.

"U.S. military activity in Japan undermines Japanese sovereignty and security."

The U.S. Should End Its Military Alliance with Japan

Joseph Gerson

In 1951, the United States and Japan signed the Mutual Security Treaty, in which the United States agreed to help protect Japan as long as U.S. troops could be based in that country. In the following viewpoint, Joseph Gerson states that this arrangement has harmed Japan, and should be ended. Gerson believes the United States has used Japan to launch military interventions in Asia, and has used its power to manipulate Japan's foreign policy. Only by ending the agreement will Japan regain control of its own foreign policy, the author concludes. Gerson is the co-editor of *The Sun Never Sets* and the peace education secretary of the American Friends Service Committee, an international organization that promotes social justice.

As you read, consider the following questions:

1. Why is the United States able to exercise so much control over Japanese politics and policies, in the author's opinion?
2. Gerson cites several situations in which the United States has successfully pressured Japan to alter its foreign policy. Name three of these situations.
3. What type of alliance does Gerson suggest could replace the Mutual Security Treaty?

Joseph Gerson, "The Troubled U.S.-Japan Alliance," *Z Magazine*, March 1992. Reprinted with permission.

For four decades leaders in Tokyo, who have enjoyed the support of the U.S., have served Washington's ambitions. They have tolerated the use of their nation as an unsinkable aircraft carrier for the U.S. in Asia. When the Reagan administration dangerously accelerated the arms race and simultaneously wounded our economy by doubling military spending, Japanese investors bailed Uncle Sam out. . . .

Since the end of the Second World War the U.S.-Japan relationship has become a profound, if troubled, alliance between economic and technological superpowers. The unequal alliance has dominated developments in the Asia/Pacific region as much as NATO has dominated the politics of Western Europe and the North Atlantic.

While public attention has been focused on growing economic tensions, successive U.S. administrations have concentrated on the military dimensions of the partnership. . . . Through the continued presence of 20 major U.S. military bases and 85 other military installations in Japan, by the fact that the U.S. controls the flow of oil from the Middle East to Japanese industry, and because Japan's history of aggression dictates that it be balanced by a U.S. presence—if it is to continue penetration of Asian and Pacific markets and politics—the U.S. continues to exercise considerable leverage over Japanese politics and policies.

The Rise of Japan

During the 1980s, when so much attention was focused on the arms race in Europe, the collapse of the Soviet empire in Europe and then of the Soviet Union itself, the North Pacific was the focal point of the world's economic growth and a related U.S. escalation of the arms race. In this period Japan was pressed to assume greater military as well as financial responsibilities as the junior partner of the U.S.-Japanese alliance. Japan's pride of place was recognized when then Prime Minister Takeshita was the first foreign head of state welcomed by President Bush in Washington in 1981. Later, prime ministers Kaifu and Miyazawa pointedly reaffirmed their allegiance to the Mutual Security Treaty (MST) within days of their elevation to office. The 1991 edition of the Japanese *Diplomatic Blue-Book*, released in December reiterates the interdependence of the U.S. and Japan and the need to maintain the global partnership. . . .

The U.S. remains deeply committed to "forward deployment" and to its military bases and installations in Japan. Since the Philippine senate voted to oust U.S. bases from their country in 1991, the Pentagon has sought to offset the loss by redeploying many forces and weapons formerly based in the Philippines to bases in Japan. While there may be some minor cutbacks over and above the 10 percent reduction announced by Secretary of

Defense Cheney in 1990, the Pentagon has been clear about its future plans: "In Japan, beyond some personnel reductions, we envision little change in current deployment patterns."

However, destabilizing and humiliating forces lie at the core of the U.S.-Japan alliance. Their interdependence is threatened by their economic rivalry and by Japan's role as the junior partner in the military alliance. Since the Mutual Security Treaty was imposed on Japan in 1951 as a condition for ending the U.S. post-war military occupation, the military dimension of U.S.-Japanese relations has remained essentially static, even as technology and targets have changed. The treaty has allowed the U.S. to use Japan as a base for forward military deployment and intervention (Korea, Taiwan, Indochina, the Philippines and Iraq), and to threaten nuclear war. Within Japan it has resulted in increasingly resented losses of sovereignty, nuclear and non-nuclear weapons accidents, assaults on basic human rights, and the destruction of the environment.

U.S. Uses Japan to Fight Wars

On the enormous U.S. Air Force base at Yokota in suburban Tokyo, headquarters not only for the Fifth Air Force but for all U.S. forces in Japan, there is a seemingly incongruous United Nations liaison office. That office is a remnant of the Korean War, which was waged under the UN flag. It is also a poignant symbol of what might have been: a genuinely multilateral peace treaty for Japan after World War II. Such a treaty just might have prevented the Korean War, the remilitarization of Japan, and the escalation of military confrontations in the Northwest Pacific. . . .

Many Japanese favored a neutral and demilitarized nation after 1945. Instead, Japan, while demilitarized for a time, was made the forward base for U.S. forces in East Asia and the staging area for the Korean War.

Alan Geyer, *The Christian Century*, April 26, 1989.

In exchange for providing Japan's "security," the United States continues to control many aspects of Japan's foreign and military policies. Japan was not permitted to recognize China before the Nixon administration did so. More recently, in response to U.S. pressure, Japan has become the number one supplier of Overseas Development Aid and other forms of financial assistance—much of it targeted to strategically important U.S. clients such as Turkey, Egypt, Jordan, the Philippines, and Panama. When the Bush administration applied highly visible pressure on the Japanese government to help finance the war against

Saddam Hussein, Prime Minister Kaifu came forward with $13 billion. And, when Secretary of State Baker weighed in with his threat that Japan could no longer get by with "checkbook diplomacy," naval mine sweepers were dispatched to the Persian Gulf in clear violation of the Japanese peace constitution. Responding to U.S. pressure and the support of conservative forces within the Japanese government and society, Prime Minister Miyazawa went still further. In the fall of 1992 he forced the Japanese Diet to adopt the Peace Keeping Operations Bill and sent Japanese troops to Cambodia, thus shatteirng the post-[Second World] War taboo against sending Japanese military forces abroad.

Before the Mutual Security Treaty was revised in 1960, it was described by Secretary of State Christian Herter as "pretty extreme from the point of an agreement between two sovereign nations." The U.S. had the right to use its bases in Japan without consulting the Japanese government. One provision authorized the U.S. to use its forces to quell disturbances within Japan. Although these provisions were removed from the treaty, U.S. military activity in Japan undermines Japanese sovereignty and security to this day. Contrary to Japan's constitution and its three "non nuclear principles" (not to manufacture, possess or introduce nuclear weapons into Japan), U.S. naval vessels and aircraft regularly bring nuclear weapons into Japan—even into Hiroshima prefecture. Low altitude military aircraft exercises regularly traumatize people in the Tokyo metropolitan area and elsewhere. In Okinawa, the site of the greatest concentration of U.S. bases in Japan, more than 20 percent of the land has been taken for U.S. bases. Farming families and villagers are frequently threatened by live-fire exercises that cannot be contained on the bases. . . .

Independence, Alliance, or Trade War

It has been argued that the U.S. has no considered policy in relation to Japan. It is muddled at best. On the one hand, . . . the goal of U.S. policymakers remains the deepening of the U.S.-Japan alliance based on the twin pillars of the Mutual Security Treaty and "managed" (not "free") trade between the two allies. Zbigniew Brzezinski has called this Amerippon, the "new global bargain" to follow the Cold War.

Modern Japan is, in many ways, a creation of the United States—from the U.S. imposed constitution and Mutual Security Treaty to the Japanese military (Self Defense Forces) and the ruling LDP organized in response to pressures and guidance from the U.S. post-war occupation. Yet, Japan's Cold War political leaders have used the unequal relationship to their advantage, accepting the military alliance and its humiliations while building a modern, competitive economy. Japan, of course, has choices. Being a sovereign nation; having the second largest, and most dynamic, economy in the world; and ranking third in world military spending, Japan has become a major power. Yet, there is deep confusion within Japan, and there is no national consensus about its role in the world.

Japan's choices will be influenced by many complicated factors. First is the relative decline of the United States and uncertainty about what the continued U.S. role in the Asia/Pacific region will be. The legacies of World War II, Hiroshima, and Nagasaki have left deep pacifist commitments among millions of Japanese and continue to play a major role in Japanese politics. Then, there are fears that the U.S. and Europe are leading the world into a new order based on fiercely competing trade zones rather than free trade among unequal powers. And Japan's history of aggression and colonization limit the initiatives this generation of Japanese can take in relation to neighboring countries.

The Consequences of Removing U.S. Troops

The departure of American troops from Japan—where they have successively symbolized wartime victory, the Occupation and the American commitment to defend their homeland—would affect deeply the psychology of the relationship, removing a sense of dependency and obligation that has existed since 1945. The common strategic objective of keeping the Soviet Union at bay, which helped contain trade disputes, would no longer exist. At the same time, ironically, major irritants caused by the troops and exploited by politicians for a generation would no longer exist either: Japanese could no longer complain about American behavior or special privileges on the bases, and American politicians would no longer be able to demand trade concessions in return for Japan's "free ride" on defense. Both the positive and negative aspects of the American troop presence would disappear—and the relationship between the two nations would change, gradually but profoundly.

Richard Holbrooke, *Foreign Affairs*, Winter 1991-92.

The confusion within Japan is marked by mixed signals and decisions, all of which are deeply influenced by the Mutual Security Treaty. With the end of the Cold War, Japanese military spending has been reduced, yet Foreign Ministry spokespeople describe the nation as "deformed" because of the severe limitations on the deployment of Japanese military forces abroad. And, while the majority of Japanese people find it difficult to

81

imagine Japan outside its MST alliance and deep integration with the United States, some leaders quietly observe that the lesson of the 1991 Gulf war was that the United States fought a war for "very narrow national interests," and that what is good for the goose is good for the gander. At the popular level, this world view is reflected in the coining of the word "kenbei" meaning "dislike of the United States."

A More Secure Future

The question thus remains open. What will the Japanese and U.S. people choose: continued alliance, trade war, or democratic independence?

Should the balance of political forces and human imagination change, the demise of the Mutual Security Treaty and the withdrawal of U.S. bases from Japan can lead to a more secure future. It need not create a vacuum to be filled by Japanese or other militarism. There are serious political visions of a Pacific Economic Community comprised of all the Pacific nations with the Pacific Ocean becoming a sea of peace, freedom, and mutual benefit. Concrete proposals have been made for the reduction of nuclear and conventional weapons in the Pacific and the creation of an internationally respected nuclear free zone. At least four models exist for different economic alliances and unions which are currently under study in Tokyo, Washington, and other Pacific Rim capitals. Such proposals can serve as the basis for debate and negotiations for the creation of a nuclear free, Mutual Security Treaty-free, independent, and economically secure Pacific Basin, which by definition includes the United States and Latin America.

The challenge to people of conscience in the U.S. is to devise a vision of, and a movement for, a third way in U.S.-Japanese relations. It is incumbent upon us to conceive a way free of military forces, alliances, intervention and military spending and which builds bridges between the people of the United States and Japan. The new relationship must not be at the expense of people in the Third World whose exploitation has helped to subsidize the American Dream and the Japanese Miracle. Similarly, it should not come at the expense of Europe, in a world of U.S. and Japanese trade zones allied against the European Common Market, a nightmare embraced by some strategic planners.

"The United States and Japan have a common interest in maintaining the current military partnership."

The U.S. Should Maintain Its Military Alliance with Japan

Seth Cropsey

Seth Cropsey, deputy undersecretary of the U.S. Navy from 1984 to 1989, is director of The Heritage Foundation's Asian Studies Center. The foundation is a conservative think tank in Washington, D.C. In the following viewpoint, Cropsey argues that the U.S.-Japan military alliance benefits both nations. Through it, the author states, Japan has a guaranteed defense without having to depend on its own people or resources and without frightening other nations with the potential of a renewed Japanese militarist threat. The United States benefits by having a military base from which it can protect American interests in Asia.

As you read, consider the following questions:

1. Japan has the resources and potential of creating a large, powerful army. Why does the author believe it would be unwise for Japan to establish such a force?
2. How has the U.S.-Japan alliance affected America's relationship with the Soviet Union, in Cropsey's opinion?
3. How does the U.S.-Japan alliance protect America's economic interests, according to the author?

From Seth Cropsey, "Uncle Samurai: America's Military Alliance with Japan." Reprinted with permission from the Fall 1991 issue of *Policy Review*, the flagship publication of the Heritage Foundation, 214 Massachusetts Ave. NE, Washington, DC 20002.

There were no aftershocks of alarm in Tokyo when Iraq invaded Kuwait in 1990. The Japanese, who rely on Middle Eastern imports for two-thirds of their energy, figured that oil is oil, and that it would find its way to market whether or not Kuwait was a sovereign nation. The land of the rising sun lay low.

Bush administration requests for Japan's assistance in transporting troops to the Persian Gulf aboard chartered airplanes elicited no response from Prime Minister Toshiki Kaifu's anxious cabinet, and polite refusals from both Japan Airlines and All-Nippon Air. By early September 1990, however, the issue could not be avoided. U.S. Secretary of the Treasury Nicholas Brady arrived in Tokyo to ask Kaifu to provide frontline countries in the Gulf and the U.S.-led coalition with $4 billion in assistance. Japan began to realize that the nations arrayed against Saddam Hussein were watching its response to the growing crisis very carefully.

What Should Be Japan's Role?

Eventually, Japan contributed $14 billion to Operation Desert Storm, and after the war was over, it sent four naval vessels to the Persian Gulf to help clear mines. Meanwhile, Japan's Asian neighbors shifted about uncomfortably at the thought of Japanese involvement once again in significant events beyond its borders. The political debate that occurred in Japan over what its role should be as a contributing member of the responsible international community continues today. As the preeminent Pacific power, as Japan's largest trading partner, and as its effective military protector, there is no nation with a keener interest in the outcome of that debate than the United States.

The United States and Japan have a common interest in maintaining the current military partnership. From it Japan derives the principal source of its security, the umbrella of U.S. military force deployed in the western Pacific. The United States, meanwhile, gets a base in Japan for protecting American influence in a region of the world whose importance will increase with time. America's superior, and Japan's subordinate, role in this security partnership are essential to the regional and global peace that both nations seek. As such, U.S. policymakers should resist isolationist and budget-driven pressures to diminish American influence in Asia. Japan's leaders, meanwhile, should hold fast to the American military umbrella by contributing to its technological and financial support as actively and greatly as possible. . . .

Asian Powderkeg

Japan's enormous national wealth, unsurpassed manufacturing capability, technological prowess, and personal industriousness would likely produce, if harnessed, an exceptionally well-organized military armed to the hilt with the most advanced equipment. Yet Japanese rearmament would cause such upheaval throughout the rest of Asia that it is almost certainly not in Japan's own interests.

Were Japan seriously to embark upon a major plan to rebuild their national defenses today, other Asian countries that have already been occupied in ambitious armament programs would redouble their efforts. A hot market in weapons would be transformed into a furnace. . . . Asia would become a powderkeg as Koreans, Chinese, and other Asians fear a resurgence of Japan as the region's preeminent military power.

Tempting as the prospect of a Japan wholly responsible for its own defense is to those in the United States who would slash the Defense Department or spend its budget on domestic priorities, it is not an option so long as a stable Asia that can go on creating wealth while it moves toward democracy remains, as it should, the U.S.'s overall policy goal for the region. Nor would rearmament be practical for the Japanese.

The Defense Relationship

The U.S.-Japan Mutual Security Treaty is the foundation upon which our bilateral relationship rests. The interests of both the United States and Japan—and, indeed, the interests of the West, of which Japan is a part—are well served by it. Our security arrangements with Japan, including the presence of our troops and facilities there, are essential for the peace and security not only of Japan but of the entire Pacific region, including, of course, the United States.

Gaston J. Sigur, *Department of State Bulletin*, May 1988.

Because Japan also remembers. Since its absolute defeat at the end of World War II, Japan has eschewed arms as passionately as it once embraced them. Article Nine of Japan's constitution, enacted in November 1946, "forever renounce[s] war as a sovereign right of the nation and the threat or use of force as a means of settling international disputes."

Successive Japanese governments have interpreted the article to allow national possession of only those weapons that are minimally necessary for self-defense. Excluded are such weapons as intercontinental ballistic missiles (ICBMs) and aircraft carriers, which are deemed offensive. Under this strict interpretation Japan has not, until spring 1991, deployed any armed forces outside its borders. It has forsworn the right of collective defense, *i.e.*, coming to the aid of allies under attack, and has steadfastly

85

refused to export weapons—to anyone.

Japan's defense budget of $30 billion is comparable to those of Britain, France, and Germany, but small relative to its GNP and its global economic importance and interests. It is also deliberately unassuming. Rejecting even the slightest appearance of military ostentation, the Japanese Self Defense Force (SDF) does not speak of its component parts as an army, navy, and air force, choosing instead to call them the ground, maritime, and air self defense forces (GSDF, MSDF, ASDF). Together they number about 249,000 active-duty troops, a little larger than the total active and reserve strength of the United States' smallest military service, the Marine Corps.

With 156,000 men, the GSDF is the largest component of Japan's military. It fields one armored and 12 infantry divisions, and would constitute the nation's final defense against a successful invasion of Japanese soil. The MSDF and ASDF divide the other 93,000 troops equally in carrying out their defensive missions. Roughly one-third of the ASDF's 365 combat aircraft are committed to the support of ground troops, with the balance assigned to defending Japanese airspace. The MSDF is built around a core of surface warships and submarines. Its principal mission is to defend the sea-lanes through which Japan's vital commercial shipping passes up to 1,000 miles from the mainland.

Beyond the 1,000-mile boundary, the U.S. Seventh Fleet, which is homeported in Yokosuka, Japan, along with its premier capital ship, the aircraft carrier USS *Independence*, assumes responsibility for patrolling the vast waters of the North Pacific and keeping open the sea lines of communication that link Japan with much of the rest of the world.

Japan's Strategic Value

Japan has benefited richly from the United States' defensive umbrella since the end of World War II. Released from the burden of acquiring a military commensurate with their dependence on the seas for delivery of raw materials and export of finished goods, the Japanese have stood out among the free nations in the relative puniness of their defense budgets. It was, for example, only in 1987 that Japan reversed a decision made 11 years earlier by Prime Minister Takeo Miki's cabinet to keep defense spending below 1 percent of gross national product. In terms of GNP, this is by far the smallest of the 20 top defense budgets in the world.

The yen saved may have contributed to the Japanese economy's position as the second largest in the world. But the use of Japan as an American base roughly 200 miles off the eastern coast of the Soviet Union has been of incalculable strategic value to the United States throughout the Cold War, and is certain to remain so unless some great event divides the two nations.

Japan's security thus has been assured without the self-effort that would have destabilized all of Asia, the United States has gained power and influence in the western Pacific while deterring war with the Soviets, and the world has been a safer place. The relationship has been mutually—and universally—beneficial. . . .

Undesired Guest

Kokusai-koken is shorthand for Japan's still-to-be-defined contribution to the emerging world order. The Gulf War helped concentrate the attention of Japanese leaders on the question. American policymakers should anticipate and debate the issue seeking to guide its resolution.

For the United States the first principle is to maintain American influence in the western Pacific and Asia. The forward-based units of the American military are essential for U.S. leverage, and the bases Japan provides and helps to provision are still central to America's military presence in the region. So long as Moscow retains powerful armed forces capable of seriously threatening vital U.S. interests around the world, American sailors, marines, soldiers, and pilots should remain in Japan as a strategic reminder to Kremlin leaders of their vulnerability to a second front. Moreover, the [former] Soviets are still modernizing their military capabilities in the Far East. U.S. forces in Japan offer the strongest bulwark in the region against that expanding threat.

A Necessary Force

The United States still has important obligations in East Asia. Northeast Asia, a perennial cockpit of great power rivalry and conflict, is today more peaceful and stable with American troops in Japan and South Korea than at any time since the beginning of the century, and those troops should not leave Japan or South Korea as long as North Korea remains a threat to peace and as long as Japan's Northern Islands, seized by the Soviet Union at the end of World War II, remain in Soviet hands. Their presence is an important factor encouraging a peaceful outcome to both problems.

Richard Holbrooke, *Foreign Affairs,* Winter 1991-92.

The second reason for preserving the U.S. defense relationship with Tokyo is economic. Japan is the heart of the Asian market that holds the fastest-growing and most dynamic economies in the world, and to which the center of international trade is shifting from the North Atlantic. As America's commerce with Asia grows, so does its interest in Asian stability. U.S. forces based in Japan assure that stability, first by protecting Japan, and second, by saving Tokyo the military exertions that would agitate other nations in the region. The rotating presence of the Yokosuka-based Seventh Fleet throughout Asia offers genuine hope for that quarter of the world's continued prosperity and its eventual progress toward democracy.

The foundation on which U.S. military presence in Japan rests is sound. Both nations benefit greatly. The fact that Japan now recognizes the need to increase its participation in shaping international events dovetails with American popular opinion that Japan should assume an even greater share of responsibility for its own defense. It should not be regarded as the first step in a reverse march of history.

a critical thinking activity

Evaluating America's Alliances

Writers often quote well-known and admired historical figures to add credibility to their arguments. When foreign policy experts debate the value of America's alliances with other nations, those who oppose such alliances often cite George Washington's September 17, 1796, farewell address to support their views. Read this excerpt from Washington's address and complete the sections that follow:

> Nothing is more essential than that permanent, inveterate antipathies against particular nations and passionate attachments for others should be excluded, and that in place of them just and amicable feelings toward all should be cultivated. The nation which indulges toward another an habitual hatred or an habitual fondness is in some degree a slave. It is a slave to its animosity or to its affection, either of which is sufficient to lead it astray from its duty and its interest. . . .

> Europe has a set of primary interests which to us have none, or a very remote relation. Hence she must be engaged in frequent controversies, the causes of which are essentially foreign to our concerns. Hence, therefore, it must be unwise in us to implicate ourselves by artificial ties in the ordinary vicissitudes of her politics, or the ordinary combinations and collisions of her friendships or enmities.

> Our detached and distant situation invites and enables us to pursue a different course. If we remain one people, under an efficient government, the period is not far off when we may defy material injury from external annoyance; when we may take such an attitude as will cause the neutrality we may at

any time resolve upon to be scrupulously respected; when belligerent nations, under the impossibility of making acquisitions upon us, will not lightly hazard the giving us provocation; when we may choose peace or war, as our interest, guided by justice, shall counsel.

Why forego the advantages of so peculiar a situation? Why quit our own to stand upon foreign ground? Why, by interweaving our destiny with that of any part of Europe, entangle our peace and prosperity in the toils of European ambition, rivalship, interest, humor, or caprice?

It is our policy to steer clear of permanent alliances with any portion of the foreign world, so far, I mean, as we are now at liberty to do it.

Part I

Answer the following questions.

1. Why does Washington warn against permanent alliances?

2. Why do you think Washington specifically points to alliances with European nations as a possible threat to American interests?

3. What does Washington cite as the benefits of neutrality?

Part II

In 1796, the United States was a small nation comprised of sixteen states and with a population of about 4,500,000. Today, it is comprised of fifty states and about 250,000,000 people. More important, whereas in 1796 the United States was a young, relatively powerless country with minimal need or ability to be deeply involved in the affairs of other nations, today it is arguably the world's leader and is involved in the affairs of many nations. America's alliances with Israel, Japan, and the nations of NATO are an expression of this involvement.

Some experts believe this involvement benefits the United States by giving it the power to control world events in its favor. Others assert that the United States should try to extricate itself from the affairs of other nations to allow it to focus on its own internal problems and prevent it from being drawn into unwanted wars and conflicts.

With these facts in mind, divide into groups and discuss the following questions:

1. After reading the viewpoints in the chapter, do you think the United States benefits from its alliances with nations such as Japan, Israel, and the members of NATO? If so, how? If not, how do you think these alliances are detrimental to the United States?

2. Do you think Washington's words of warning concerning alliances are still valid today? Why or why not?

Periodical Bibliography

The following articles have been selected to supplement the diverse views presented in this chapter.

George Bush — "Great Promise for U.S.-Japan Relations," *U.S. Department of State Dispatch*, July 6, 1992.

Steven R. David — "Bosom of Abraham," *Policy Review*, Winter 1991.

Gerald Frost — "Americana and Her Friends," *National Review*, May 27, 1991.

Clyde Haberman — "Israelis Worry if World's New Epoch Will Find Them Shunted Aside by U.S.," *The New York Times*, August 3, 1992.

Seigi Hinata — "An Optimist's View of Japan-U.S. Relations," *Vital Speeches of the Day*, December 1, 1991.

Richard Holbrooke — "Japan and the United States: Ending the Unequal Partnership," *Foreign Affairs*, Winter 1991-92.

Charles Kimball — "A Push for Peace in the Middle East," *Sojourners*, December 1991.

Robin Knight — "Alliance Without an Enemy," *U.S. News & World Report*, November 11, 1991.

Edward N. Luttwak — "The U.S.-Japanese Crisis," *The Washington Quarterly*, Autumn 1992. Available from MIT Press Journals, 55 Hayward St., Cambridge, MA 02142.

Elichi Nakao — "Japan's Role in the 1990s," *Vital Speeches of the Day*, July 1, 1991.

Richard Nixon — "Is America Part of Europe?" *National Review*, March 2, 1992.

Norman Podhoretz — "America and Israel: An Ominous Change," *Commentary*, January 1992.

Dan Quayle — "The United States and Israel: An Unshakable Alliance," *U.S. Department of State Dispatch*, April 13, 1992.

Jed C. Snyder — "NATO: What Now?" *The American Enterprise*, September/October 1991.

Scott Sullivan — "The Birth of a New NATO," *Newsweek*, November 18, 1991.

Is U.S. Intervention in Other Countries Justified?

AMERICAN
FOREIGN POLICY

Chapter Preface

In 1991-92, civil war and drought caused widespread famine in the east African nation of Somalia. Although international relief organizations sent food and medical aid, rebels confiscated or destroyed most of these supplies. By late 1992 the nation was in complete anarchy, and hundreds of thousands of Somalians were dying, either from starvation and dehydration, or in the fighting. In response, a U.N.-sanctioned U.S. military force entered Somalia to try to restore order and ensure that suffering Somalians received food and medical care.

Because this U.S. intervention was motivated by humanitarianism, it seemed justified to most Americans. The justness of other types of intervention, however, has not always been as clear. This is because intervention due to strategic, economic, or political interests seems less altruistic and therefore more questionable. For example, President George Bush cited economic, strategic, and humanitarian reasons when he led the effort for a U.N.-sanctioned military intervention in the 1991 Persian Gulf War. Whether one believed the war was justified depended upon whether one accepted any or all of the reasons given for the intervention.

The motivation for U.S. interventions is important to many Americans for one main reason: America has always ascribed to certain ideals in its foreign policy goals, in particular, helping the oppressed and spreading democracy. Consequently, in cases in which an altruistic motive is absent, a president risks losing the support of the American people. For example, the Vietnam War was initially motivated by the altruistic goal of protecting the Vietnamese from communism. At first, Americans supported this goal and the war. As the war dragged on, however, many Americans perceived that the war was harming, not helping, the Vietnamese and that American soldiers were dying for no clear objective. Americans' belief in the altruistic motives of the war eroded, as did their support for President Lyndon Johnson.

What motivates a particular U.S. intervention is not always easy to determine. For this reason, responses to American intervention run the gamut, from unwavering support to vehement opposition. The authors in the following chapter present their views concerning when and where, if ever, it is appropriate for America to intervene in the affairs of other nations.

> *"Intervention is . . . permissible if the action under consideration will promote the cause of freedom."*

U.S. Intervention Is Sometimes Justified

James Robbins

The goal of American foreign policy should be to promote democracy throughout the world, James Robbins states in the following viewpoint. Robbins argues that, while it is best to achieve this goal through example and diplomatic efforts, sometimes military intervention is required to help liberate foreign peoples. Robbins cites U.S. actions in Grenada and Panama as examples of justified military intervention. Robbins is assistant editor of *Liberty*, a bimonthly journal of libertarian views on politics and culture.

As you read, consider the following questions:

1. What broad foreign policy guidelines does the author believe the United States should follow?
2. Why does Robbins believe that isolationism is appealing to Americans?
3. What are three marks of a successful military intervention, in the author's opinion?

From James Robbins, "A New Approach to Foreign Policy." This article originally appeared in the Fall 1991 issue of *Orbis: A Journal of World Affairs*, published by the Foreign Policy Research Institute and is reprinted with permission.

The overall goal of American foreign policy should be to promote, by properly adapted means, the creation and survival of liberal societies and governments throughout the world. The distinction between societies and governments is important, however. A state may have a government with liberal mechanisms, and yet its society may lack a liberal spirit. Weimar Germany is an example. In such cases, there is no reason to expect the state will have a special predilection for either peace or stability. Nevertheless, so long as liberal governmental mechanisms exist to some degree, it is usually best that no overt interference take place and that the society be allowed to evolve on its own. In extreme circumstances, however, it may be worthwhile to impose liberal governmental mechanisms on a fundamentally illiberal society, in the hope that people will grasp the benefits of such institutions and come to adopt a liberal spirit. The experience of the United States with postwar Germany and Japan is instructive in this regard.

Standards for Activism

Once the link between classical liberalism and peace is recognized, U.S. policy should follow these broad guidelines:

• If U.S. interests are threatened directly, through a possible armed attack on the American homeland, a major threat to citizens or property abroad, or similar circumstances, then state action is mandatory, in proportion to the threat.

• If U.S. interests are not threatened directly, intervention is still permissible if the action under consideration will promote the cause of freedom, and if the United States has the capacity to take this action with a good chance of success.

These conditions would give American foreign policy a principled underpinning, sensitive to the cause of limited government and to liberal internationalism. The result would be a foreign policy that was normative without being utopian, and realistic without falling into amoral realism.

Critics of such principled internationalism point out that the United States cannot or will not right every wrong, the implication being that it is hypocritical to intervene for ideological purposes in some conflicts but not in others. This objection has been raised by comparing the Iraqi invasion of Kuwait with the Soviet crackdown in the Baltic states. "Why hasn't the United States sent half a million troops to Lithuania?" detractors ask, implying that Washington's (or the U.N.'s) "response to aggression" is only a cover for state-interested motives.

But as Charles Krauthammer has pointed out, "legitimacy is a necessary, not a sufficient, condition for intervention." Internationalism must be both principled and prudent. Washington should not react uniformly to every case of aggression, but should discriminate between those cases in which action can make a positive difference and those in which it can not. Thus, the United States did not deploy to Lithuania because the consequences might have included a nuclear exchange, which would have served no discernible purpose, and certainly would not have advanced the cause of freedom.

Instruments of Policy

When setting down the guidelines for a foreign policy acceptable to classical liberalism, therefore, the means are as important as the ends. The use of certain means, in certain circumstances, would vitiate the ends sought; and insufficient means naturally lead to frustrated ends. The key is finding a correct balance of means to ends, not counting any means in or out, except in relation to policy goals.

Force. The most controversial tool, and the one most opposed by neutralists, is military force. But force, if used judiciously and in proportion to the threat or goal, is often an important aspect of an activist foreign policy. For the past forty years, it was in large part through strong, forward-based defenses that the Western world was protected and aggressors deterred. Moreover, military force is occasionally a useful instrument in the extension of freedom, as was shown in Grenada and Panama. . . .

Neutralist classical liberals commonly protest that activism violates the "isolationist tradition" of the United States. Obviously, this is an America-centered argument; Europeans in the classical liberal tradition, lacking broad oceans between themselves and their neighbors, looked to international cooperation, not to self-imposed isolation, as the preferred alternative to war.

That said, isolationism undoubtedly makes a strong appeal to Americans. For many years, the Atlantic and Pacific Oceans rendered isolation a physical reality and thus a habit of thought. Moreover, the country was founded by people who, in large measure, defined themselves by contrast to European statesmen. As a consequence, Alexis de Tocqueville observed that early American foreign policy consisted "more in abstaining than acting."

But noninvolvement existed only as a prudential, not a creedal, policy. Before the twentieth century, the United States had fewer reasons to act. U.S. overseas economic interests were indirectly protected by the *Pax Britannica*. When American policy makers thought they needed to take action, they did so. International cooperation began with the Revolution, during which the Continentals were allied with France, Spain, and the Netherlands. Washington's Farewell Address—famous for warning against entangling alliances—was directed in large part against one specific alliance, namely, the alliance with France that Jeffersonians were thought to be contemplating.

Under Jefferson, of course, America purchased the Louisiana Territory, an arguably unconstitutional bit of activism that was nevertheless a foreign policy triumph. Had America's prototypical liberal not been expansionist-minded and willing to involve himself with the foreign powers that owned the rest of the continent, America today would terminate at the Mississippi.

The U.S. Is the World's Leader

America . . . is the only nation capable of mobilizing effective international coalitions to tackle the post-Cold War problems that will arise.

U.S. military strength is the backbone of any collective response. The United States is still the world's leading military power. And we must keep it that way. One of America's chief foreign-policy goals thus ought to be to ensure that no nation will ever be allowed to threaten the world the way the Soviet Union did.

Winston Lord, *Los Angeles Times*, September 17, 1992.

As a matter of fact, Jefferson looked forward to a day when Americans would bring democracy and the English language to the entire hemisphere. The Monroe Doctrine, formulated by Secretary of State John Quincy Adams to prevent European intervention in the Western Hemisphere, is a nineteenth-century policy that neutralists often claim as their own. They take it to imply the United States would not stray from this hemisphere. Yet, contemporaries of the doctrine sometimes asserted it was interventionist, because it committed the United States to defending far-flung Latin America. . . .

Of course, many past American interventions would not qualify as just under the guidelines laid out earlier in this article, nor is their enumeration meant to be a justification for activism. Rather, the purpose here is to show that arguments stemming from a neutralist tradition *per se* are fraught with difficulties.

Tactical Blunders

A second common objection to foreign policy activism is that it backfires, leaving Washington in a situation worse than if it had taken no action. To this it may be said that, obviously, some foreign policy initiatives fail. But some succeed, and that should not be ignored. The early Reagan administration provides useful examples on each side: intervention in the Lebanese conflict, and the invasion of Grenada. The former was a failure, the latter a major success.

Lebanon. Since 1975, Lebanon had been in a state of civil war as various ethnic, religious, and political groups contended for power. Syria and Israel used the conflict to further their own designs, Syria shifting support to keep any single group from becoming too powerful (thus ensuring Syrian influence), and Israel pommeling the PLO, which was based in southern Lebanon. This objective led Israel to invade Lebanon in June 1982, and, with Syrian forces already present, fears arose of a new Arab-Israel conflict.

In August 1982, the United States joined France and Italy in a Multinational Force (MNF), with the mission of evacuating the PLO army from Beirut, in order to prevent a destructive, house-to-house battle with the Israelis. The MNF ferried PLO fighters onto ships and dispersed them (solving another problem at the same time). By September 14 the MNF had left, with its mission accomplished.

A Fiasco

But the situation did not stabilize, and a week later the MNF returned. Its new mission was unclear, however. President Reagan said it would "give a kind of support and stability while the Lebanese government seeks to reunite its people." Worse still, this second MNF lacked the firepower to be militarily effective, and, since it was now taking sides, it and other American targets came under attack, the two worst attacks being the bombings of the American Embassy in April 1983 and of the Marine barracks in October 1983. These bombings led to escalation as air and naval forces were brought to bear, yet it was escalation without purpose or effect. Eventually, West Beirut was cut off from the airport, negating the MNF's one clear mission. With an election year looming and criticism increasing, President Reagan withdrew the troops on February 26, 1984.

The intervention in Lebanon thus turned into a fiasco. The policy behind it had no clear goal, and no discernible American interests were involved. It should never have taken place.

Grenada. But mere days after the bombing of the Marine barracks in Beirut, the Reagan administration enjoyed a foreign policy triumph, Operation Urgent Fury, the invasion of Grenada.

In 1979, the island of Grenada had fallen victim to a Cuban-backed coup, and a socialistic People's Revolutionary Government immediately began to integrate the country into a growing Caribbean socialist alliance. The most alarming development was the construction of an airstrip on the island, capable of basing high-performance military aircraft, though the ostensible purpose was to promote tourism. On October 19, 1983, a struggle within the government led to the violent deaths of Prime Minister Maurice Bishop and his followers, who were succeeded by an even more hard-line faction. The island seemed to be in chaos, and so arose an additional danger—the threat of harm to U.S. medical students studying on the island. With the possibility of a new hostage crisis looming, and with Lebanon-bound Marines in the area, President Reagan hastily assembled an invasion force and unleashed it on Grenada. Within days the socialist government had been removed and the students rescued.

The invasion of Grenada illustrated three marks of a successful military intervention. The first is a clearly defined, legitimate interest, or multiple interests. In this case, state interests were served by diminishing the strategic threat of an anti-U.S. Caribbean alliance. Moreover, U.S. citizens were rescued from danger, a primary state function. Finally, the cause of freedom was advanced by the liberation of the Grenadian people from an oppressive socialist regime.

A Clear Goal

The second mark of a successful military intervention is a definite mission. In the case of Grenada, this was the direct and complete excision of the People's Revolutionary Government, and the rescue of the students.

The third mark is the effective use of forces proportional to the mission. In Grenada, no more force was used than was necessary to accomplish U.S. objectives, and as a result, there were few U.S. and civilian casualties and little destruction of property. The use of too much force in a military action can have negative consequences on the people that the United States is trying to free, thus making them less amenable to the liberalism that the United States represents. On the other hand, indecisive or inept use of force often results in the failure of an operation.

In sum, where the Lebanese intervention met none of the conditions for a satisfactory military intervention, Urgent Fury met them all, and this was reflected in the favorable outcome of the operation. When these three elements (clear, legitimate interests; a well-defined mission; and the use of an appropriate force level) are present, classical liberals should have no tactical objections to state action.

==========

*"The costs of intervention may have outweighed
any specific benefits that the United States could
plausibly have realized."*

==========

Intervention
Harms the U.S.

Alan Tonelson

Alan Tonelson is the research director of the Economic Strategy
Institute, a Washington, D.C., think tank. In addition to writing
many essays on American politics and foreign policy, Tonelson
co-edited the book *Powernomics: Economics and Strategy After the
Cold War.* In the following viewpoint, Tonelson expresses his belief that America's internationalist foreign policy has led the
United States to intervene militarily in other nations, and that
these interventions have harmed America economically and politically. Tonelson defines internationalism as the belief that the
security of all other nations is vital to America's own security.

As you read, consider the following questions:

1. Why does Tonelson believe Americans should not celebrate
   U.S. victories in the Cold War and the Gulf War?
2. Why is internationalism's focus on the future harmful to
   America, in the author's opinion?
3. What does the author believe will happen if America
   continues to fail to achieve its foreign policy goals?

Alan Tonelson, "What Is the National Interest?" *The Atlantic*, July 1991. Reprinted with
permission.

For the first time since the end of the Second World War the United States faces the need to redefine the international requirements for its security and prosperity. Circumstances today demand that the United States rethink the ends of its foreign policy—that is to say, its national interests.

With the recent victories in the Cold War and the Gulf War, those who have been responsible for U.S. foreign policy are in a triumphant mood. There is little reason for it. The world continues to fray; ever more threatening weapons become ever more widely available. The gap between the stated ends of U.S. foreign policy and the means to achieve and pay for them remains wide and unbridgeable, as it has been for decades. Nor is it clear that the ends of U.S. foreign policy, when they are achieved, do more good than harm—for ourselves or for those we seek to assist. Perhaps most important, the recent victories have brought few benefits to the home front; indeed, they seem scarcely relevant to the daily lives and pressing concerns of most Americans today, or to the economic and social problems that bedevil the nation. The disconnection between the nation's needs at home and its ambitions abroad is at once bizarre and dangerous.

And yet, faced with all these facts, much of the nation's foreign-policy elite has chosen variously to ignore them or to berate those who have called attention to them.

Three Crucial Lessons

Since the end of the Second World War, Americans have by and large defined their foreign-policy objectives in what may be called globalist or internationalist terms. Internationalism has been protean enough—liberal and conservative, hawkish and dovish, unilateralist and multilateralist—to have commanded the loyalty of figures as different as Ronald Reagan and Jimmy Carter. But its essence springs from three crucial lessons learned by most Americans and their leaders from the Great Depression and the rise of fascism during the 1930s, from the global conflagration that those events helped produce, and from the emergence of a new totalitarian threat almost immediately after that war.

The first lesson was that the United States would never know genuine security, lasting peace, and sustained prosperity unless the rest of the world also became secure, peaceful, and prosperous. The second lesson was that international security was indivisible—that the discontent that produced political extremism and, inevitably, aggression was highly contagious and bound to spread around the world no matter where it broke out. The third lesson was that the only way to achieve these fundamental goals and prevent these deadly dangers was to eliminate the conditions that breed extremism wherever they exist, and some-

101

how to impose norms of peaceful behavior on all states.

The result of all this was a global definition of vital U.S. foreign-policy interests, with globalist international-security and economic structures to back it up. The United States supported the United Nations and forged alliances with scores of countries to guarantee security in all major regions and to deter aggression everywhere. In the process Washington expanded the definition of the U.S. defense perimeter to encompass literally every country outside the Communist world. At the same time, the imperative of resisting subversion as well as aggression everywhere in the world created an equally vital interest in the political and economic health of all these countries, which was fostered by U.S. foreign-aid programs and by an international economic system built on such mechanisms as the International Monetary Fund, the World Bank, and the General Agreement on Tariffs and Trade.

The internationalist approach led U.S. foreign-policy makers to insist that no corner of the world was so remote or insignificant that it could be ignored. Of course, not all parts of the world were given equal attention or resources. But disparities emerged not because foreign-policy makers viewed certain regions as expendable but because they perceived no serious threat either to these regions per se or to crucial international norms at the moment. Whenever a serious threat did appear, America's leaders usually favored a prompt response. The power of internationalist impulses has been underscored by military interventions, paramilitary operations, peace-keeping missions, and diplomatic initiatives in marginal countries and regions such as Angola, the Horn of Africa, and Lebanon, and also by a foreign-aid program that continuously sprinkles funds on virtually every Third World mini-state, micro-state, and basket case that has won its independence since 1945.

The Costs of Intervention

Internationalism has insisted that U.S. foreign policy should aim at manipulating and shaping the global environment as a whole rather than at securing or protecting a finite number of assets within that environment. It has yoked America's safety and well-being not to surviving and prospering in the here and now but to turning the world into something significantly better in the indefinite future—into a place where the forces that drive nations to clash in the first place no longer exist. Internationalism, moreover, has insisted that America has no choice but to "pay any price, bear any burden" to achieve these conditions, even though humanity has never come close to bringing them about. In so doing internationalism has sidestepped all questions of risk and cost. In fact, it has defined them out of existence.

Yet even before the Gorbachev revolution in Soviet foreign policy—during the Cold War years, when the case could be made for a total response to the ostensibly total Soviet threat—the problems created by the internationalist approach to foreign policy were beginning to loom as large as those that it was meant to solve. Militarily and strategically, internationalism identified America's foreign-policy challenges in such a way as to turn any instance of aggression into an intolerable threat to America's own security, whether or not tangible U.S. interests were at stake, and no matter how greatly the costs of intervention may have outweighed any specific benefits that the United States could plausibly have realized. Vietnam is the classic example. Internationalism also drew America into nuclear alliances—notably, in Europe—deliberately structured to entrap the country in nuclear conflict even in cases when our own national security had not been directly affected. . . .

The Risks of Intervention

The object of foreign policy cannot be to transform societies or to change men's hearts. Defending America's security by containing, deterring and fighting a hostile country is one thing; attempting that defense by fundamentally influencing internal change is quite another. When America has attempted to do so in the past—in the Philippines, in Iran, in Vietnam, in Lebanon—the results have been spectacular failure.

Enforcing acceptable behavior in foreign lands is a burden best not taken up. It is ironic that, while the impetus for such attempts may largely arise from a desire for a kinder, gentler world, the moral risks of intervention are at least as great as the palpable ones. By defining instability and injustice as a threat, the United States will perforce adopt a posture approximating paranoia in what promises to be a chaotic world. And, in making others the objects of our generous interests, we will almost inevitably succumb to making them the objects of our coercion. President Bush spoke at the Naval Academy of America's global role, dictated by a "moral force that's born of its founding ideals." But perhaps America's founders enjoined us not to go abroad in search of monsters to destroy for fear of the monster we may create at home.

Benjamin Schwarz, *Los Angeles Times*, June 8, 1992.

Internationalism continues to deny us a strategic basis for selectivity, a way of thinking about our international goals that would enable our leaders to resist the temptation to plunge into every crisis and right every wrong that life brings along, and to stand aside without being perceived by the American people as impotent or callous.

In fact, internationalism dismisses as morally reprehensible questions that other nations ask routinely in order to inject some discipline into their decision-making: What is it that we need to do in the world to secure a certain level of material and psychological well-being? What is it that we simply would like to do in the world? What are we able to do? How can we pursue our objectives without wrecking our economy, overloading our political system, or convulsing our society?

Calamitous Consequences

At best, post-Cold War internationalism is a recipe for intense, genuinely worrisome domestic political frustrations. Repeated failure to achieve declared foreign-policy goals and especially to avert foreign-policy outcomes officially characterized as intolerable or disastrous could poison and destabilize American politics and democracy. A string of such failures could bring calamitous international consequences by undermining America's ability to conduct a minimally responsible, rational foreign policy. At worst, internationalism raises the threat of drawing the nation into dangerous conflicts for the slightest of stakes. And even if such political and military disasters are somehow avoided, internationalism will continue to drain the nation to its core, especially if U.S. allies do not lend enough help.

Internationalism has not only locked the foreign policy of this nation of self-avowed pragmatists into a utopian mold; it has led directly to the primacy of foreign policy in American life and to the consequent neglect of domestic problems which has characterized the past fifty years. Internationalism encourages us to think more about the possible world of tomorrow than about the real world of today. Thus the strange irrelevance of our recent foreign policy, and even its victories, to the concerns of most Americans.

"The Gulf War showed that it is possible to fight a contemporary war within the bounds of the just war principles."

The Gulf War Proves that Intervention Is Justified

James Turner Johnson

James Turner Johnson is university director of international programs, professor of religion, and associate member of the graduate department of political science at Rutgers University in New Brunswick, New Jersey. He is the editor and author of numerous books, including *Can Modern War Be Just?* In the following viewpoint, Johnson determines that the 1991 Persian Gulf War, in which a U.S.-led coalition defeated Iraq, meets the criteria of a "just war." Johnson concludes that the United States had a moral obligation to stop Iraq's aggression, and that America must continue to use its military and political power to influence world events.

As you read, consider the following questions:

1. Why does Johnson believe the Persian Gulf War met "just cause" criteria?
2. What is the proportionality concept of a just war, according to the author?
3. Why does Johnson believe the United States must continue to exert its influence in world affairs?

From James Turner Johnson, "The Just War Tradition and the American Military," in *Just War and the Gulf War*, James Turner Johnson and George Weigel, eds. Washington, DC: Ethics and Public Policy Center, 1991. Reprinted with permission.

American political debate over the use of military force is full of arguments and appeals rooted in moral concerns. Indeed, far from being irrelevant to the political process, such concerns have historically played a major role in American political life. Americans want their nation's actions to be moral; it is part of the legacy of that tradition by which this country is "a city set on a hill," a model for other nations to follow. . . .

This essay examines one particular element in the moral debate over American use of military force against Iraq in the Gulf War: the justifiability of that action in terms of the just war tradition of Western culture. This tradition has deep roots in both the ancient Hebraic and the classical Greek and Roman foundations of the West. It has developed over history in both religious and non-religious strands and takes contemporary form in religious doctrine, in international law on war, in codes of military conduct, and in underlying values regarding human rights and the rights of nations. . . .

Justifiable Resort to Force

Examining the Gulf War in just war terms requires standing back from the narrowly political, economic, and ideological arguments that were advanced between August 2, 1990 and January 16, 1991 and concentrating instead on the implications of the criteria for judgment contained in this moral tradition. . . .

The just war tradition has arrived at seven criteria that must be satisfied to justify resort to military force. These include just cause, right authority for the use of such force, right intention, the goal of restoring peace, overall proportionality of good over evil, a reasonable hope of success, and a situation of last resort. I will define each criterion more fully, and then examine each in the context of the decision to use force against Iraq.

The Notion of Just Cause

Just cause classically included one or more of three conditions: defense against an attack, recovery of something wrongly taken, or punishment of evil. . . .

In order to avoid defining evil in ideological terms, recent just war theorists have tended to focus on one particular evil, the aggressive use of force by a people or nation against another. . . .

When Iraq invaded Kuwait on August 2, 1990, and declared that the territory that was "formerly Kuwait" was "irrevocably" part of Iraq, a just cause for use of force against Iraq came into being. This was a flagrant case of aggression, one that violated the most fundamental norms of international order, and it was quickly recognized as such by the United States, by the United Nations Security Council, and also by the overwhelming majority of nations of the world. Not only did Iraq's action blatantly violate the letter of Article 2 of the U.N. Charter (prohibiting "use of force against the territorial integrity [and] political independence" of another country), but, more profoundly, it showed utter disregard for the very norm on which the state system, and through it the United Nations itself, stands: a *de facto* acceptance of every state's right to exist.

The presence of just cause alone is not sufficient to justify resort to force; yet this was as clear and unambiguous a case as one could hope to find in the real world, and the brazenness of Iraq's action remained on public display even as the international community tried to expel the Iraqis through a variety of non-military means. . . .

Action by Right Authority

The second criterion for justified use of force is that such action be undertaken by a *right authority*. . . . The criterion of right authority seeks to minimize the frequency of resort to force, by limiting it to the political leadership of a sovereign state duly authorized by the legitimate political processes of that state. (The concept of such authority has been extended also to the U.N. Security Council under the conditions specified in the Charter.)

In the case of the Gulf War, right authority for use of force by the coalition of nations cooperating to undo Iraq's aggression was manifest at both the international and national levels. Internationally, such authority was provided by Resolution 678 of the United Nations Security Council. Within the United States, right authority derived first from the president's powers as defined by the Constitution and the War Powers Act, then by the congressional resolutions adopted on January 12 and 13 authorizing use of U.S. military force against Iraq. . . .

Aspects of Right Intention

Right intention, the third notion bearing on the just war decision to resort to force, was classically defined in two ways: positively, by considering whether the other just war criteria were present; and negatively, by distinguishing itself from *wrong* intentions such as those enumerated by Augustine: "the love of violence, revengeful cruelty, fierce and implacable enmity, wild resistance and the lust for power, and such like.". . . The concept of right intention . . . centers, positively, on such goals as protection or restoration of national, civil, and human rights and other values, reestablishment of order and stability, and the promotion of peace. Negatively, right intention today involves avoiding taking another state's territory, violating the rights of individuals or nations, and deliberately depriving a nation of peace and stability.

All these conditions existed when the United States and allied forces decided to take military action against Iraq. . . .

The existence of a right intention on the part of the coalition in this case also substantially satisfied the requirement that the use of force *aim at achieving peace*. . . .

In the case of the Gulf War, the goal of peace was closely tied to the concept of right intention: rolling back Iraqi aggression and restoring Kuwaiti territory and sovereignty (right order and justice), deterring such aggression in the future, restoring the shattered peace of the region, and attempting to set in place safeguards to protect that peace in the future. . . .

© 1991 Brookins/*Richmond Times-Dispatch*. Reprinted with permission.

The next just war concept to be examined is the criterion of *proportionality*, which refers to the effort to calculate the overall balance of good versus evil in deciding whether to use force to right a wrong. One must first assess the evil that has already been done—damage to lives and property, as well as harm to the more intangible values of human rights, self-government, and a peaceful and stable world order. Second, one must calculate the costs of allowing the situation of wrongdoing to continue. Finally, one must evaluate the various means of righting these wrongs in terms of their own costs, as well as the benefits they might produce. . . .

The decision to resort to force, to be justified, must also rest on a conviction that military action will have a *reasonable hope of success.* Clearly this, too, is a matter for prudential judgment, since "success" can be interpreted in many ways. . . .

"Reasonable hope of success" turns on the understanding of just cause and right intention, and includes not only achieving the goals thus established but also observing the limits on means. What is called for, in short, is a reasonable hope of doing what is justified by these moral criteria within the moral limits they define.

War as Last Resort

Finally, before engaging in military action, a government should determine whether the wrongs involved can be redressed by means other than force. It is important to note that the criterion of last resort does not mean that all possible non-military options that may be conceived of must first be tried; rather, a prudential judgment must be made as to whether *only* a rightly authorized use of force can, in the given circumstances, achieve the goods defined by the ideas of just cause, right intention, and the goal of peace, at a proportionate cost, and with reasonable hope of success. Other methods *may* be tried first, if time permits and if they also satisfy these moral criteria; yet this is not mandated by the criterion of last resort —and "last resort" certainly does not mean that other methods must be tried indefinitely.

The Case of Iraq

It is my judgment that all the just war criteria providing guidance on the justified use of force were amply satisfied in the case of the decision to use military force against Iraq. The decision not to continue with negotiations or economic sanctions after January 15, 1991, did not violate the criterion of "last resort." The failure of the Geneva talks, the continued intransigence of Saddam Hussein, the ongoing process of military buildup by Iraqi forces, the continuing systematic rape of Kuwait, the history of Iraq's relations with its own dissident population and its neighbors, and threats of violence by Iraq against those neighbors all provided ample reasons to conclude that non-military means held little possibility of success, and that the continuing atrocities in Kuwait necessitated action.

Indeed, Iraq was an easy case. Most instances are fraught with much more ambiguity. There was no moral equivalence between Iraq and Kuwait, for example, or between Iraq and the coalition nations. Iraq's actions flagrantly violated both international law and the deeper international conscience expressed in the idea of a peaceful and stable world order. Nor were military forces committed by the United States or the other coalition nations behind closed doors; the authorization was public, was worked out in debate, and, when it came, clearly represented the will of the authorizing bodies. The critics' charges of a hidden American agenda were not borne out, either during or after the fact. The use of force was proportionate, given the wrongs that were to be righted. The continual aggression on the part of Saddam Hussein swept away, one by one, other possible means of resolving the crisis short of force. The judgment of a reasonable hope of success was eminently sound. The coalition's military action was motivated by the desire to lay a foundation for peace. While the final establishment of peace in the Gulf region and throughout the Middle East clearly remains to be accomplished, that is the proper task for statecraft, and exceeds the bounds of what military force alone can ever achieve. . . .

A Necessary War

The main result of the war was to restore the independence of Kuwait and to reduce Iraq's ability to threaten its neighbors for a decade or so. . . .

Much of the argument against the U.S. role hinges on the belief that another outcome to the crisis was possible. The alternative to the U.S. and its allies joining the war was to leave Hussein in Kuwait, on the grounds that the cost of war would have been higher. But, on the evidence available, it cannot be argued that there was another way to get Iraq out of Kuwait. Sanctions would not have worked, since they assumed that Hussein would yield in the face of the hardship on his people, something he had never done before and has not done since the war ended. Negotiation would not have worked, since Hussein did not believe he would be attacked. Those who say the war was illegitimate because oil was involved simplify the questions—there was plenty of oil around in the outbreak of the war in December 1941 without this making the U.S. conflict with Japan illegitimate.

Fred Halliday, *In These Times*, January 15-21, 1992.

The Gulf War showed that it is possible to fight a contemporary war within the bounds of the just war principles of discrimination and proportionality of means, and that the decision to do so is a moral judgment on the part of the belligerents involved, not a choice forced on them by contemporary weapons. There is, I think, a lesson to be drawn from this: we need to put aside our fears that contemporary war must, by its very nature, be an indiscriminate, disproportionate holocaust, and move on to deliberate the best ways of developing means of force that may be used morally if military action is necessary. In contrast to the destructiveness exemplified in World War II's carpet-bombing of cities and Vietnam's free-fire zones, the Gulf War showed that highly accurate weapons and appropriate plans and policies for their use can limit the overall destructiveness of contemporary war. The Gulf War, in short, is a real-life example of what just war tradition has always held to be true in principle: war is an enterprise capable of being conducted morally or immorally, depending on human decisions. . . .

We seem to have moved into a cycle of limited warfare, having passed through a period of world-wide conflicts. Whether this is a genuine cycle or not, or whether total war and limited war are always parallel options, we would do well to note William V. O'Brien's observation that limited war represents the practical application of the just war idea. Whereas the Cold War, as well as the models of the two World Wars, encouraged those engaged in the moral debate to focus on an image of total war, the Gulf War provides a powerful historical example to buttress the moral argument for military preparedness oriented to limited and humanly controllable forms of warfare. . . .

America's Role in the World

America today stands in a position of unrivaled strength among world powers, and it is clearly the object of much envy on the part of people around the world. While no country can single-handedly deal with all the world's problems, the leadership role the United States has assumed in the Middle East since August 2, 1990, suggests that Americans might now do a great deal more in the international arena than was conceivable so long as the Cold War lasted. American leadership might be exercised through the United Nations, whose Security Council functioned in the Gulf crisis as it was designed to function but had not since 1945; American leadership might be exercised through alliances or coalitions of nations dealing with regional problems; or, on rare occasions, America may need to exercise its influence alone.

Keeping the Debate Alive

Using influence does not necessarily mean taking military action, although, the exercise of statecraft inevitably involves the use of national power, and the military represents a component of such power. Thus it is important to keep the just war debate alive in this post-Gulf War era, for its categories may need to be drawn on again in assessing our proper response to crises that may erupt in the future. As the Gulf crisis has shown, it is also important to think of the contemporary meaning of this moral tradition not simply in terms of the debate over nuclear weapons and deterrence, which preoccupied just war theorists for most of three decades from 1945 until the end of the Cold War, but also in terms of weapons-planning and development, strategic and tactical thought, and the socialization and training of military personnel. In short, it is time to rethink our moral tradition of statecraft and force it back to its roots, and to reconsider the tradition's implications for present and future policy, anticipating an active American role in the developing world order that lies ahead.

"If the war against Iraq serves as a guide, then the new world order the United States is constructing prefers military solutions [and] scorns diplomacy."

The Gulf War Proves that Intervention Is Harmful

Jack Nelson-Pallmeyer

In the following viewpoint, Jack Nelson-Pallmeyer states that the 1991 Persian Gulf War was just one in a string of unjust U.S. interventions in the Third World. He believes it is wrong for the United States to attack and devastate nations such as Iraq simply to further U.S. interests. Nelson-Pallmeyer concludes that the Persian Gulf War is just the beginning of U.S. plans to oppress the Third World and manipulate world affairs for its own gain. The author's books include *War Against the Poor: Low-Intensity Conflict and Christian Faith*, *The Politics of Compassion*, and *Hunger for Justice*.

As you read, consider the following questions:

1. What six principal reasons for the Gulf War does the author cite?
2. Why does the United States defend oppressive governments, in Nelson-Pallmeyer's opinion?
3. What will be the characteristics of a U.S.-led new world order, in the author's opinion?

From Jack Nelson-Pallmeyer, *Brave New World Order*. Maryknoll, NY: Orbis Books, 1992.

The brave new world order being fashioned by the United States is based on clearly defined roles. U.S. leaders are "predestined" to be world controllers. Poor people in and outside of the United States are being "conditioned" to accept their place as the equivalent of "future sewage workers" in Aldous Huxley's novel. President Bush has suggested that in the new world order the weak must learn to trust the mercy of the strong. Unfortunately, as we will see, the weak can expect neither mercy nor justice in the new order. . . .

The new order, like the old, is concerned with the relative distribution of wealth and power. The old order's most powerful players are struggling to adapt to changing circumstances. These circumstances include the decline of the Soviet Union, reduced East-West tensions, growing conflict between the developed nations of the North and the underdeveloped nations of the South, unrestrained U.S. military power, regional conflicts in the Third World, and economic realignment among Western nations, including the economic decline of the United States. In addition to the obvious shift in the balance of military power in the post-Cold War period there are three major economic trends that are shaking the foundations of the old order. Each involves a massive transfer of wealth:

• from poor nations to rich nations;
• from U.S. poor and working-class people, and from future generations, to U.S elites; and,
• from the United States to Japan and Western Europe.

Shifts in the balance of military and economic power, which confront U.S. leaders with numerous problems and contradictions, hold the key to unmasking the motivation of U.S. leaders during the Gulf War and to understanding the broader policy objectives of the United States within the new world order. . . .

The Predominance of Military Power

The Commandant of the Marine Corps told Congress in March 1990 that "the people of our great Nation continue to demand that we maintain our status as a superpower." In fact, through the Gulf crisis the U.S. military and broader National Security Establishment took steps to ensure that the United States would shape a new world order in which the principal U.S. role is that of a *military* superpower. Michael Klare captured the underlying issues in a talk at the University of Minnesota in October 1990.

> Something else is also at work here [in the Persian Gulf], something more visceral . . . than the protection merely of vital interests. I believe that many American leaders are motivated by a psychological need to preserve America's role as a global superpower in the post Cold War era, and to retain

thereby their power and prestige as the managers of the National Security Establishment. This preoccupation with . . . global dominance emerges out of the changing global landscape and the crisis in American leadership brought about by the end of the Cold War. For years Americans reveled in our status as the leaders of the so-called free world even if it meant squandering our wealth on military forces while Japan and Germany devoted their wealth to economic primacy. But with the end of the Cold War our claim to superpower status is put in jeopardy.

The U.S. National Security Establishment, with leadership from President Bush, orchestrated the Gulf crisis. It was a ticket to remaining a superpower and shaping a new world order in which military power mattered more than the economic health of the country.

Opportunity Lost

The end of the Cold War offered the possibility for U.S. economic revitalization and for a world order in which conflicts could be resolved through negotiations rather than violence. The Gulf War closed the door on these new possibilities. . . .

The numerous tragedies of the Gulf War and its aftermath, including U.S. war crimes, were products of a war that should never have been fought. General Schwarzkopf returned to a hero's welcome to address a joint session of Congress on May 8, 1991. "We were the thunder and lightning of Desert Storm," he shouted. "We were the United States military and damn proud of it." He then repeated the greatest deception of the Gulf War:

We left our homes and our families and traveled thousands of miles away and fought in places whose names we could not pronounce simply because you asked us to, and it therefore became our duty, because that's what your military does.

The war in the Gulf was the product of a National Security State. The U.S. military and National Security Establishment did not respond to a Congressional call. It created and manipulated a crisis. It wasn't a war fought to free Kuwait, to uphold international law, to demonstrate that big countries can't bully little ones, to usher in a new world order of peace and stability. It was fought by and for the U.S. military and the broader National Security Establishment.

Reasons for the War

A brief examination of whose interests were served by the Gulf War demonstrates that the military and broader National Security Establishment were the biggest winners. In my view there were six principal reasons for the Gulf War.

One reason, although not the most important, is oil. Two-thirds of the world's known oil reserves are located in the Middle East.

The U.S. State Department has called this oil "a stupendous source of strategic power" and "one of the greatest material prizes in world history." The United States is committed to maintaining control over governments in the region who exercise nominal control over the resources within their borders. Saddam Hussein, despite a long history of human rights abuses, was a favored U.S. ally until he demonstrated that he could not be trusted to follow U.S. directives. Middle Eastern oil is important to the United States in another way as well. Japan and Western Europe are far more dependent on oil from this region than the United States. As the United States sinks further behind these economic powerhouses it hopes to use its control over Middle Eastern oil supplies as leverage against its allies.

© Joel Pett/*Lexington Herald-Leader*. Reprinted with permission.

A second factor contributing to the Gulf War is U.S. dependency on surplus oil revenues from the Middle East. The Gulf War occurred in the context of huge U.S. budget deficits, the Savings and Loan scandal, a deeper crisis affecting the U.S. banking industry, and the beginning of an economic recession. Middle East expert Joel Beinin describes the importance of recycled petro-dollars to the U.S. economy:

> Both the Saudis and the Kuwaitis pursue a policy of recycling petro-dollars in the economies of Western Europe and North

America. That means that most of the profits that are made from the sale of oil by the Kuwaitis and by the Saudis are reinvested in the stock market, in the purchase of real estate, in the purchase of United States government treasury bonds. . . . Saudi Arabia has about $400 billion invested in the economies of Western Europe and North America and Kuwait has between $100 and $150 billion invested in those economies. Since the mid-1980s . . . Kuwait's income from its investment portfolio has been larger than its income from the sale of oil.

The United States is committed to maintaining governments in the Middle East and elsewhere that are committed to highly unequal societies. Saddam Hussein, like all the other leaders in the region, ruled in a dictatorial fashion. This was not a problem for the United States. Iraq squandered enormous wealth in the war with Iran. This also was not a problem, because Iran was an enemy of the West and because the war lined the pockets of arms manufacturers. Iraq was a problem because its oil revenues belonged to the state and not to royal families. It provided universal health and education programs for its people, and Saddam Hussein was inflaming Arab masses by raising uncomfortable issues concerning inequalities within and between various countries in the region. . . . The United States defends governments that maintain highly unequal societies because they use "surplus" oil revenues to finance the U.S. budget deficit and U.S. businesses and banks rather than to improve the living standards of the majority of their impoverished populations.

A Diversionary Tactic

The third reason for the Gulf crisis was that it took attention away from domestic problems. Washington Post columnist David Broder offered the following explanation as to why so little attention was paid to a deepening recession:

> Why has it taken so long for something so obvious on Main Street to be recognized on Pennsylvania Avenue? You can blame much of the inattention on the Persian Gulf crisis. Kuwait and Saddam Hussein became the preoccupation of the president and his top advisors, the Congress and the mass media, consuming time and energy that would otherwise have been spent on the slump. The boom on Wall Street also masked the urgency that might otherwise have been felt about the drop in retail sales and manufacturing.

Broder almost got it right when he suggested a relationship between the Gulf War and the recession. However, he ignored one important detail: The recession began one month *before* the beginning of the Gulf crisis. The Gulf War fulfilled part of its intended purpose when it diverted attention, not only from the recession, but from a far deeper economic crisis in which "the boom on Wall Street" had little relationship to the actual economic health of the country.

A fourth reason for the Gulf War was intimidation. General Colin Powell, on the eve of the U.S. invasion of Panama, reportedly said that "we have to put a shingle outside our door saying superpower lives here no matter what the Soviets do, even if they evacuate from all of Eastern Europe." The Gulf War, like Panama, sent a clear message to friends and foes alike. "The U.S. war in the Persian Gulf," writes James Petras, "was an attempt to recreate Washington's role as world policeman, to resubordinate Europe to U.S. power and to intimidate the Third World into submission." The war not only intimidated third-world leaders who thought they might have more freedom to maneuver in the aftermath of the Cold War; it also sent a clear message to Europe: economic power may be important but it is military power that guarantees global predominance. . . .

No More Dividend

The fifth reason for the Gulf crisis was to foreclose on the peace dividend. Andrew and Leslie Cockburn write:

> Short-term domestic political considerations aside, there were very important institutional imperatives behind the push toward military confrontation in the Gulf. . . . In April 1990 a seasoned Pentagon official lamented in casual conversation that the atmosphere at his place of employment was dire. "No one knows what to do over here," he sighed. "The [Soviet] threat has melted down on us, and what else do we have? The Navy's been going up to the Hill to talk about the threat of the Indian Navy in the Indian Ocean. Some people are talking about the threat of the Colombian drug cartels. But we can't keep a $300 billion budget afloat on that stuff. There's only one place that will do as a threat: Iraq." Iraq, he explained, was a long way away, which justified the budget for military airlift. It had a large air force, which would keep the United States Air Force happy, and the huge numbers of tanks in Saddam's army were more than enough to satisfy the requirements of the U.S. ground forces.

This indicates that Iraq was targeted by the U.S. National Security Establishment as a useful enemy months before Iraq's invasion of Kuwait. The Gulf crisis as it unfolded proved so successful in eliminating the peace dividend that within the Pentagon "Desert Shield" was referred to as "Budget Shield.". . .

This leads to the final reason for the Gulf War: the desire of the National Security Establishment to create a world order in which U.S. military power guarantees superpower status. The Gulf War reestablished the primacy of the military in U.S. and global affairs. Senator John McCain of Arizona, eight months prior to the Iraqi invasion of Kuwait, argued that the United States had an enforcer role to play in the post-Cold War period. "No other allied nation will suddenly develop power projection forces, and . . . it would not be in our interest to encourage other nations to assume this role," he wrote in the *Armed Forces Journal.* "The U.S. may not be the 'world's policeman,' but its power projection forces will remain the free world's insurance policy.". . .

Third World Wars

Ever since Vietnam, American leaders have been looking for a formula that would permit the use of force in the Third World but avoid the semblance of war. . . .

Saddam Hussein was portrayed as a potent military threat to oil and Israel. A security interest was claimed, tied to the likelihood that Iraq would soon possess a nuclear bomb. As we now know, the "war" was not a war at all; it had the one-sidedness of torture. Casualty ratios approached 1,000 to 1. . . . No losses Iraq inflicted seemed real in a military sense to Americans, who could satisfy a thirst for victory and revel in the superiority of U.S. military technology. We could view Saddam as a demon who deserved devastation and the Iraqi people as part of the Islamic horde that had given rise to anti-Western terrorism.

Richard Falk, *The Nation*, February 3, 1992.

Michael Klare describes what it means for the United States to maintain its "superpower status" in light of its decision to forego economic revitalization and assume the role of global enforcer:

[To be a superpower] according to the national security leadership of the United States is to assume leadership in the struggle against the South [and] to assume responsibility for the protection of the Western World's economic resources in return for the continuing profession of our leadership by our esteemed erstwhile allies in Europe and Japan who will continue to need us because we will protect their supply of oil and other strategic raw materials.

Just how entrenched the role of global cop had become after the U.S. "victory" in the Gulf was illustrated in a single sentence in *Newsweek*: "The idea that economic power is what counts most in today's world, so fashionable before this war began, now seems woefully shortsighted."

The "New" World Order

During and after the war against Iraq, the United States grounded its actions in rhetoric of high moral purpose. Peace, justice, international cooperation, and diplomacy were to be the fruits of this war and the new world order in process of formation. However, the means employed point elsewhere. If the war against Iraq serves as a guide, then the new world order the United States is constructing prefers military solutions, scorns diplomacy, selectively obeys and enforces international law, respects human rights only when politically expedient, vilifies enemies, censors the press (which seems all too willing to confine its role to that of patriotic cheerleader), promotes uncritical patriotism, cultivates religious legitimacy, and manipulates the United Nations. It is also thoroughly racist and is willing to inflict unprecedented violence on third-world countries of "strategic" importance to the United States and other industrial nations of the North.

The U.S. National Security Establishment was the only clear winner in the Gulf War. With stunning speed it erased the prospects for a significant peace dividend; fashioned a world order based on "military power projection" rather than negotiations; carried out a press-sanctioned and presidentially-led "military coup"; intimidated potential adversaries and discouraged alternative visions of an authentically new order; showcased weapons and thereby dramatically improved prospects for global weapons sales; garnered support for other weapons systems, such as "star wars"; paved the way for a permanent U.S. military presence in the Gulf; and made significant strides in overcoming the Vietnam Syndrome.

The victory was both illusionary and costly. The cracks in the U.S. economy grew wider during the Gulf War and hopes for economic revitalization and the creation of an authentically new world order vanished. The U.S. and third-world poor were relegated to places of permanent marginalization. The United States set a course for itself rooted in violence, U.S. democracy also failed a crucial test; it was now clearly subordinate to the priorities of a National Security State.

a critical thinking activity

Distinguishing Between Fact and Opinion

This activity is designed to help develop the basic reading and thinking skill of distinguishing between fact and opinion. Consider the following statement as an example: "In 1991, the United States led a United Nations coalition in the Persian Gulf War." This is a factual statement because it could be checked by looking at news magazines or newspapers from 1991. But the statement "The Persian Gulf War was fought to continue America's domination of the Third World" is an opinion. Many people believe the war was fought to prevent Iraq from controlling the Middle East and to rescue Kuwait from Iraqi aggression.

When investigating controversial issues, it is important that one be able to distinguish between statements of fact and statements of opinion. It is also important to recognize that not all statements of fact are true. They may appear to be true, but some are based on inaccurate or false information. For this activity, however, we are concerned with understanding the difference between those statements that appear to be factual and those that appear to be based primarily on opinion.

Most of the following statements are taken from the viewpoints in this chapter. Consider each statement carefully. *Mark O for any statement you believe is an opinion or interpretation of facts. Mark F for any statement you believe is a fact. Mark I for any statement you believe is impossible to judge.*

If you are doing this activity as a member of a class or group, compare your answers with those of other class or group members. Be able to defend your answers. You may discover that others come to different conclusions than you do. Listening to the reasons others present for their answers may give you valuable insights into distinguishing between fact and opinion.

O = *opinion*
F = *fact*
I = *impossible to judge*

121

1. Under Thomas Jefferson, America purchased the Louisiana Territory.

2. The Monroe Doctrine was formulated by Secretary of State John Quincy Adams to prevent European intervention in the Western Hemisphere.

3. The United States supported the United Nations and forged alliances with scores of countries to guarantee security in all major regions and to deter aggression everywhere.

4. All the just war criteria were amply satisfied in the case of the decision to use military force against Iraq.

5. The cause of freedom was advanced by the liberation of the Grenadian people from an oppressive socialist regime.

6. In August 1982, the United States joined France and Italy in a multinational force with the mission of evacuating the PLO army from Beirut.

7. Indecisive or inept use of force often results in the failure of a military operation.

8. Middle Eastern oil is important to the United States.

9. America's founders enjoined us not to go abroad in search of monsters to destroy.

10. America is clearly the object of much envy on the part of people throughout the world.

11. The just war tradition of Western culture has deep roots in both the ancient Hebraic and the classical Greek and Roman foundations of the West.

12. The overall goal of American foreign policy should be to promote the creation and survival of liberal societies.

13. It is hypocritical to intervene for ideological purposes in some conflicts but not in others.

14. The Gulf War should never have been fought.

15. Saddam Hussein was a favored U.S. ally until he demonstrated that he could not be trusted to follow U.S. directives.

Periodical Bibliography

The following articles have been selected to supplement the diverse views presented in this chapter.

James A. Baker III
"A Summons to Leadership," *U.S. Department of State Dispatch*, April 27, 1992.

Doug Bandow
"Keep the Troops and Money at Home," *Orbis*, Fall 1991. Available from Kraus Reprint and Periodicals, Route 100, Millwood, NY 10546.

Ted Galen Carpenter
"Beyond Intervention," *Reason*, October 1992.

Angelo Codevilla
"Magnificent, but Was It War?" *Commentary*, April 1992.

Lawrence Eagleburger
"Engagement vs. Withdrawal: U.S. Foreign Policy After the Cold War," *U.S. Department of State Dispatch*, October 7, 1991.

Richard Falk
"What War?" *The Nation*, February 3, 1992.

Graham E. Fuller
"The Breaking of Nations—and the Threat to Ours," *The National Interest*, Winter 1991-92. Available from Dept. NI, PO Box 3000, Denville, NJ 07834.

Janet Geovanis
"Disquiet on the American Front," *In These Times*, April 1-7, 1992.

Richard N. Haas
"One Year After the Gulf War: Prospects for Peace," *U.S. Department of State Dispatch*, April 13, 1992.

Leon Hadar
"Extricating the U.S. from Middle Eastern Entanglements," *USA Today*, September 1992.

Fred Halliday
"Looking Back Without Anger: Myths on the Left Obscure Gulf War Gains," *In These Times*, January 15-21, 1992.

George Kenney
"See No Evil, Make No Policy," *The Washington Monthly*, November 1992.

Louise Lief and Bruce Auster
"Defusing New Threats," *U.S. News & World Report*, September 21, 1992.

What Are the Effects of U.S. Foreign Aid?

AMERICAN
FOREIGN POLICY

Chapter Preface

Approximately 1 percent of the U.S. annual budget is devoted to foreign aid. In 1991, this sum amounted to just under $17 billion.

Many Americans, upon hearing this figure, react with indignation. They ask why the United States is giving money to foreigners when it has so many problems at home that could benefit from $17 billion. They often perceive foreign aid as a misplaced expression of American generosity.

The motivations behind U.S. foreign aid, however, are more complex than this. The United States provides many types of aid, for many different reasons. Although some American aid, such as the medical and food supplies sent to Armenia after its devastating 1988 earthquake, is purely humanitarian, aid may be given to further strategic, economic, or political interests as well. For example, during the cold war the United States provided military aid to nations in the Middle East, Africa, and Central America as a way to help these nations fend off communist movements. This aid was motivated by America's ideological and strategic interests.

The United States has also used aid or its withdrawal as a tool to force nations to improve their human rights records, or to effect other types of policies. For example, in 1992 the United States withheld $10 million in loan guarantees—a form of economic aid—from Israel in the hope of forcing Israel to cease building settlements in the occupied territories. (The settlements had exacerbated the already heightened tensions between Israelis and Palestinians, and the Bush administration believed that stopping the construction was a necessity if any progress toward peace was to be achieved.) Although Israel desperately needed the aid, prime minister Yitzhak Shamir refused to comply. Many believe that his unwillingness to acquiesce to U.S. demands contributed to his defeat in Israel's June 1992 election. The nations's new leader, Yitzhak Rabin, agreed to reduce the number of settlements in the territories.

Americans vary in their opinions concerning use of aid in this way. Some vehemently oppose America's manipulation of aid as a tool to influence the policies of other nations. Others, however, maintain that the United States must consider its own interests when it aids a foreign nation. Finally, some Americans oppose all aid, regardless of its motivations, believing that if the United States desires to be generous, it should first be generous with the poor and needy at home. These diverse opinions are reflected in the viewpoints presented in the following chapter.

"In addition to helping countries help themselves *through economic growth, A.I.D. directly intervenes to save lives and educate people. "*

U.S. Foreign Aid Benefits Other Nations

U.S. Agency for International Development

The U.S. Agency for International Development (U.S. AID) is the government agency that administers foreign aid programs. In the following viewpoint, U.S. AID explains how American assistance helps ease economic, political, educational, and health care problems in foreign nations. The United States has always been known for its generosity, the authors contend, and AID programs help promote this view of America throughout the world.

As you read, consider the following questions:

1. Why have Americans given aid in the past, according to the author?
2. In what specific ways has American aid helped reduce population growth throughout the world, according to U.S. AID?
3. In the author's opinion, how does U.S. foreign aid help bring stability to the world?

From *Why Foreign Aid?* by the U.S. Agency for International Development, February 1992.

Among all the nations of the world only a handful choose to give substantial amounts of their material and intellectual wealth to relatively less well-off nations. No nation has done so for as long as the United States, and none has transferred so much wealth and knowledge to less fortunate nations as we have. It is sometimes suggested that American foreign assistance has been simply an extension of the Cold War by other means and that the wellsprings of our assistance programs found their source in the containment of the Soviet Union. This view reflects a poor appreciation of American history and of the American spirit. As we ponder a new age freed from the terrors of the Cold War, we suggest that it is equally appropriate to look back over our history of moral and economic support to peoples and nations in need.

To answer the question, "Why do the American people provide assistance to foreign nations?", we must look to the intellectual and moral roots of the American republic.

Early Assistance

American independence was forged in a crucible of tolerant and generous principles that valued individual initiative and valued the institutions that permit individuals to realize their full potential. It is no accident that the young republic—when it was less than 10 years old—America sent relief assistance to refugees from oppression in Santo Domingo. America responded to the Greek struggle for independence with economic assistance in the 1820s and with food and money for the victims of famine in Ireland in the 1840s. In the first years of the 20th century, hundreds of New England's "best and brightest" volunteered to carry literacy and literature throughout the Philippine islands as part of what became known as the Thomasite movement. In 15 years they transformed the largely illiterate population into the most educated population in tropical Asia.

In the 1920s President Hoover epitomized the ability of Americans to put individuals ahead of sectarian and ideological concerns when he mounted a program to send food and relief supplies to hundreds of thousands of Russians facing starvation.

When General Marshall and President Truman agreed to undertake the largest foreign assistance program ever mounted to restart the world economy in the aftermath of World War II, they were not acting in a vacuum. They were providing leadership and vision to a nation richly endowed with a historic tradition of generosity and international concern.

The Marshall Plan and its successors over the 1950s translated into action the longstanding conviction of our nation that continued American economic and moral leadership is vital to a peaceful and prosperous world.

For the American people our investments in foreign assistance have not been seen as Machiavellian transactions in which each dollar of aid was measured against a known and certain return. Rather, Americans have provided foreign assistance in much the same spirit that they pledge some share of their personal income to their church or charity—we give our assistance with expectations akin to those that guide us to replant trees in our great American forests—with the confidence that over the long term these small investments will pay great and lasting dividends to all of us.

Aid Reflects American Values

Looking back across the span of America's last two centuries, the answer to the question about the reasons for our international assistance becomes clearer. They form part of a pattern of classical liberal values in which open and unfettered trade and intercourse among nations are understood as the mainspring of international prosperity. Americans are willing to accept as a matter of common sense the idea that our own best interests are well served in a world where nations are freed from poverty, ignorance and malnutrition.

The laws of our nation and the decisions of our Presidents have assigned the stewardship of this tradition of generous and enlightened self-interest to the U.S. Agency for International Development. We have an honorable and proud role in sustaining these historic American values and translating them into tangible actions around the world. A.I.D. is charged with bringing together the essence of American concern and American self-interest by assisting developing countries to realize their full national potential through the development of open and democratic societies and through the dynamism of free markets and individual initiative. As an agency, we give expression to the vision of the 18th century philosophers who inspired our republic with their faith in the perfectibility of the human condition as we assist nations throughout the world to improve the quality of human life and to expand the range of individual opportunities. . . .

The American Tradition of Concern and Generosity

Foreign aid is the conscious, vigorous advancement of *American values and interests*. The programs below support development of healthy, educated people—an essential ingredient in creation of markets. In most of the world, per capita income is less than $500 per year. 440 million people live in the 42 least developed countries. Their per capita income is just above $200 per year (in 1980 dollars). $200 is barely 2 percent of the income in developed countries. During the past 25 years, A.I.D. has responded to more than *1,000 disasters in more than 135 nations.* A.I.D. is still in the forefront of responding to human suffering during times of urgent need.

• In 1991, we provided $275.8 million in *humanitarian assistance* during the long-term drought in the Horn of Africa. This effort saved millions of people from sure starvation.

• In 1985, A.I.D. helped prevent more than *20 million people* in Sahelian sub-Saharan Africa from starving to death.

• We have helped the survivors of earthquakes, volcanos and storms all over the world from Armenia to Bangladesh to the Philippines to Peru.

• And on the smallest scale, the United States helped finance the opening of the Young Muslim Women's Association Furniture Factory in Jordan, which employs about 25 handicapped young women who make furniture.

The need for our assistance is still great. In addition to *helping countries help themselves* through economic growth, A.I.D. directly intervenes to save lives and educate people. In this fashion, A.I.D. also helps their economies because a healthy, educated population is necessary for economic growth.

• Since 1985, *A.I.D. has invested more than $1.1 billion* in child survival programs, resulting in dramatic increases in vaccination rates, declines in infant mortality and improved nutrition among mothers and children.

• A.I.D.-funded immunization programs and treatment of diarrheal diseases are *saving the lives of more than 3 million children* a year. In 1980, only 20 percent of the world's children were fully immunized. Today, 80 percent are.

• Infant mortality rates have declined worldwide, from 106 deaths per 1,000 live births in 1980, to 83 deaths per 1,000 live births in 1991. *In several A.I.D.-assisted countries, the percentage decline has been over 50 percent.*

• With U.S. support, four out of five of the world's children now have access to at least some aspect of modern health services. . . .

Family Planning

A.I.D. provides 45 percent of all the family planning funds in the world. High rates of population growth can have a devastating effect on economic development, the environment, available resources and the health of mothers and children.

• In 1990, well over 30 million couples used family planning as a direct result of A.I.D.'s program.

Family planning programs work: A study of the demographic impact of family planning programs finds that these programs:

• have *speeded fertility decline* in developing countries by almost 10 years, bringing fertility down to 4.2 percent in 1980-85 rather than in 1990-95, which would have been expected in the absence of organized efforts;

• have produced a *population reduction of 412 million* through 1990; and,

• will have an even more dramatic effect on fertility in the future.

Demographic successes: In the 28 countries with the largest A.I.D.-sponsored family planning programs, the average number of children per family has dropped from 6.1 in the mid-1960s to 4.2 today. . . .

Contraceptive provision: A.I.D. is the *leading donor of contraceptive supplies* for family planning programs worldwide, contributing about *75 percent* of donor-provided contraceptives. . . .

Aid to Primary Education Programs

A.I.D. educational assistance accounts for about *40 percent of all grant assistance.* Without an educated population, there can be no hope for the growth in incomes necessary to improve their own lives and to provide markets for U.S. products.

• Primary school enrollment in A.I.D.-assisted countries has increased by half and enrollment for girls has doubled.

• In El Salvador, A.I.D. built or reconstructed *400 classrooms* and provided basic furniture and supplies to *2,400 classrooms.* A.I.D. implemented a school maintenance program in *3,200 communities.* It printed *3.5 million textbooks.*

• In Guatemala, A.I.D. improved education for the neglected Mayan population. The full curriculum was implemented in *400 schools* and a pre-primary program in *400 schools.*

  • *85,000 children* are now receiving education in their native language and Spanish, and A.I.D. is working to reach another *900 schools.*

• A.I.D. constructed *classrooms for thousands* of rural Egyptian children who had no access to primary education. Female *primary school attendance has increased* by 30 percent over the last five years and male attendance by 20 percent. A.I.D. constructed *1,200 primary schools* serving more than *600,000 students* and trained more than *10,000 teachers* and technicians. . . .

Transnational Problems

There are some problems that must be addressed internationally, for example, narcotics trafficking, environmental pollution and the disease of AIDS.

Environment: Our assistance *prevents the destruction of millions of acres of tropical forest* and preserves species through programs emphasizing education, development of alternatives and collaboration with a network of international institutions.

• *Foreign assistance helps our own environment.* The practices of a slash-and-burn farmer in Brazil and a power plant operator in Poland can have a direct effect on the world in which we live and breathe.

Agency for International Development-Administered Assistance Programs

($ in thousands)	FY 1991 Actual	FY 1992 Estimate	FY 1993 Request
Development Assistance	—	1,277,000	1,265,500
Agriculture, Rural Development & Nutrition	463,063		
Population	244,253		
Health	131,897		
Child Survival Fund	97,701		
AIDS Prevention & Control	50,805		
Education & Human Resources	115,716		
Private Sector, Env. & Energy	146,074		
Science & Technology	8,624		
Deobligation/Reobligation Authority	56,574	36,000	21,500
Total: Development Assistance	1,314,707	1,313,000	1,287,000
Development Fund for Africa	800,000	800,000	775,600
Capital Projects	—	—	100,000
Other A.I.D. Activities	700,798	662,753	715,652
Economic Support Fund	4,036,491	3,240,000	3,123,000
Special Assistance Initiatives	529,675	560,000	530,000
Humanitarian Aid to Former Soviet Union	0	150,000	350,000
Demobilization & Transition Fund (Contras)	13,000	0	0
Food for Peace (PL 480)	1,230,889	1,043,681	966,500
A.I.D. Total	8,625,560	7,769,434	7,847,752

NOTE—FY 1991 Food for Peace includes 3 months of Title I activities.

• *Foreign assistance preserves the potential* for medical, agricultural and biological discoveries in the future. A.I.D. helps research institutions collect and store diverse genetic material thereby helping ensure biodiversity for future generations. . . .

U.S. Assistance Fights AIDS.

• From 8 million to 10 million people are estimated to be afflicted by AIDS. 100,000 have already died in the U.S. The World Health Organization estimates between 25 million—30 million adults will be infected with the HIV virus by the year 2000.

131

• *650 A.I.D. activities in 74 countries* help both governments and individuals respond to this epidemic through educational and technical support.

• A.I.D. has supplied more than 374 million condoms and is supporting programs to promote their use to prevent HIV infection or other sexually transmitted diseases.

• A.I.D. supports education and counseling to change behavior, including training for educators and clinic-based professionals.

• A.I.D. finances improved diagnosis and treatment of sexually transmitted diseases as a way to slow the spread of the AIDS virus.

A.I.D. Is Fighting Narcotics Trafficking

It has supported counter-narcotics efforts in Asian and Latin American countries since the mid-1970s. Helping control the supply at its source is an important part of the overall strategy to reduce the use of illegal drugs in the United States.

• The United States is providing *economic alternatives—new crops and new industries—and education* in narcotics producing countries.

• The *Andean Counter-Drug Initiative* of 1990 proposes nearly $1 billion over five years to help Bolivia, Colombia and Peru reduce their dependence on coca revenues. Sustained, vigorous law enforcement can disrupt the coca market, while A.I.D. acts to stimulate legitimate economic growth. Together, these programs make alternative economic opportunities viable. . . .

World Stability

Foreign aid creates economic and political stability—making the world safer for us and our children.

• *While communism is shattered, its debris remains toxic.* If progress is not made, reversion to totalitarianism is possible. A.I.D.'s goal in former communist nations is to foster democratic pluralism, market-oriented reforms, respect for human rights and friendly relations with the United States.

• *Economic and political stability reduce the threat of military conflict and promote economic trade for the United States.* Efforts in Eastern and Central Europe and the republics of the former Soviet Union continue what has been a long-term part of the foreign assistance program. . . .

• A.I.D. assistance has helped ensure free and fair elections in Nicaragua, El Salvador, Chile, Honduras, Paraguay, Panama, Zambia, Mali, Bulgaria, Poland, Hungary, Czechoslovakia and other emerging democracies. A.I.D. is currently working on developing a program for free elections in Cambodia.

• A.I.D. supplies training and technical assistance in such areas as legislative organization and management, the administra-

132

tion of justice and financial management systems.

• Special courts in Colombia, assisted by A.I.D., have tried over 700 drug cases, in which 60 percent of the defendants have been found guilty.

• A.I.D. supports a free press and media, "think tanks," labor unions, business organizations and other grassroots and civic organizations that are all essential to a fully functioning democracy.

A.I.D.'s Budget

Public opinion polls show that many in the general public assume that "foreign aid" makes up as much as 15 or more percent of the budget. In its broadest sense, it actually makes up just about 1 percent, and the Agency for International Development's budget is less than one-half of 1 percent of the total federal budget.

The total international relations budget request for fiscal year 1993 is $20 billion. Foreign assistance totals to $13.2 billion. The balance of the money is devoted to running the State Department including buildings and missions, programs like the Voice of America and the National Endowment for Democracy and the Export-Import Bank.

All of the components of foreign aid, add up to barely more than 1 percent. A.I.D.'s budget of over $7 billion was less than one-half of 1 percent of the total budget. By comparison, during the four years of the Marshall Plan (1948-52), the U.S. spent $13.3 billion dollars, the equivalent of about $52 billion today, and a much larger part of our GNP.

===
"The worth of development aid is not self-evident."
===

U.S. Foreign Aid Harms Other Nations

Peter Bauer and Anthony Daniels

Peter Bauer is professor emeritus of development economics at the London School of Economics, and the author of *The Development Frontier*. Anthony Daniels, a physician who worked for two years in Tanzania, is the author of *The Wilder Shores of Marx*. In the following viewpoint, Bauer and Daniels state that U.S. foreign aid props up oppressive governments and inefficient, socialist economic policies in other nations. Aid, the authors believe, creates dependence, worsens poverty, and does nothing to help nations become self-sufficient and prosperous.

As you read, consider the following questions:

1. What are the two main arguments in favor of aid, according to the authors? How do the authors refute these arguments?
2. What examples do Bauer and Daniels give to show that aid causes poverty?
3. How can the United States aid nations such as Russia, in the authors' opinion?

Peter Bauer and Anthony Daniels, "No Aid at All," *The Spectator*, September 7, 1991. Reprinted with permission.

Now that Russia has finally joined the Third World by accepting the Third World's only unifying principle, the need for and right to large subventions from the West, popular sentiment toward it has softened considerably. The Russian bear has become the Russian beggar, and who can so harden his heart as to refuse to give?

No sooner had Mr. Gorbachev been temporarily ousted from power by hard-liners, than there was speculation in the West that the "real" cause of the coup was the West's refusal to provide Mr. Gorbachev with sufficient aid. Economic conditions had deteriorated, not improved, under perestroika; the West had failed to rescue the reforms, and thereby delivered the country to the dinosaurs. The lesson drawn from the coup was that, if disaster were to be averted, there must be aid on a scale commensurate with the size of the country and its problems.

The word *aid* pre-empts sensible discussion. Who can be against giving aid to the less fortunate? Those who advocate giving aid therefore claim a monopoly of compassion; indeed, the extent of one's compassion can be measured by the amount of aid one advocates.

Alas, we live in an age of euphemism, when words have more power than ever to disguise the nature of things. Aid is not a direct charitable donation to the poor and unfortunate by the rich and fortunate; it is the subsidy of one government by another. And subsidies tend to have lamentable economic and social effects; like certain drugs, they are habit-forming.

Arguments for Aid

There are two main arguments in favor of aid, the first moral and the second prudential. Here a distinction is granted between Russia and the rest of the Third World. The case for aid to Russia is primarily prudential, while that for aid to Africa, Latin America and those parts of Asia that are not about to overtake the donor countries is primarily moral.

The moral argument, where it does not rest upon the open-ended duty of the rich to assist the poor regardless of the cause of their poverty, rests upon the premise that some countries are rich because others are poor. The rich countries play bourgeoisie to the poor countries' proletariat, extracting surplus value from them and condemning them to constant immiseration, à la Marx and Nyerere. Aid, therefore, is restitution, and the poor countries have a right to expect it.

There are so many misconceptions in that argument that only its fulfillment of some deep psychological need could explain its continued popularity among academics and the *lumpenintelligentsia*. It relies upon a clear-cut distinction between rich and poor, when in fact there is a continuum of national income and level of development among nations. (Only people fundamentally uninterested in reality could fail to notice the difference between Colombia and Chad, for example.) It ignores the fact that there are many rich people and groups in Third World countries. It does not explain how some countries have managed, in less than half a century, to move from great poverty to considerable prosperity. It ignores the fact that Latin America as a whole, despite its problems, has become very much richer, not poorer, since the 19th century. It predicts that those countries with the most trade should be the poorest, when the very opposite is palpably the case. In short, the argument is a farrago of guilt-ridden nonsense.

Little Progress

The United States Agency for International Development (AID) has for three decades administered America's foreign aid programs. Yet AID's efforts have done little to alleviate poverty in the Third World. Not surprisingly, there is widespread criticism of AID's record. Even AID itself has admitted that little, if any, economic improvement has resulted from its programs. States a 1989 AID report, entitled *Development in the National Interest*:

> All too often, dependency seems to have won out over development . . . U.S. development assistance, overall, has played a secondary role and has not always succeeded in fostering growth-oriented policies among recipient states. . . .

Demands for increased assistance funding and tied-aid overlook the fact that AID projects consistently have been poorly designed, wasteful and subject to fraud.

Bryan T. Johnson, The Heritage Foundation *Backgrounder*, May 6, 1991.

There are very few, however, who would claim that Russia's poverty, in certain respects worse and more intractable than that of Guatemala or Malaysia, is the result of an unjust world economic order. Since it is axiomatic that aid is a Good Thing, in the Sellar and Yeatman sense, the argument for giving aid to Russia is of necessity different. It is the prudential argument that unless we give aid, it will be the worse for us.

That, of course, is precisely the point Mr. Gorbachev was making when he attempted—shortly before the coup—to extort more money from the West. Essentially, Mr. Gorbachev reiterated the moral at the end of Hilaire Belloc's "Jim, Who Ran Away from His Nurse, and Was Eaten by a Lion":

. . . always keep a hold of Nurse
For fear of finding something worse.

In that alarming vision, the reactionary communist generals and party functionaries played Lion to Mr. Gorbachev's Nurse.

To the extent that famine and economic chaos in Russia might result in a Bourbon restoration, or in a massive efflux of refugees, or in a violently xenophobic regime, Mr. Gorbachev had a point. The transition from a planned to a market economy is bound to produce dislocations and hardships, including unemployment and abrupt price increases (previously disguised by over-manning and shortages). No one wants to see the Russian people, who have suffered in this century almost as no other, face yet another famine. There is, therefore, a good case for short-term donations of food and other essentials to alleviate the inevitable suffering caused by the transition. Those donations, however, should as far as possible avoid official channels, and they should be stringently conditional upon the genuine implementation of reform. On no account should they be used as a means of buying time for the old system and methods.

The provision of relief from a crisis, however, is a far cry from development aid as normally conceived. The latter is ostensibly designed to help countries whose economic problems are thought to result from a shortage of capital for investment. With regard to Russia, figures of $30 billion a year for five years have already been bruited with abandon by everyone except the people who will actually contribute the money (i.e., the taxpayers of the West). Such discussion as there is concerns only the amount of aid to be given, not the worth of aid per se, which is assumed to be, like man's right to life, liberty, and the pursuit of happiness, self-evident.

Creating Wealth

A moment's reflection, however, is sufficient to demonstrate that the worth of development aid is not self-evident. Poverty is not caused by lack of capital; if it were, men would still live in caves. Moreover, countless individuals and numerous societies have, over a few decades, become rich starting out from poverty. All that was necessary for them was incentive, inclination, and opportunity (that is to say, a lack of obstruction, especially by governmental policy). The international economic pecking order is not immutably fixed by the current presence or absence of capital; if it were, how could large parts of Asia and West Africa have moved from grinding poverty to appreciable wealth in the relatively few years from the end of the 19th century to the middle of the 20th without aid?

But even if an external source of capital *were* required for a society or country to make economic progress, the worth of intergovernmental subsidies would still not be established, for there are other sources of capital—direct private investment, for example, or commercial loans. It is commonly asserted that such sources will not fund the expensive infrastructure necessary for economic development, but that is surely to misunderstand the nature of the relation of infrastructure to the rest of the economy. No country develops by establishing an infrastructure and then finding an economic use to which to put it. In normal circumstances, the infrastructure grows organically, pari passu with the rest of the economy. The world is replete with giant infrastructural projects without economic justification, many of them financed by development aid. Such projects are not merely useless; they are harmful.

Those who advocate development aid surely have a duty to examine its practical consequences. In an increasingly psychotherapeutic cultural milieu, little distinction is drawn between doing good and feeling good, but it is as well to remember that what are small sums for rich governments may be huge sums for poor governments. It is not sufficient to assume that aid—those few billions the rich countries will not miss— can do no harm and may do some good. Casual sentimentality among the rich can devastate the poor.

The pauperizing effects of subventions to poor countries are seen in sharpest relief in Tanzania. For many years, aid has provided Tanzania with more than twice as much foreign currency as its own exports. Satire is redundant where Tanzania and its Western (notably Scandinavian and World Bank) supporters are concerned; the reality is truly Swiftian.

Subsidizing Horrors

It was aid that made possible the resettlement at gunpoint of a considerable proportion of Tanzania's rural population within two years, with many millions of poor peasants herded into villages against their will to the hosannahs of the compassionate of Uppsala, Copenhagen, and Sussex University; it was aid that paid Nyerere and his self-appointed elite to extend their ruthless control over every aspect of life in Tanzania; it was aid that built the factories that, at immense expense, not only failed to provide anything but drained the rest of the economy; it was aid that paid the deficits of the state-owned agricultural procurement corporations whose position of monopsony made it uneconomic for the peasants to grow produce for export; it was aid that allowed the gross overvaluation of the Tanzanian currency, to the great advantage of the rulers and their favored groups who had access to dollars at the official exchange rate, and to the detriment of everyone else; and it was aid and only aid, that made possible the continuation of policies for 20 years that were predictably disastrous even before they were implemented.

The solution to Tanzania's pauperization is, of course, more aid, as advocated recently by former UN Secretary-General Javier Perez de Cuellar. That neatly demonstrates the tendency of aid to reward impoverishing policies: the worse everything gets, the better for the aid agencies.

It might be argued that the effects of aid in Tanzania are peculiar to it and that elsewhere the effects have been different. But that is not so. Aid goes to and through governments and, therefore, increases the powers of patronage of politicians, civil servants, and their associates—a patronage that is at the very heart of the problem of countries ranging from Peru, where state enterprises lose the equivalent of an eighth of the annual GNP, to the Soviet Union, and from Mozambique to India. The resultant politicization of life diverts the energies and resources of people from economic activity to politicking and raises the stakes—for both winners and losers—in the struggle for power. People's economic and even physical survival comes to depend on the outcome of the political struggle and on administrative decisions.

U.S. Aid

U.S. foreign aid, in millions of dollars.

	1991	1992*	1993*
Economic and Humanitarian	4,246	4,750	5,020
Security	10,060	7,857	7,536
Multilateral Banks	1,256	1,571	1,487
International Organizations	1,184	1,567	1,642
Total Foreign Aid	16,746	15,745	15,685
Percentage of U.S. Budget	1.3%	1.1%	1.0%

*Estimated

Source: The Carnegie Endowment for International Peace.

Furthermore, aid in practice provides no worthwhile political leverage; there is no country whose government is so vile, so incompetent, so callous in its disregard of the welfare of its people, so anti-Western that it has not received aid from the West, whether bilateral or multilateral. While Syria's Hafez al-Assad was gassing the people of Hamaa and blowing up civilian aircraft, his government received large subventions ($1,736 million between 1986 and 1989). The same is true of former Ethiopian president Mengistu Haile Mariam while he was engaged in a near-genocidal war and behaved with insensate brutality

139

($2,941 million between 1986 and 1989). Burma, whose vicious military socialist government has reduced its country to the nadir of poverty, has not been starved of funds ($1,455 million between 1986 and 1989). Zaire, the fortune of whose president is said to equal the external debt, received $2,288 million in the same period. Even Saddam Hussein's Iraq, despite its military excesses and wasted oil revenues, received $139 million during those four years.

There is thus no reason to suppose that subventions will help Russia climb out of the pit of Lenin's making. If it consistently and unequivocally pursues market-orientated policies, it will be able to attract direct investment and to raise loans; if it does not, no amount of aid will rescue it. Indeed, aid might then be harmful, for it would reinforce the policies that made aid allegedly necessary in the first place.

Intergovernmental subsidies are demonstrably neither necessary nor sufficient for the creation of prosperity. It is not possible to prove conclusively that they have done, or will do, harm in every case; but they have done enough harm in enough cases to raise serious doubts about them.

Why the Support for Aid?

In the light of those doubts, it is curious to note the virtually unanimous acceptance of the benefits of aid. Such near unanimity invites inquiry as to its cause, although such speculation cannot in itself shed light on the value of aid.

In the first place, there are powerful interest groups, in both the public and the private sectors, in favor of aid. There are large bureaucracies who administer it, both at home and overseas. Jobs depend upon the continuation and, if possible, the expansion of aid. As the American professor of economics, Thomas Sowell, puts it:

> To be blunt, the poor are a goldmine. By the time they are studied, advised, experimented with and administered to, the poor have helped many a middle-class liberal to attain affluence with government money.

And since much aid is granted on condition that it be spent on goods and services from the donor's country, contractors may bid without fear of foreign competition.

Better to Be Evil Than Insignificant

But there is something deeper than mere financial interest at stake. The argument that poor countries are poor because the rich are rich satisfies the widespread craving for personal transcendence in a post-colonial and post-religious age. If Western civilization can no longer be considered the fount of all that is good in the world, it can at least be considered the fount

140

of all that is bad. For many, it may be more satisfying to be bad on a cosmic scale than to be merely insignificant.

As to Russia, it is gratifying for some to think that that great country, with its highly talented people, needs us for its redemption. But it is surely presumptuous and condescending to imagine that people who crave material progress cannot achieve it without our handouts. We would help them more by opening our markets to their produce than by turning them into our pensioners.

3

"Foreign aid is a springboard allowing Americans, American ideas, and American products to compete and thrive in a tough global marketplace."

Foreign Aid Benefits the United States

Richard Bissell

Foreign aid is an inexpensive way for America to influence the political and economic policies of developing nations, Richard Bissell argues in the following viewpoint. Bissell contends that through foreign assistance, the United States can help establish free market economies and democratic governments in developing nations. These new markets would be open to American products and services, and would consequently help strengthen America's economy. Bissell is the assistant administrator for research and development with U.S. AID, the U.S. government agency that administers foreign aid programs.

As you read, consider the following questions:

1. What does Bissell believe is America's chief national security concern?
2. How has U.S. aid to Latin America benefited the United States, according to Bissell?
3. Why does the author argue that it is now more important than ever for the United States to be actively involved in world affairs?

Richard Bissell, "Foreign Aid and the American Interest." This article appeared in the May 1992 issue of, and is reprinted with permission from, *The World & I*, a publication of The Washington Times Corporation, copyright © 1992.

As Congress begins hearings on the U.S. foreign assistance program, calls for "America First" are increasing. The isolationist chorus is a puzzling phenomenon because it comes at a time of great success for U.S. foreign policy. Our worldwide engagement during the past four decades has resulted in the global ascendance of American political and economic principles. What folly it would be for our nation to turn away from the international community now, in an atmosphere of lessened world tension—to say nothing of vindication—as the whole world looks to the United States for leadership.

Today's world is one where nations are increasingly—and irreversibly—bound together, a truly global village encircled by telephone lines and videotapes, fax machines and satellites; where once-rigid boundaries have faded and action by one nation produces consequences influencing many other nations.

Certainly, the U.S. foreign economic assistance program was part of the Cold War world. It was an instrument, sometimes as effective as arms, in confronting and containing communism in the main streets and remote corners of the world.

Now that communism has been nearly extinguished and the importance of political and ideological concerns begins to recede, a question persists in this post-Cold War world: What constitutes "American interests" and how do they join those of the developing world? The answer is twofold.

Why Foreign Aid?

First, foreign aid remains an extension of the American character; we are a compassionate people who find it morally indefensible to accept poverty, sickness, and unfulfilled human potential. In responding to natural and man-made disasters, U.S. assistance—yes, our tax dollars—has saved the lives of millions of children, promoted freedom, and prevented tens of millions of people from starving to death. America's generosity toward fellow nations is quite simply unprecedented in the history of the world. At the same time, that "generous" foreign assistance effort presently constitutes less than one-half of 1 percent of the federal budget.

Second, the transformation in the economic balance of power among nations can be considered the chief national security concern. Our nation's overall economic health is the No. 1 issue. Foreign aid is a springboard allowing Americans, American ideas, and American products to compete and thrive in a tough global marketplace. Increasingly, the job market in Massachusetts or Texas is going to be linked to economic growth in the developing world. That is where four out of five of the world's consumers will soon be living—and that is where free-market and free-government principles, based on our American model, are taking hold.

Economic considerations have always played a significant role in the diverse U.S. foreign assistance effort. After all, only economically strong nations can hold their own or build expanding markets for U.S. exports.

Free Markets and Free Governments

That is why, in recent years, the U.S. Agency for International Development (USAID) has placed special emphasis on promoting market economies and entrepreneurship, democracy and political participation.

Aid Strengthens U.S. Alliances

In 1991, the United States provided some form of foreign assistance to more than 125 countries. The top 15 recipients of U.S. foreign assistance in that year (in millions of dollars) were:

Israel	$3,650.0
Egypt	2,300.2
Turkey	804.0
Philippines	551.1
Greece	350.6
Eastern Europe	304.9
El Salvador	291.6
Nicaragua	263.6
Peru	183.7
Bolivia	182.1
Honduras	151.3
Portugal	143.6
Morocco	133.8
India	108.6
Bangladesh	107.5

Congressional Digest, August/September 1992.

Free markets and free governments have created significant payoffs to the U.S. economy. Between 1983 and 1990, for example, American exports to countries with USAID programs grew by nearly 40 percent. U.S. annual private-sector investment in the developing world has expanded to 13 times the annual USAID budget; more than half of our agricultural exports now go to the developing world, and about 40 percent of total U.S. exports end up there too—about $127 billion annually. This is more than all our exports to Western Europe and almost three times greater than our exports to Japan.

Latin America provides an ideal example: In this region, U.S. foreign assistance contributes to political and economic stability, and stability, in turn, produces a huge demand for U.S. goods and the foreign exchange necessary to buy those goods. Overall, U.S. exports to Latin America have risen consistently for the last two decades. The share of U.S. exports in relation to total exports from all countries to Latin America has risen from almost 48 percent to 68 percent. Moreover, in 1983, U.S. exports to Latin America were worth approximately $26 billion. In 1990, those exports totaled $55 billion. That means orders for American goods and services, and it means jobs for American workers.

This lesson has not been lost on other nations. Certainly, it is not, strictly speaking, humanitarianism that prompts the Japanese to pour $2 billion in foreign aid annually into Indonesia, the fourth most populous nation on earth and a mineral- and oil-rich nation. In fact, Japan's total foreign aid budget is nearly equal to our own. Germany, the United Kingdom, the Netherlands, and every other industrialized country provide hefty amounts of assistance to the developing world as well.

What USAID Offers U.S. Business

USAID is an untapped resource for American business and the U.S. economy. Its 30 years of overseas work has produced a large network of USAID personnel in the field. USAID professionals know the host country's language, culture, geography, and economy. These characteristics of foreign markets are supposed obstacles that American businesspeople understandably find daunting. Often, its work with developing countries is aimed at making the business environment hospitable to the United States.

USAID also helps U.S. business in far more subtle ways. The agency trains foreign students at U.S. universities and colleges and in U.S. businesses themselves. These trainees are an invaluable investment for America. U.S. companies that help train nationals of developing countries make valuable international business contacts. And because the participants are trained here with U.S. equipment, techniques, and business practices, the program promotes a preference and continuing international demand for U.S.-made products and services. Moreover, USAID personnel are very familiar with the political and economic leaders of more than 80 host nations, and in many cases, the agency delivers the most important commodity of all—access to the leaders.

Beyond Economics

But the American interest in building a safe and livable world involves more than promoting the ideas behind the *Federalist* papers and *The Art of the Deal*. The agency improves other areas of life linked to material progress. You cannot, for instance, have long-term economic growth in a country whose citizens are perpetually sick and hungry and unable to care for themselves. Social stability will not endure if people are uneducated. Nor will political reform take root if governments and elections are not open and fair.

Perhaps it is unfortunate—even unfair—that the international AIDS epidemic, narcotics production, and severe environmental damage in developing countries affect "American interests," but that they do is a fact of life.

Advancing American Interests

Many well-informed and well-intentioned Americans question the purpose, the size, the extent, or the character of our foreign assistance programs. Perhaps the full importance of our programs is not clearly understood, nor the modest cost we pay to achieve important benefits generally known. I would assert quite unequivocally that, dollar for dollar, our foreign assistance program is a low-cost, high-return means of advancing our national interests abroad. . . .

Seventy percent of the money appropriated for bilateral foreign assistance is spent in the United States, not abroad. American firms supply commodities, equipment, consulting services, and other expertise to foreign assistance projects, which are then exported. . . .

The economic growth of developing countries contributes to our own prosperity. American corporations that profit from exports or foreign investments depend on the stable conditions and economic growth in the Third World that foreign assistance promotes. As developing countries prosper and modernize, our trade with them increases, creating new job opportunities for our labor force. . . .

America's foreign assistance programs enhance regional security, promote economic development, encourage the growth of democratic institutions, stimulate commercial relations with the Third World, and alleviate human suffering. They help our friends and allies help us while helping themselves.

Michael H. Armacost, address before the Regional Foreign Policy Conference in Kansas City, Missouri, September 11, 1985.

There are those in the United States—some are called isolationist, others, protectionist—who don't see, or don't want to see, a world shaped by, and needing, American engagement. Nor do they understand this increased international economic competition on the horizon. Perhaps they forget that the last time the United States averted its gaze from the globe, there was world war. Worldwide depression ensued the last time this country misunderstood the interrelation of the global economy. As President Bush noted, "We invested so much to win the Cold War. We must invest what is necessary to win the peace. If we fail, we will create new and profound problems for our security and that of Europe and Asia."

Today, the United States must be involved. As Secretary of State James Baker has said: "Geographically, we stand apart from much of the world, separated by the Atlantic and Pacific. But politically, economically, and socially, there are no oceans. And in a world without oceans, a policy of isolation is no option at all. Only American engagement can shape the world we so deeply desire." Part of that engagement is a foreign assistance program benefiting the U.S. economy.

Foreign economic assistance, that one-half of 1 percent of the federal budget, was an important portion of the long, drawn-out struggles of the Cold War. Now, as America's international interests become increasingly economic in nature, foreign assistance can play an important role in advancing those interests.

> *"Foreign aid programs . . . have won us few friends, but have helped to increase the size of the national debt . . . and to strengthen foreign competition."*

Foreign Aid Harms the United States

Robert W. Lee

By assisting foreign nations, the United States depletes its own financial resources, neglects its domestic problems, and bolsters the economies of its competitors, Robert W. Lee asserts in the following viewpoint. If the United States is to remain the world's economic leader, it must invest its money at home, not abroad, Lee believes. Lee, a regular contributor to the conservative periodical *The New American*, is the author of the book *United Nations Conspiracy*.

As you read, consider the following questions:

1. Why is foreign aid so unpopular with Americans, in Lee's opinion?
2. Proponents of aid often cite four goals of U.S. assistance. Why does the author believe these goals are illogical?
3. What is the relationship between socialism and U.S. aid, in Lee's opinion?

Robert W. Lee, "International Welfare," *The New American*, March 23, 1992. Reprinted with permission.

The hundreds of billions of dollars expended on foreign aid programs over the past five decades have won us few friends, but have helped to increase the size of the national debt, to prop up socialist regimes unfriendly to the United States, and to strengthen foreign competition to American-made products. American workers can compete when the competition is fair, but the competition is hardly fair when it is subsidized by American taxpayers.

No wonder foreign aid ranks as one of the most unpopular government programs ever inflicted on the beleaguered U.S. taxpayers! A representative of the Washington-based Elections Research Center told the Senate Foreign Relations Committee in 1975 that it was "almost a bemusing fact of our political system that . . . you have been able, in the U.S. Congress, to maintain a program of foreign aid against the manifest opposition of the great majority. One might even go so far as to say . . . that was undemocratic."

An Unpopular Program

In part because of the unpopularity of the program, no foreign aid authorization bill has been enacted since 1985. Both the House and the Senate approved legislation in 1991 authorizing expenditures totaling $25 billion in fiscal years 1992 and 1993, but the House subsequently balked at the final version of this legislation, known as the conference report. As the authoritative *Congressional Quarterly* noted, the legislation "fell victim to an intense backlash against foreign aid." It was little more than politically expedient posturing, however, since both houses had a few days earlier approved a massive stop-gap appropriations bill that included among its many provisions foreign aid funding through March 31, 1992. Many of the same congressmen who voted against the foreign aid bill supported this stop-gap funding measure. And undoubtedly, many of these same congressmen will boast to their constituents that they voted against foreign aid.

The unpopularity of the foreign aid program has also delayed a $12 billion funding increase for the International Monetary Fund, according to IMF officials. As reported by the February 23, 1992 issue of the *New York Times*, "Bush Administration officials say they have urged Congress to approve the $12 billion in funding, although members of Congress say the Administration's pleas have been neither loud nor persistent. . . . Officials of the I.M.F. attribute the delay to a desire by the White House and Congress not to offend the electorate by voting billions of dollars more in foreign aid when the economy is in recession."

But the unpopularity of foreign aid has not resulted in the abolition of the program. Most Americans view foreign aid as a gigantic waste of money and have difficulty understanding why their lawmakers continue to promote it. But the architects of U.S. foreign policy have established the U.S. foreign aid program for a reason, and that reason has to do with realizing their long-sought-after goal of a new world order.

Proponents of a new world order view America's wealth, not as the exclusive property of Americans, but of the entire world. They see foreign aid as a useful tool for redistributing this wealth, taking it from the "have" countries and giving it to the "have not" countries. These new world order advocates, many of them members of the world-government-promoting Council on Foreign Relations (CFR), are not about to abandon their vision of an interdependent and socialist world. Because these Establishment Insiders have been able to influence government decision-making, they have generally gotten their way.

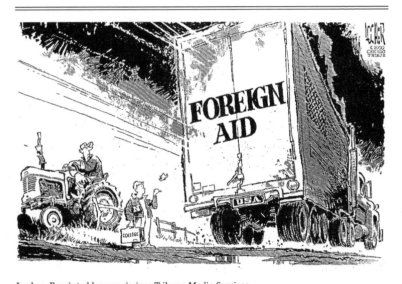

Locher. Reprinted by permission: Tribune Media Services.

In spite of strong public sentiment against the foreign aid program, the Bush administration is a big promoter of it. On January 22, 1992, for example, President Bush offered a $645 million increase in U.S. assistance to the Commonwealth of Independent States (CIS), boosting the U.S. commitment to the former Soviet Union to more than $5 billion, mostly in loans to finance the purchase of U.S. agricultural products.

Aid to Russia is being "sold" to Westerners on humanitarian grounds. Nevertheless, even though Russia has set aside—at least for the time being—socialism in its militant form (communism), it still clings to socialism in its nonmilitant form. Socialism is economic control of the people by government. So long as Russia remains socialist, our foreign aid will primarily help the government, not the people. As economist Dr. Paul Craig Roberts notes, while our "leaders want to rush aid to Russia, along with an economic reform program sponsored by the International Monetary Fund, to quickly build new bureaucratic structures to bring order out of chaos," the main result "would be to create new elites endowed with Western financial and political backing. Soon these new elites would be sewing up the system with rules and regulations that benefit them. Entrepreneurs would be hemmed in by red tape and governmental authority, and Russia would settle down into predictable stagnation, forever dependent on foreign aid.". . .

Only by abandoning socialism, and embracing genuine freedom, can the Russian people truly benefit. The freedom to produce and to keep the fruits of your labor, not more handouts, is the answer. . . .

Hidden Aid

Foreign aid is channeled through such a multitude of domestic and international organizations and projects that the average citizen finds it impossible to determine the full extent of the problem. For example, much of the money is given to countries in the form of "loans," even in cases where there is no realistic expectation of repayment. During World War II, "lend-lease" countries were loaned a total of $42 billion. Eight years after the war a mere $49 million (0.1 percent) of that amount was actually repaid. The Soviets had repaid $36 million (0.3 percent) of the $11.1 billion in lend-lease aid that they had received, when in 1975 they refused to make any more payments. More recently, we forgave Egypt's $6.7 billion debt to the United States as a means of winning their backing in the Persian Gulf crisis.

We may not have forgiven Iraq's foreign aid debt yet, but Saddam is refusing to pay and the U.S. taxpayers will likely get stuck with the tab. During fiscal years 1983 through 1990, we granted around $5 billion in agricultural export credit guarantees to Iraq. The Agriculture Department's risk analysis documents for fiscal years 1989 and 1990 rated Iraq as a high-risk market for granting substantial credit guarantees, but the credits continued to flow to Saddam Hussein's regime until August 2, 1990, when Iraq invaded Kuwait. At that point, the Commodity Credit Corporation, a U.S. government agency, had a $2 billion loan liability to Iraq.

Although the total cost of our foreign aid program cannot be determined precisely, information is still available confirming that it runs into the hundreds of billions and even trillions of dollars. According to the 1991 edition of the *Statistical Abstract of the United States,* official U.S. foreign economic and military aid programs from 1946 to 1989 totalled $358,386,000,000. In 1992, the cumulative amount since 1946 will exceed $400 billion, since we are providing assistance at the rate of about $15 billion annually.

But the actual costs are much higher than this official amount. During most of the years from 1946 to the present, the U.S. government has operated in the red. Thus, the government has had to go further in debt in order to finance the foreign aid program. When the compounding interest on the money that had to be borrowed for the giveaways is taken into account, it is likely that the actual foreign aid bill exceeds our entire federal debt of $3.5 trillion! For the years 1946 through 1980, for instance, figures compiled by the Library of Congress in 1982 pegged total foreign aid expenditures at $2.3 trillion, including $286.5 billion in principal and $2 trillion-plus in interest.

Other Forms of Aid

But even these calculations do not tell the whole story. In addition to official foreign aid programs, the U.S. government operates other programs that assist foreign countries, yet are not considered part of the foreign aid budget. U.S. participation in NATO, for example, is officially a defense program, not a foreign aid program. Yet, even though NATO was established for the stated purpose of protecting Western Europe from the Soviet threat, the practical effect of this military alliance has been to shift the burden of Western Europe's defense cost from European taxpayers to American taxpayers. This subsidy has enabled European countries to devote a larger percentage of their resources to their economies, making them more competitive in the world market. Studies indicate that about half of our entire defense budget has been spent to protect other nations.

We invested some $5 billion in buildings and other improvements in Europe after World War II. The Pentagon surveyed the situation and reported that the only thing the U.S. actually owned was a schoolhouse in Belgium. With the military preparing to cut troops in Europe by at least one-half by 1995, the lack of U.S.-owned assets means that we will not have the bargaining power such assets would provide. As one congressional aide noted, "We have title to nothing, even though since World War II we've spent about $1 trillion on the defense of Europe. The land belongs to them, and everything we built on it belongs to them. We figure we'll end up paying several billion dollars to leave" the 200 or so facilities.

Proponents of the foreign aid program have claimed at various times that foreign aid is necessary in order to oppose communism, avoid future wars, provide jobs, and raise the standards of living in other countries. But these claims could not be further from the truth.

Too Much Aid

Our first duty is to put our own country in the sort of state that it ought to be in before we get carried away by giving large financial aid anywhere else in the world. . . . I think we give too much of it away already.

George Kennan, quoted in *Conservative Chronicle*, January 31, 1990.

Certainly the Soviet Union benefitted immensely from our multi-billion-dollar lend-lease giveaway during WW II. Much of this aid was not military equipment to fight Hitler but the wherewithal to industrialize after the war, including entire industrial plants, oil refineries, railroad rolling stock, merchant ships, etc. But even during the Cold War period that followed, foreign aid programs that were sold to the American people as "anti-communist" did not hurt the communists at all, but did foster more socialism and interdependence while draining the economic lifeblood of the United States. . . .

"Peace" Pretext

The early advocates of foreign aid claimed that it would help keep us out of war. To the contrary, it has played a key role in instigating wars. Without U.S. aid, many other nations could not afford the expensive, destructive conflicts which they have been fighting. During the India-Pakistan war of the early 1960s, we supplied aid to both sides, which used U.S.-supplied weapons against each other, each side hating us for helping the other side. India moved closer to communism than she already was, while Pakistan (which was previously considered one of our staunchest friends in Asia) denounced us and snuggled up to Red China. . . .

"Freedom" Pretext

Although foreign aid advocates claim that the aid is needed to maintain freedom, it has instead fostered socialism. Because foreign aid is given to the *governments* of the recipient countries, it enables government to become more powerful. Even when governmental leaders, who benefit most from foreign aid, allow it to filter down to the people, the handouts create dependency, which in turn leads to a larger welfare state and bigger government. . . .

Foreign aid handouts to a socialist country will not benefit that country over the long term so long as socialism remains in place. Dan Smoot reminds us that our spectacular growth was made possible "because we adopted a political system which gave us freedom—freedom from our own government. . . . Our growth was achieved by private, not governmental, effort. This is the only safe and effective way for any nation to achieve industrial growth.". . .

University of London economics professor Dr. Peter Bauer, one of the world's leading authorities on the subject, has noted that foreign aid "is clearly not necessary for progress, nor is it sufficient. If the personal and social conditions of material progress (capacities, motivations, mores, and institutions) are not present, aid will be ineffective. What holds back many poor countries is the people who live there, including their governments. A society which cannot develop without external gifts is altogether unlikely to do so with them. . . . If the conditions for development other than capital are present, capital will be generated locally or supplied to governments or to business commercially from abroad. If the required conditions are not present, aid will be unproductive and therefore ineffective. Where the mainsprings of progress are present, material progress will come about without foreign aid. Where they are absent, no amount of aid will help.". . .

Does the U.S. government have a moral obligation to help other nations? Not at all! Individuals and private enterprises and charitable organizations may have a moral responsibility for international development, but there is nothing in the Constitution, in the writings of the Founding Fathers, in our historic political policy, or in the generally accepted theory of international relations, to suggest that our government (or any government for that matter) has a responsibility to develop another country. After all, the essence of sovereignty is independence, and independence is seriously undermined whenever one government undertakes responsibility for the public welfare of citizens in another.

Foreign aid is not charity from rich people to poor people. It is money extracted by government coercion from working-class Americans and sent to ruling elites. Or, as liberal former Congressman Clarence Long (D-MD) once phrased it, economic development aid "is a device for taking money from poor people in rich countries and giving it to rich people in poor countries."

"Jobs" Pretext

Advocates of foreign aid argue that the program creates and maintains jobs for Americans because (in the words of one Agency for International Development publication) "more than 70 cents of every dollar committed for goods and services is spent in the United States." It is a ludicrous contention, since a full dollar kept and spent at home in the first place would obviously do more to create employment than would the 70 cents that AID claimed comes back after being sent abroad. A transfusion from one arm to the other through a leaky tube is hardly the path to recovery. As Professor Peter Bauer notes, "To argue that aid helps our domestic economy is like saying that a shopkeeper benefits from being burgled if the burglar spends part of the loot in the victim's shop."

Often, nations which receive our aid buy goods from other nations which receive our aid, because the latter have lower production costs and selling prices, thanks to our aid. . . .

Simply stated: Foreign aid provides the means for financing the growth of socialism worldwide while levelling national economies (including our own), thereby creating the conditions necessary for imposition of a collectivist world government, euphemistically known as a "new world order." It also enables a redistribution of wealth from countries that "have" to countries that "have not," in accord with the Marxist principle, "From each according to his abilities to each according to his needs.". . .

Stop All Foreign Aid!

Opponents of foreign aid are often branded "isolationist" by internationalists. Yet, they simply favor the foreign policy followed throughout most of our history, which entails avoiding meddling in the political and military affairs of other nations, staying out of foreign wars, and allowing private citizens and enterprises maximum freedom to engage in economic transactions with other countries. . . .

It is time to elect a Congress that will bring an end to the destructive drive to drag America into a new world order by forcing it to bankroll the world. It is time to *Stop All Foreign Aid!*

Recognizing Statements That Are Provable

We are constantly confronted with statements and generalizations about social and moral problems. In order to think clearly about these problems, it is useful if one can make a basic distinction between statements for which evidence can be found and other statements that cannot be verified or proved because evidence is not available or the issue is so controversial that it cannot be definitely proved.

Readers should be aware that magazines, newspapers, and other sources often contain statements of a controversial nature. The following activity is designed to allow experimentation with statements that are provable and those that are not.

The following statements are taken from the viewpoints in this chapter. Consider each statement carefully. *Mark P for any statement you believe is provable. Mark U for any statement you feel is unprovable because of the lack of evidence. Mark C for any statement you think is too controversial to be proved to everyone's satisfaction.*

If you are doing this activity as a member of a class or group, compare your answers with those of other class or group members. Be able to defend your answers. You may discover that others come to different conclusions than you do. Listening to the reasons others present for their answers may give you valuable insights into recognizing statements that are provable.

P = *provable*
U = *unprovable*
C = *too controversial*

156

1. No nation has transferred so much wealth and knowledge to less fortunate nations as has the United States.

2. There are those in the United States who do not see, or do not want to see, a world shaped by, and needing, American engagement.

3. Family planning programs will have a dramatic effect on fertility in the future.

4. Some Third World countries have managed, in less than half a century, to move from great poverty to considerable prosperity.

5. Public opinion polls show that many in the general public assume that foreign aid makes up as much as 15 or more percent of the budget.

6. Economic chaos in Russia might result in a Bourbon restoration, or in a massive efflux of refugees, or in a violently xenophobic regime.

7. U.S. assistance has saved the lives of millions of children, promoted freedom, and prevented tens of millions of people from starving to death.

8. Foreign aid is a springboard allowing Americans, American ideas, and American products to compete and thrive in a tough global marketplace.

9. Iraq, despite its military excesses and wasted oil revenues, received $139 million in aid between 1986 and 1989.

10. During the past twenty-five years, AID has responded to more than one thousand disasters in more than 135 nations.

11. Aid in practice provides no worthwhile political leverage.

12. There are powerful interest groups, in both the public and private sectors, in favor of aid.

13. Jobs depend upon the continuation and, if possible, the expansion of aid.

14. High rates of population can have a devastating effect on economic development, the environment, available resources, and the health of mothers and children.

15. From eight million to ten million people are estimated to be afflicted by AIDS.

16. Foreign aid is the conscious, vigorous advancement of American values and interests.

17. Americans are a compassionate people who find it morally indefensible to accept poverty, sickness, and unfulfilled human potential.

18. The hundreds of billions of dollars expended on foreign aid programs have helped increase the size of the national debt.

Periodical Bibliography

The following articles have been selected to supplement the diverse views presented in this chapter.

Steve Askin
"U.S. Aid: Who Gets What—and Why," *Toward Freedom*, June/July 1991.

Richard E. Bissell
"After Foreign Aid—What?" *The Washington Quarterly*, Summer 1991. Available from MIT Press Journals, 55 Hayward St., Cambridge, MA 02142.

Cato Policy Report
"Are Third World Countries Hooked on Foreign Aid?" July/August 1991. Available from 224 Second St. SE, Washington, DC 20003.

Drew Christiansen
"Establishing Foreign Aid Priorities," *Origins*, October 24, 1991. Available from the Catholic News Service, 3211 Fourth St. NE, Washington, DC 20017-1100.

Nicholas Eberstadt
"How Not to Aid Eastern Europe," *Commentary*, November 1991.

Harvard International Review
"Foreign Aid in the 1990s," entire section on foreign aid, vol. 15, no. 1, Fall 1992. Available from the Harvard International Relations Council, PO Box 401, Cambridge, MA 02238.

Heather Hill
"The Cycle of Dependency," *Africa Report*, January/February 1992.

Paul Craig Roberts
"U.S. Foreign Aid Programs: Problem or Solution?" *New Dimensions*, February 1991. Available from 874 NE 7th St., Grants Pass, OR 97526-0069.

Peter Faesch Schaefer
"Foreign Policy: Repairing the Damage, Rethinking the Mandate, Rewriting the Law," *The American Enterprise*, November/December 1992.

John W. Sewell
"Foreign Aid for a New World Order," *The Washington Quarterly*, Summer 1991.

Laurence R. Simon
"Making Foreign Aid Work," *Tikkun*, May/June 1991.

5 CHAPTER

How Should the U.S. Deal with the Former Soviet Republics?

AMERICAN
FOREIGN POLICY

Chapter Preface

For decades the Soviet Union and the United States were enemies and American foreign policy centered on either how to contain Soviet expansion or on ensuring that U.S. defenses were more than sufficient to deter a Soviet attack.

With the collapse of the Soviet Union in 1991, American foreign policy toward the former Soviet republics is much less clear. First, the United States is no longer dealing with a single monolithic government; it must now work with fifteen separate nations, twelve of which have formed a loose confederation as the Commonwealth of Independent States. These states, which were once held together by totalitarianism, are diverse regions with distinct languages, cultures, and goals, and consequently the United States will be required to set up a new, distinct relationship with each.

Second, Americans must struggle with the concept of how to deal with a former enemy who has yet to be completely defined as an ally. While most Americans agree that it is in America's interest to foster friendship with the young republics, they disagree about how to achieve this. If assisting and befriending the emerging republics will help them build strong democracies, most believe it is clearly in America's interests to do so. But not all American leaders believe that a great deal of aid and a hand extended in friendship are the answers. These leaders favor a more cautious approach to U.S. relations with the former Soviets. As U.S. democratic senator Barbara Mikulski of Maryland states: "As a Polish-American, I have a deep distrust of the people who imposed communism on Eastern Europe and the Baltic states for two generations. . . . I cannot forget the history of the past seventy-five years. I . . . continue to regard the former Soviets with caution and skepticism."

No matter which approach U.S. leaders take in the future, they will no longer be able to rely on the policies of their predecessors. The collapse of the Soviet Union has forced the United States to completely reexamine its policies toward the region. The authors in the following chapter offer their opinions concerning what these policies should be and how they will affect the future of America's relations with the former Soviet republics.

"The U.S. must take the lead in putting together a bridge loan to help Russia make the transition from its old system to its new economy."

The U.S. Should Aid the Former Soviet Republics

Bill Clinton

Bill Clinton was elected president of the United States in November 1992. In the following viewpoint, Clinton states that U.S. economic assistance to the former Soviet republics would help these new nations form strong capitalist economies and establish democracy. Clinton believes that if the United States neglects to aid the republics, they will be unable to form stable governments and economies and will once again resort to totalitarian regimes that could threaten America.

As you read, consider the following questions:

1. How will the Information Age affect America's ability to spread democracy around the world, in Clinton's opinion?
2. How will a democratic Russia benefit the United States, according to the author?
3. What does Clinton believe Russia must do in order for it to receive U.S. aid?

From Bill Clinton, "A Strategy for Foreign Policy," speech delivered to the Foreign Policy Association, April 1, 1992.

Perhaps once in a generation, history presents us with a moment of monumental importance. In the aftermath of World War I, our country chose to retreat from the world, with tragic consequences. After World War II, we chose instead to lead the world and take responsibility for shaping the post-war era.

I am literally a child of the Cold War, born as it was just beginning. My parents' generation wanted nothing more than to return from a world war to the joys of work and home and family. Yet it was no ordinary moment, and history would not let them rest. Overnight, an expansionist Soviet Union summoned them into a new struggle. Fortunately, America had farsighted and courageous leaders like Harry Truman and George Marshall, who recognized the gravity of the moment and roused our battle-weary nation to the challenge. Under their leadership, we helped Europe and Japan rebuild their economies, organized a great military coalition of free nations, and defended our democratic principles against yet another totalitarian threat.

Now, we face our own moment of great change and enormous opportunity. The end of the Cold War and collapse of the Soviet empire pose an unprecedented opportunity to make our future more prosperous and secure.

It reminds us, too, of our duty to prevent the tragedies of the 20th Century—cataclysmic wars and the fear of nuclear annihilation—from recurring in the 21st Century. . . .

An Urgent Issue

Today I want to discuss what America must do to secure democracy's triumph around the world, and most of all, in the former Soviet empire. No national security issue is more urgent, nowhere is our country's imperative more clear. I believe it is time for America to lead a global alliance for democracy as united and steadfast as the global alliance that defeated communism.

If we don't take the lead, no one else can, and no one else will. As we proceed, we must keep in mind these realities:

First, the end of the Cold War does not mean the end of danger in the world. Even as we restructure our defenses, we must prepare for new threats.

Where might these threats arise? From armed conflict within and among the former Soviet republics, four of which have nuclear weapons. From the spread of nuclear, chemical, and biological weapons. From regional tensions on the Korean Peninsula and in the Middle East. From terrorist attacks on Americans abroad. And from the growing intensity of ethnic rivalry and separatist violence, which could spill across borders in Yugoslavia and elsewhere.

I have laid out a defense blueprint for replacing our Cold War military structure with a more flexible mix of forces better suited to the dangers we will face in the new era. We can and must substantially reduce forces originally designed to counter the Soviet threat. But the level of defense spending must be based on protecting our enduring interests and preserving our comparative advantage in training, mobility and advanced military technology. And though we will continue to reduce our nuclear arms in tandem with Russia and the other republics, we must retain a survivable nuclear force to deter any conceivable threat.

The Commander in Chief must be prepared to act, with force if necessary, when our country's interests and values are threatened, as they were in the Gulf War. I will not shrink from using military force responsibly, and I will maintain the forces we need to win, and win decisively, should that necessity arise.

An Easier Job

A second reality is that the irresistible power of ideas will shape the world in the Information Age. Television, cassette tapes and the fax machine helped ideas to pierce the Berlin Wall and bring it down. Look at the defining images of the past decade: Lech Walesa scaling the fence at the Lenin Shipyard; Vaclav Havel sounding the call for freedom at Wenceslas Square; Chinese students marching in Tienanmen Square; Nelson Mandela walking out of prison a free man; Boris Yeltsin standing defiantly atop a tank to face down the coup. These pictures speak of people willing to fight against all odds for their convictions, their freedom, and the right to control their own destiny.

This means that we are in a position to do more with less than at any time in our recent history. During the Cold War, we spent trillions to protect freedom where it was threatened. In this post Cold War era, the West can spend a fraction of that amount to nurture democracy where it never before existed.

America's challenge in this era is not to bear every burden, but to tip the balance. Only America has the global reach and influence to lead on the great issues confronting the world. . . .

Rebirth of Isolationism

The President kept America largely on the sidelines in the democratic revolution that toppled the Soviet empire and is transforming the face of world politics. Time and again, the administration sided with stability over democratic change. President Bush aligned the U.S. with Mikhail Gorbachev's efforts to prop up the stagnant and despised Soviet center, long after it was apparent that hopes for democratic reform had shifted to Boris Yeltsin and the republics. Similarly, he poured cold water on Baltic and Ukrainian aspirations for independence and still has not recognized Croatia and Slovenia despite prodding from our European allies.

By failing to offer a compelling rationale for America's continued engagement in the world, the administration has invited a new birth of isolationism on the left and the right, especially at this time of economic duress, when most Americans are properly demanding that we devote more attention and money to our needs here at home. But putting our own people first cannot mean an uncritical withdrawal from the world. That's why we need a clear statement of purpose.

America deserves better than activism without vision, prudence without purpose, and tactics without strategy. America needs leadership of vision, values and conviction. . . .

We need to respond forcefully to one of the greatest security challenges of our time, to help the people of the former Soviet bloc demilitarize their societies and build free political and economic institutions. We have a chance to engage the Russian people in the West for the first time in their history.

A Democratic Revolution

The stakes are high. The collapse of communism is not an isolated event; it's part of a worldwide march toward democracy whose outcome will shape the next century. For ourselves and for millions of people who seek to live in freedom and prosperity, this revolution must not fail.

I know it isn't popular today to call for foreign assistance of any kind. It's harder when Americans are hurting, as millions are today. But I believe it is deeply irresponsible to forgo this short-term investment in our long-term security. Being penny wise and pound foolish will cost us more in the long run in higher defense budgets and lost economic opportunities.

What does a democratic Russia mean to Americans? Lower defense spending. A reduced nuclear threat. A diminished risk of environmental disasters. Fewer arms exports and less proliferation. Access to Russia's vast resources through peaceful commerce. And, the creation of a major new market for American goods and services.

As I said at Georgetown in December 1991,

> We owe it to the people who defeated communism, the people who defeated the coup. And we owe it to ourselves. . . . Having won the Cold War, we must not now lose the peace.

Already, chaos has threatened to engulf Russia. Its old economy lies in ruins, staples remain scarce and lawless behavior is spreading. The immediate danger is not a resurgence of communism, but the emergence of an aggressively nationalistic regime that could menace the other republics and revive the old political and nuclear threats to the West.

Boris Yeltsin has embarked on a radical course of economic reform, freeing prices, selling off state properties and cutting wasteful public subsidies. Hopes for a democratic Russia ride on these efforts, which must produce positive results before economic deprivation wears down the people's patience.

I believe America needs to organize and lead a long-term western strategy of engagement for democracy. From Russia to Central Europe, from Ukraine to the Baltics, the U.S. and our allies need to speed the transition to democracy and capitalism by keeping our markets open to these countries' products, offering food and technical assistance, and helping them privatize key industries, convert military production to civilian uses, and employ weapons experts in peaceful pursuits.

Make no mistake: Our help should be strictly conditioned on

an unswerving commitment by the republics to comprehensive economic reform and on continued reductions in the former Soviet nuclear arsenal.

Russia faces two economic challenges. The short-term challenge is to stabilize the economy and stem hyperinflation, so that Russia doesn't go the way of Weimar Germany. The long-term challenge is to build a market system from the ground up—to establish private property rights, create a banking system, and modernize its antiquated capital stock, which outside the defense sector lags behind world standards.

Russia is intrinsically a rich country. What it needs is not charity but trade and investment on a massive scale. What the major financial powers can do together is help the Russians help themselves. If we do, Russia's future holds the possibility of a stronger democracy rather than a resurgent dictatorship, and a new American market rather than a new American nightmare.

We should look at this assistance not as a bail out, but a bridge loan, much as a family gets from the bank when it buys a new house before selling their old house. I propose that the U.S. must take the lead in putting together a bridge loan to help Russia make the transition from its old system to its new economy.

We must have no illusions: The West cannot guarantee Russia's prosperity. Even with our help, the future of Russia and the other republics is uncertain. But we can give President Yeltsin's reforms and Russian democracy a fighting chance.

An Economic Net

The West should establish a $6 billion fund to help stabilize the Russian ruble. Without this fund, the ruble will continue to lose its exchange value and inflation will continue to soar. America's share would be about $1 billion, in the form of a loan, not a gift. In return, Russian leaders have to agree to tough conditions. They must rein in public spending and stop excessive printing of money. A fund of this kind is like a net for acrobats. By building confidence, it reduces the chance it will ever be used.

Russia also needs to import food, medicine and the materials required to keep the economy functioning. According to the IMF, which has just endorsed Russia's economic reform program, that country needs a minimum of $12 billion in financial assistance in 1992 to do so, primarily in the form of loans. Without this, Russia faces more than a 20 percent drop in GNP in 1992—a bigger drop than America suffered in any year of the Great Depression. This assistance should be carefully aimed at those sectors where it can do the most good, and should come from the western democracies, including Japan, and perhaps also from other countries like Saudi Arabia, Kuwait, South

Korea and Taiwan. The U.S. share of these loans would be roughly 10 percent.

Finally, it is also crucial to give Russia some breathing space for servicing its external debts, at a time when it doesn't have the money to stabilize its currency or import goods.

An Affordable Investment

Let me be clear: Our nation can afford this. This is not an exorbitant price to pay for a chance to create new American markets and anchor a revitalized Russia firmly in the democratic camp. The amount of money we need is available from defense and other foreign aid savings that the end of the Cold War makes possible. If Boris Yeltsin and his economic advisers stay the course, the chances are good that Russia will be in a position to pay us back in full by the latter part of the decade. Nevertheless, passing such aid will require an act of political will by the Congress and the President, and the kind of leadership from the White House we have not previously seen.

Guiding Russia to Democracy

Now the cold war is over and the West has won, but the victory will seem hollow if the peace is lost. The fulfillment of the policy course set in the 1940s arrives not when Russia is on the brink of collapse, but when it enters the community of democratic free-market nations. The communist system has been defeated, but that is no guarantee that Russia will become a lot more liberal and a lot more democratic than it has ever been in its thousand years of history. Which is where the West must come in. The timing may not be ideal for the president, who does not want U.S. voters to see him adding to the $5.2 billion aid package already offered Russia; or for most of Europe and Japan, where recession is also biting. Nevertheless, the argument is compelling that the West must see beyond the moment and do more to assist Russia through its metamorphosis.

Bruce W. Nelan, *Time*, March 16, 1992.

I also strongly support fulfilling the commitment America has made to our share of the IMF quota increase. Of a total increase of $60 billion, our share is 19 percent, or roughly $12 billion. But we are not talking about giving the $12 billion away. It is like a line of credit in a cooperative bank, and we earn interest on it. The quota increase was voted in 1990. It was necessary to help emerging democracies in Eastern Europe. It is all the more urgent now, with Ukraine, the Baltics, and other newly independent nations whose economic fate depends on it. Every other country in the IMF has agreed to pay their share, except the U.S. Why? Because our President has not taken the lead in persuading the Congress to authorize the necessary funds. We need a President who doesn't mind taking a little flak to seize this moment in history.

At the same time, we should encourage private American investment in the former Soviet Union. The newly independent republics, after all, are rich in human and natural resources. One day, they and Eastern Europe could be lucrative markets.

Americans Must Help

But Russia needs to do more than make the transition from state socialism to free markets. Constitutional democracy must take root firmly there as well. The popular movement for Russian democracy has been held together more by anti-communism than by a clear or common understanding of how to build a democratic society. Democracy remains an abstract and theoretical notion; there is an enormous deficit of knowledge in the former Soviet Union about the texture and dynamics of a free society.

No one on earth can fill that gap better than Americans. We need to make our engagement for Russian democracy a matter for people, not just governments. We need person-to-person contacts: a Democracy Corps, as Rep. Dave McCurdy has proposed, to send Americans over there; a crash program as others have proposed to bring tens of thousands of Russians and others here to learn how free institutions work; and a strong National Endowment for Democracy to lead the way in spreading American values. Promoting democracy is not just a task for the American government. For years, labor unions, universities, and volunteer organizations in this country have nurtured the democratic revolution around the world.

Without democratic institutions and values, economic reforms will not succeed. Our nation's greatest resource is ultimately not our dollars nor our technical expertise, but our values of pluralism and enterprise and freedom and the rule of law—and our centuries of experience in making those values work. In an era of fledgling democracies, those values can be our proudest export and our most effective tool of foreign policy.

2

"We must take care of . . . our own people, who, after all, are the ones whose shirts are being offered to the peoples of the former Soviet states."

The U.S. Should Not Aid the Former Soviet Republics

Dennis DeConcini and Robert C. Byrd

U.S. senators Dennis DeConcini and Robert C. Byrd are Democrats. DeConcini represents Arizona, while Byrd represents West Virginia. In the following two-part viewpoint, DeConcini and Byrd oppose U.S. aid to the former Soviet republics. DeConcini argues that as long as Russian troops illegally occupy the Baltics, the United States should refrain from aiding Russia. Byrd believes that other nations, especially the Persian Gulf states, are in a much better position to aid the republics than is the United States. Both senators maintain that U.S. tax money should go to solve the nation's serious domestic problems.

As you read, consider the following questions:

1. What are some of the domestic problems the United States faces, according to DeConcini?
2. Why should the nations of the Persian Gulf feel grateful to the former Soviet republics, in Byrd's opinion?
3. What comparison does Byrd make between U.S. aid to the republics and aid given by Japan and Europe?

From Dennis DeConcini and Robert C. Byrd, remarks from the Senate floor debate of July 2, 1992, on S 2532, the Freedom for Russia and Emerging Eurasian Democracies and Open Markets Support Act.

I

The events that have transpired on the Eurasian continent over the past few years can easily be described as incredible. We have witnessed the fall of the Berlin Wall and the subsequent reunification of Germany. We have witnessed the end of the Warsaw Pact and the break-up of the once mighty superpower, the Soviet Union. Each of these events was considered a fantasy only a few short years ago. Now they are a reality, and it is our task to deal with them as such.

The bipartisan, five-decade-long battle against communism is over. We prevailed in our long nightmare and we stand on the threshold of a new era.

This momentous event signaled the end of a military rivalry that has lasted since before the end of World War II. The collapse of communism preceded the fall of the Soviet Union, leaving the United States as the lone victor of the Cold War. But does that make it our responsibility to provide billions of dollars to Russia? The answer, for this senator at least, is a resounding no. Before we pour more money into solving the problems abroad, we must turn our attention to the long neglected problems here at home.

A Wise Way to Spend Tax Dollars?

The Freedom Support Act is an honest attempt at tackling a difficult problem facing this Congress and President Bush. I sincerely appreciate the major effort undertaken in drafting this legislation and recognize the daunting task facing the emerging democracies in the former Soviet Union as they begin rebuilding their nations. But we as elected officials have been entrusted with the responsibility of seeing that the American tax dollar is wisely spent.

How can we honestly explain to the American public that their hard-earned tax dollars are now being sent to a country which we have called our enemy for over 40 years, when in our own country we are experiencing record unemployment, increased racial tension, skyrocketing infant mortality rates, woeful underfunding of education and a crumbling national infrastructure? To top it all off, we have record budget deficits which mortgage not only our grandchildren's future, but also the future of our grandchildren's grandchildren. If this government has the billions called for in this bill to spend abroad, then why are Americans suffering at home?

In addition to our domestic problems, there are issues within the CIS [Commonwealth of Independent States], and within the bill itself, which must be carefully considered. I am confounded that President Bush is urging this Congress and the American people to provide aid to Russia while Russian troops continue to illegally occupy the independent countries of Estonia, Latvia and Lithuania, and while Russian troops are intervening in internal disputes in Moldova in much the same manner as Serbian forces are intervening in Bosnia. The Russian government agreed to withdraw its forces from the independent Baltic states through attrition. However, in a report that I previously submitted for the [*Congressional*] *Record*, military activity is increasing, while the Russian troops are not leaving the Baltic nations. Indeed, as troops are mustered out at the end of their draft period, more troops are being rotated into these sovereign nations. I attempted to condition all but humanitarian assistance for Russia—and prevent it from being extended—until President Bush certified that significant progress toward removal of Russian or CIS troops from Estonia, Latvia and Lithuania had been achieved. My amendment was ultimately watered down by an amendment from the Foreign Relations Committee, but I will continue to oppose this package and any new aid for Russia until the Baltics are truly free. . . .

I wonder why we cannot start with a small aid program, using our current unpopular foreign aid authorities, to begin addressing this problem and, if necessary, expand the program slowly. . . . To throw money into a new, untested program will not solve the problems that new democracies face. If it is irresponsible to throw billions of dollars at domestic problems, as many of the supporters of this bill have argued, then why is it not irresponsible to throw billions of dollars at a new foreign aid program? . . .

Domestic Needs Must Be Addressed

My colleagues have made many eloquent and cogent arguments in support of this sweeping legislation. They are correct in the statement that it is in our best interests to ensure that the dramatic changes now taking place in the former Soviet Union achieve the desired end of creating free, independent, vibrant, democratic, market-oriented nations where once there existed only a monolithic, totalitarian dictatorship.

But the Freedom Support Act is overly broad and nebulous. We still are unable to determine exactly how much aid, through various government agencies and programs, will be provided for the states of the CIS.

The bill provides foreign aid to a country which illegally occupies other countries. We opposed Iraq's occupation of Kuwait. Why then do we tolerate Russia's occupation of Estonia?

The bill does not focus sufficient attention—even as amended—on the need for private sector investment and technical assistance.

Finally, the bill ignores the reality of our long-neglected domestic needs. We must first address the many problems facing our Nation before we turn our attention to more of the world's problems.

II

The Senate recently spent several days debating proposed solutions to the deficit problems confronting the United States. In the course of that discussion, we heard great floods of information detailing the fiscal woes facing the United States. Our own economic situation creates a difficult environment in which to talk about foreign aid programs, even worthy aid programs.

Thompson/Copley News Service. Reprinted with permission.

There is no doubt that Russia and the former Soviet states face severe economic problems, but we cannot ignore the fact that we have severe economic and unemployment problems right here at home. It seems to me that the Administration is always ready with a handout to foreign countries, but it turns a blind eye to the problems in our own Nation.

We don't have to go overseas to find poverty, unemployment, homelessness, or lack of hope and opportunity—those problems are epidemic in many of our Nation's urban and rural areas. I well know that in West Virginia, as in other States, people face unemployment, critical needs for basic infrastructure improvements, including better roads, bridges and sewer and water systems. The human toll of our domestic economic problems—measured in terms of education, health care, research advances and family services—may be devastating to the Nation in the long run. Clearly, it is in the best interests of the United States for democracy and stability to prevail in the former Soviet Union and throughout the world, but we simply cannot afford to bankroll the economies of foreign countries at a time when we have so many critical unmet needs within our own borders. . . .

Where Is Aid from the Persian Gulf?

It is worth exploring the contributions that ought to be made to Russia and the new independent republics by the oil-rich states of the Persian Gulf. They should be feeling grateful to the former Soviet states. After all, the Soviets were not, for the first time in decades, putting pressure on our allies in the region, and so they were not distracted from prosecuting the war with us. It is clear that a hands-off Russia is in the interests of the oil-rich Persian Gulf states. Those are states where the coffers overflow with black gold, day in and day out.

What financial resources are those states contributing to this effort? Here's the answer—nothing. This is not surprising. The Congress had to pass legislation, authored by the Appropriations Subcommittee, to hold up arms sales to Saudi Arabia, Kuwait and the United Arab Emirates until they paid their large past due balances to the United States, balances on their promised contributions for our bailing them out from Iraqi aggression. They paid, finally, but many months late, after a long, slow roll, and only after direct legislative action to buy more arms. It is not surprising, then, that we are faced again with the same situation. The American economy is on the ropes while the economies of the Persian Gulf states are doing very nicely, as usual. We are contemplating new billions in aid programs for the former Soviet Union. But those Gulf states are not contributing. What are they doing? They are considering, thinking about, sending delegations to Russia to assess the situation.

This slow roll by the Persian Gulf states is not unusual, but I don't hear anything from the White House about leadership of a coalition to gather up some of that black gold for Russian aid. It is certainly in the direct national interests of those states to put the Russian economy onto a solid footing. I am informed by the State Department that we have been trying to stimulate the interest of the Middle East states in such an effort. Apparently we have to be the stimulator, but we have not gotten their juices running very fast.

The United States should not pay for our generous spirit and our concern for suffering around the world by being played for a sucker. We have already pledged more than two and one-half times as much in total aid to the former Soviet states than has Japan. We have already pledged $6.9 billion for their assistance, while Japan has only pledged $2.7 billion. Of that, tellingly, the United States has pledged almost 23 times as much in technical assistance than has Japan. Japan has pledged a mere $5 million in technical assistance to help the former Soviet states in their transition to a market economy.

Caution Required

I am reluctant to commit the United States to a broad and generous aid program while many of the same old comrades are running today's bureaucracy in the Commonwealth of Independent States. As a Polish-American, I have a deep distrust of the people who imposed communism on Eastern Europe and the Baltic states for two generations. . . .

Before we provide new economic opportunity to the people in the former Soviet Union, we should provide a helping hand to the people at home.

In my home town of Baltimore there are 40,000 families on the waiting list for Federal housing assistance. Even in affluent Montgomery County there is a waiting list of 12,000. . . .

President Boris Yeltsin's June 1992 speech to the Congress was full of hope and promise. I was moved by it. But I cannot forget the history of the past 75 years. I urge my colleagues to continue to regard the former Soviets with caution and skepticism.

Barbara A. Mikulski, before the U.S. Senate, July 2, 1992.

The United States total in pledged aid to date, $6.9 billion, is 60 percent above the amount pledged by the European Community Commission—a group of states that also must surely have a direct and vested interest in seeing stability and democracy emerge in the former Soviet states. But the European Community Commission has pledged only $4.03 billion to help their struggling neighbors. As we debate the additional spending envisioned in this bill, we should not forget these numbers. How is it somehow so much more in our interest to help these struggling states than it is in the interest of our fellow industrialized nations? How is it somehow more in our interest to foster democracy and market reforms in the hope of creating stability and economic prosperity in the former Soviet states than it is for those nations who so recently expressed fears of having their own borders crossed by Soviet troops?

The United States should not, I believe, be digging more deeply into our own pockets than are other nations with equal interest in establishing democracy and market-based economies in the states of the former Soviet Union digging into theirs. If we give them the shirts off of our backs, we may be left shirtless ourselves. And I, for one, am not entirely confident that the rest of the world would leap to our aid any faster than they are leaping to the aid of the former Soviet states. We must not rob ourselves blind. We must take care of our own long-term economic health and our own people, who, after all, are the ones whose shirts are being offered to the peoples of the former Soviet states.

3

*"U.S. economic aid to the former Soviet republics
will increase political stability."*

U.S. Aid Will Strengthen
the Republics' Economies

James L. Hecht

James L. Hecht is the editor of the book *Rubles and Dollars:
Strategies for Doing Business in the Soviet Union*. In the following
viewpoint, Hecht states that U.S. aid to the former Soviet republics will strengthen the new nations economically and politically. The former Soviets will use the aid to make the transition
from totalitarian, centrally planned states to democratic capitalist states, he believes. Hecht maintains that U.S. aid will help
America in the long run by creating new markets and trading
partners in the republics.

As you read, consider the following questions:

1. In what three ways will aid to the republics benefit the
   United States, in the author's opinion?
2. Why does Hecht believe the U.S. government should provide
   incentives to U.S. companies doing business in the former
   republics?
3. Why may the former Soviets have difficulty learning market-
   oriented business practices, according to Hecht?

Despite critical U.S. domestic needs, Christians have a clear mandate to support aid to the former Soviet Union—or the Commonwealth of Independent States, as most of that vast land encompassing 11 time zones is now being called. But the question of how much support should be given and how that support should be provided is complex. Our government has much too little money to meet all needs, and difficult choices must be made. Smart, cost-effective programs are required. The case for aid to the former Soviet Union is strong because our own interests are deeply involved.

First, U.S. military expenditures could be greatly reduced. Most of the $300 billion a year being spent on defense has been justified on the basis of the need to counter Soviet military power. Aid to the former Soviet Union would accelerate disarmament, providing jobs and housing for persons being shifted from military to civilian activities. In addition, if economic assistance were traded for political concessions, the U.S. might be able to reduce military spending by tens of billions of dollars more.

Second, economic aid can benefit the U.S. economy as well as the new Commonwealth's. Some of the most effective aid will advance the interests of U.S. business. Many countries already use economic assistance programs to help their own economies. The billions in economic aid recently given by Germany to the Soviet Union were largely tied to benefits for German companies.

Finally, U.S. economic aid to the former Soviet republics will increase political stability. If economic decline is not countered in the Commonwealth, there may be internal fighting, environmental catastrophes, aggression against bordering countries and—although a remote possibility—resort to the use of nuclear weapons.

The Failures of a Command Economy

The desperate need for economic aid by the new republics stems from the fact that the old command economy has broken down, but a new market economy has not replaced it. Most Americans understand that the old system was bad, but only those who have studied the Soviet Union realize how absurd it was. Under the command system the central authorities in Moscow told each enterprise what to make, paid the costs of making it, and purchased all of the production. Products were then sold to consumers at prices that often bore little relation to production costs, and hence required heavy governmental subsidizing. Thus bread was sold at less than the cost of the grain used to make it.

Wages were set by the state, and when production goals were exceeded, workers were given a bonus. However, there was no managerial incentive to increase productivity or to save energy, since an enterprise did not need to make money. There also was no incentive to make a product deemed superior by the user since all product was bought by the state. As a result, virtually no Soviet enterprises are competitive with similar enterprises in the West.

Still, the command system worked to a certain extent. It allowed the Soviet Union to invest a large percentage of its gross national product in new production facilities—a larger percentage than most other nations put into economic growth. The U.S.S.R.'s well-educated work force and immense natural resources helped make up for the failings of the command system. However, when the central authorities began to lose control, the command economy disintegrated. In a country with acute shortages, enterprises were no longer willing to give their products to the state for the low prices previously paid; they would sell or trade part or all of their production to the highest bidder they could find. This meant not only empty state stores but idle factories as well, because vital raw materials or manufactured components were no longer available.

Most observers outside of the Commonwealth, and most experts and officials within it, see the long-range solution to its economic ills in the transition to a free market. However, since virtually no enterprise in the former Soviet Union can compete with any in the West, if the republics move too quickly to a market economy, widespread bankruptcies will occur. This, of course, is what happened in East Germany; almost one-third of the workers in East Germany lost their jobs, and it has a stronger industrial base than the Commonwealth. Moreover, East Germany is a relatively small country that has had special help from West Germany. The former Soviets are not so lucky. They must chart an economic course which has no precedent. No transitional program will succeed that does not involve establishing many world-class enterprises.

The Benefits of Joint Ventures

The ideal way to create competitive enterprises is through joint ventures between foreign companies and Commonwealth partners. The former Soviets might obtain the huge amounts of capital necessary in other ways, but without foreign partners they will not gain the necessary know-how. Private investment has best met this need for world-class technology and know-how as well as for capital itself, and has proved to be the engine for economic growth in both the industrial nations and developing countries.

The U.S.S.R. has permitted joint ventures with foreign partners since 1987, but few are operating. Many possible ventures fall by the wayside because of the inadequate communication and transportation systems. Moreover, most of those ventures that are feasible get stalled because a gap exists between what a U.S. company wants to gain and what the Soviets are willing to give. The Commonwealth partners fear exploitation by foreigners and do not understand the high rate of return most Western companies require for risk capital.

The Majority of Americans Support Aid to Republics

Response to the question: "Do you feel the United States should or should not help the Soviet Union in strengthening its economy?"

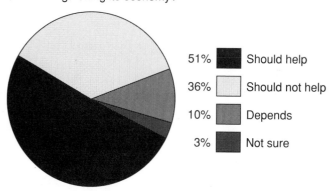

51% Should help
36% Should not help
10% Depends
3%   Not sure

Source: NBC News/*The Wall Street Journal*, August 28, 1991.

Government incentives to U.S. companies investing in the Soviet Union could bridge the gap. Incentives to encourage private investments consistent with national goals have been used successfully many times in the past. An unfortunate result of such incentives has been that corporate executives with good political connections frequently are favored. To avoid this, the incentives could be in the form of a tax rebate on U.S. earnings of between 5 and 50 percent of an approved hard-currency investment, with approvals awarded in a quarterly auction to those companies requesting the lowest percentage of U.S. government support. Thus the recipients would be determined entirely by the bidding, not by government bureaucrats. In addition, the aid would go only to projects which one judged economically viable by successful companies willing to invest their own money. Another advantage of providing the incentive as a tax rebate on profits is that it would prevent the business practice in which new companies are formed for the specific purpose of making high-risk, high-gain investments in the Commonwealth. Such companies use relatively little of their own money and, should the outcome prove unfavorable, quickly declare bankruptcy.

The incentive program outlined might appear an unnecessary handout to profitable corporations. Probably some participants could make investments which would yield acceptable levels of profitability without the incentive of a tax rebate. But on the other side, at present hardly any U.S. companies are willing to make more than token investments in the former Soviet Union. The risks are not considered worth the gains when compared to investment opportunities elsewhere. When that perception changes, the incentive program could be phased out, but until that happens, about $2 billion a year to encourage investment could change the course of history. Just as sales are used to persuade people to try a new store, an incentive program of the type described will get American business into the Commonwealth states.

Oil and Food

The chances of success will be greatly enhanced if large U.S. investments are made initially in two key sectors: oil recovery and food production. In order to be certain that this happens, it might be desirable to give investments in these two areas a 5 to 10 percent "bonus" at the beginning of the program.

The Soviet Union is the world's largest producer of oil, and while its proven reserves are less than one-half those of Saudi Arabia, many geologists believe that its huge land mass may eventually yield more oil than the Arabian desert. However, the Soviets have squandered this natural resource. It has been estimated that for every barrel of oil recovered, another barrel is either lost or will need to be obtained by an expensive secondary recovery process. American technology, know-how and investment could quickly allow the oil-rich republics to increase their exports of oil, thereby generating at least $20 billion a year in hard currency which could be invested in developing other parts of their economy. And unlike most industries in which the former Soviets cannot contribute much of real value to the capital required by the enterprise, in the case of oil they can contribute a very valuable asset—the natural resource. Bringing the Commonwealth's oil recovery up to world standards is a practical way to jump-start the rest of its economy, with the additional benefit that it will stretch out the world's dwindling supply of oil and make the U.S. and other Western countries less dependent on oil from the Middle East.

Emphasizing food production—from farm to market—is another practical way of launching the economy as well as helping to remove a potential source of political instability. As in the case of oil, the Soviets have managed food production very

badly. About 30 percent of what is actually produced rots before
it reaches the consumer. Given the natural resource of huge
acreage, including large areas of extremely fertile land, the former Soviet republics should be a major exporter of food instead
of a Commonwealth which spends much of its hard currency on
feeding its people. Because of the value of farmland, the republics can contribute capital assets of value. U.S. companies
can provide machinery for production and packaging, geneti-
cally superior seeds, and the know-how that makes the U.S. the
world's foremost producer of food products.

A Unique Challenge

We now have the opportunity, so fervently pursued for generations, to guarantee a peaceful transition to democracy. America
must respond to this challenge, as we have so many times before,
through leadership of an international coalition to secure the success of reform in Russia and the other states of the former Soviet
Union.

Richard M. Nixon, Gerald R. Ford, Jimmy Carter, Ronald Reagan, letter to the U.S.
Congress, July 1992.

A second type of aid that the U.S. can give which would be
very effective yet reasonable in cost is management training. A
market economy cannot succeed in a country where hardly anyone understands the free-enterprise system. The magnitude of
the problem is not always grasped. In an article in *Harvard
Business Review*, Jeffrey Hertzfeld, an attorney with more than
20 years' experience representing Western companies in the
Soviet Union, observed, "There probably aren't 300 Soviets out
of 300 million who know how to read a P&L [profit and loss]
statement." When Robert Schmidt, a vice-president of the
Control Data Corporation, tried to negotiate an agreement in
which the Soviets would partially pay for Control Data products
with Soviet-made greeting cards, the Soviets insisted they receive the retail price.

Addressing such problems is only part of the need. Soviet
managers have developed skills in purchasemanship but not
salesmanship. Securing supplies and services was very difficult,
but it never was necessary to sell anything. Innovation was sti-
fled by a bizarre system in which few rewards were offered for
major improvements, but careers were ruined when production
quotas were not met. Soviet managers saw little reason to decrease costs or improve quality, yet securing recreational facilities for employees might help advance a career.

In the West successful management depends on developing alternatives and then making the best choice. But since Soviet society seldom offered choices, managers educated in that environment are understandably unprepared to deal with alternatives. Clearly, Commonwealth managers are not going to function effectively in a market economy after a one-week seminar. Their unpreparedness is far greater than that of managers from the Eastern bloc countries where 40 years of communism was not enough to wipe out the precommunist business culture.

Training the Soviets

How to train these managers is a challenge. A range of programs will be needed. For some, a few lectures plus books and video cassettes will have to suffice. A four-month full-time program would be far better, and for future business leaders a two-year program would be desirable. Necessity requires providing most of this training in the Soviet Union with visiting lecturers, but we should also bring large numbers of Soviets to the U.S. to experience our business culture and our way of life. To the extent possible, those coming to the U.S. should have classroom training supplemented by internships with American companies. During the past several years a few Soviets have come to the U.S. for management training in programs of varying length and effectiveness. One of these is a three-week program coordinated by Elisa B. Miller of the University of Washington. This program includes sessions on the language of business (e.g., financial statements) and on how markets work. A very significant part of the program is TOPEXEC, a computer simulation game. Participants form executive teams which manage a business enterprise and compete with other teams running similar enterprises. TOPEXEC and all materials for the other sessions are in Russian.

Incentives for investment and training will take time to have an effect and will not help the critical problems faced by the people in the former Soviet Union. Humanitarian aid, such as delivering food and medicines to places where they are needed, must be supplied generously. This aid needs to be much more than the level required to prevent people from dying; otherwise the pain of the transition may be politically unacceptable, and the reforms that are in progress will be reversed. Immediate needs obviously must be met, but the guiding principle for the long term should be that it is far better to teach persons to fish than to feed them. Our assistance should be aimed at helping the new republics help themselves.

Longer term consequences should be carefully considered before enacting "quick-fix" solutions to economic problems in these regions. A number of economists advocating market reforms have placed a high priority on giving immediate aid in the form of a ruble stabilization fund to allow the ruble to become a convertible currency. Without question, the ruble eventually must become freely convertible, but as pointed out earlier, if this is done before the former Soviet republics have developed a base of world-class enterprises, many employers will not be able to compete unless there are barriers to imports. Also, with a freely convertible ruble there probably would need to be restrictions on the purchase by foreigners of assets in the republics; otherwise the Commonwealth will resemble a giant garage sale. Thus, while the lack of a freely convertible ruble has negatives, it may be a lesser evil than the alternatives.

Aid Is Worth the Cost

The cost of these suggested programs, somewhere between $3 and $6 billion a year for three to six years, is a lot more than most people supporting aid are willing to spend. Even with this amount of aid it would be many years before the Commonwealth's economy could approach that of the West. The republics will need to invest at least $2 trillion to do that. Yet the aid levels proposed can easily be justified. It is worth spending $10 billion on aid to save $160 billion in military spending. Moreover, after the $10 billion has been spent a couple of times, the $160 billion will be saved every year, and will be available for many of our other domestic needs.

"The economic assistance programs now under consideration in the West may not only prove to be wasteful, but may even ultimately retard reform."

U.S. Aid May Not Strengthen the Republics' Economies

Nicholas Eberstadt

Rather than strengthening nations, U.S. foreign aid often causes these nations to become dependent on America and incapable of rising out of poverty, Nicholas Eberstadt asserts in the following viewpoint. Eberstadt believes that economic aid to the Soviet republics will simply repeat this trend. Only when the republics make definite strides toward market economies should the United States provide assistance, the author concludes. Eberstadt is a researcher with the Harvard Center for Population and Development Studies in Cambridge, Massachusetts, and with the American Enterprise Institute, a Washington, D.C., think tank. He is the author of the books *The Poverty of Communism* and *Foreign Aid and American Purpose*.

As you read, consider the following questions:

1. Why does Eberstadt believe it would be foolish to stabilize the economies of the former Soviet republics?
2. What evidence does the author give to show that Russia's attempts at privatization have been weak?
3. What kind of aid should the United States give Russia, in the author's opinion?

From Nicholas Eberstadt, "A Skeptical Look at Aid to Russia," © *The National Interest*, No. 29, Fall 1992. Washington, D.C. Reprinted by permission.

If Western leaders press forward with their present plans, the principal focus for international development assistance in the 1990s promises to be the former Soviet Union. Indeed, the scale of aid now being contemplated could easily make the CIS the largest single recipient of development assistance transfers. At the Munich economic summit in July 1992, the leaders of the seven major industrial democracies ratified a $24 billion aid program—a one-year package, and for Russia alone. "Never before," noted analysts at Germany's Deutsche Bank, "has a comparable amount been made available to one single country."

Yet the initiative for Russia is merely meant to be a beginning. The managing director of the International Monetary Fund, for example, stated that the fifteen countries from the former Soviet Union will require an average of at least $25 billion a year in economic aid at least until 1996—and by implication very possibly longer. Such a sum would substantially exceed the present volume of aid for all of sub-Saharan Africa or for all of low-income Asia. In fact, a program of that size would absorb nearly half of all Western "official development assistance" (ODA) disbursement at current levels of giving.

What Are Goals of Aid?

Whether such an ambitious international aid program can actually be arranged and approved, of course, remains to be seen. But the ultimate magnitude of the West's pending bequest is by no means the only question that arises in reviewing the many plans and packages for CIS aid now under discussion. One major question can be posed bluntly: Apart from the immediate symbolism of the gesture, just what is Western "development assistance" to the former Soviet Union supposed to accomplish, and exactly how is it expected to achieve these results?

Obvious as the question may appear, it is not easily answered, for this particular aspect of the various aid initiatives in question seems to have received remarkably little consideration from prospective donor governments. The oversight in itself is revealing. And unfortunately, it is consistent with a pattern that is all too familiar.

To a disturbing degree, Western bilateral and multilateral aid agencies treat objectives and strategy as peripheral to the real business at hand. Throughout the so-called "donor community" there is a pervasive tendency to equate performance with "moving money": to judge aid not by the effectiveness with which it is spent, but simply by the *fact* that it is spent. Needless to say, this does not augur well for the impact of development assistance on recipient economies.

Examined in its particulars, the actual record of bilateral and multilateral development assistance should not inspire confidence among potential new "beneficiary" populations. In recent decades the international aid community has subsidized wasteful or even positively destructive economic policies in many countries; it has underwritten a transition to self-sustaining economic growth in very few. By comparison with most developing economies, moreover, the task of restoring economic health to the CIS states looks truly imposing. Why the "donor community" should be expected to succeed in this challenge when it has conspicuously failed in many easier tests is far from obvious. . . .

The Stabilization Myth

Russia and the other former Soviet republics are today wandering in a no-man's land between Leninist central planning and the market order. As a system, these current arrangements are inherently unstable; it is far from obvious why one should wish to "stabilize" them. In its IMF and World Bank usage, however, stabilization has a more limited focus: it refers to the objective of restoring a balance or reducing volatility in specific macroeconomic indicators, such as aggregate output, price levels, and external accounts. Traditionally, the IMF has underwritten stabilization programs that move recipients toward economic health through austerity measures (such as budget cuts, elimination of subsidies, and devaluation). Traditional stabilization policies, unfortunately, are fundamentally miscast for economies like those of the CIS. The reason is simple: economic activity in these countries is dominated by state-owned enterprises which do not behave like firms in a competitive market setting. In these post-communist societies, the macro-response to stabilization policies will be different from those evinced in a market-oriented society precisely because their macro-environments are so very different.

Poland already offers an example of what can be expected from "stabilization without privatization" in a post-communist economy. Two-and-a-half years ago, the Polish government embarked upon a bold program of "shock therapy." Prices were decontrolled, the budget was very nearly balanced, and a trade surplus was achieved. Despite strenuous stabilization efforts, however, the Polish economy has not yet been stabilized. By the IMF's reckoning, inflation in Poland in early 1992 was running at over 60 percent a year—a much more rapid pace than in Mexico or Venezuela. Though technically convertible (for transactions within Poland), the zloty has weakened almost continuously against all the major currencies, and a balance of trade deficit has emerged. Official data suggest that Poland's GNP continues its decline, and that industrial production may have fallen by nearly half since 1989.

Why has this shock therapy ushered in such disappointing results in Poland? In the main, it is because the country's vast and predominant network of state-owned enterprises was neither constrained nor motivated by the rules of the market. Accountable essentially only to themselves, the enterprises could grant themselves credit as they saw fit, thus thwarting the government's monetary policies. Similarly, they could refuse to pay their bills with impunity, thereby adding to the budgetary burden. Producing for themselves rather than their customers, they proved to be largely indifferent to the incentives and signals evoked by price decontrol. And by continuing to suck capital into money-losing activities, they effectively strangled much of the supply-response that would have been expected from Poland's competitive private sector.

Prospects for stabilization are hardly more auspicious for the CIS states than they were for Poland. To the contrary: the economic situation in the former Soviet Union is, if anything, even more thoroughly distorted. Unlike Poland, the CIS states own the farms as well as the factories. And an arrangement linking (at this writing) fourteen separate central banks and fourteen separate budgets to a single currency creates a situation in which the temptations of "beggar thy neighbor" policies may prove overwhelming. Even the comparatively modest objective of moving the ruble to the status of technical convertibility within Russia may prove elusive in the absence of a far-reaching privatization and genuine economic reform.

A Poor Investment

To throw money at the former Soviet Union as it exists now, without any statutory conditions, would give us meager results at a very high price. We should not forget that between September 1990 and January 1992, a number of industrialized countries delivered or pledged about $80 billion to Russia and its sister republics. But the return on this investment has been dismal.

John Seymour, debate before the U.S. Senate, July 2, 1992.

To be sure, under current conditions Western stabilization aid (or other sorts of balance-of-payments support) could have an immediate impact on the economies of Russia and the other CIS states. It could pay for imports from abroad. It could subsidize local consumption. It might even provide the illusion of price stability and ruble convertibility until the stabilization funds or balance-of-payments supports run out. But until and unless there is domestic and international confidence in the governments—and the economic arrangements—*behind the ruble*, neither convertibility nor stabilization can be feasible propositions. Without the sorts of measures that would lend credibility to Russia's money and her economy, stabilization aid, no matter how generously it is provided, can only postpone the ultimate hour of reckoning.

The Policy Reform Myth

The other concrete suggestions for economic aid to Russia concern subventions for policy reform. By offering the CIS governments assistance as they privatize state assets, eliminate expensive subsidies, and veer toward more liberal economic arrangements, it is argued, Western governments can help speed the transition to a market economy and reduce the attendant social pains.

In the abstract, one may wonder why it should be necessary to reward governments for desisting from demonstrably unwise economic practices, or for embracing policies that stand to improve the well being of their citizens. Such philosophical issues notwithstanding, it is far from obvious that policy reform aid for the former Soviet Union is capable of achieving its desired results.

Unlike dams, irrigation networks, or even family-planning programs, policy reform aid is not associated with a tangible "product." When such aid is extended in the form of subsidized loans—as is the common practice at the World Bank and some other institutions—these loans are contracted without identifiable collateral. In return for immediate infusions of cash into their treasuries, recipient governments simply promise to amend their current practices.

Since policy reform aid is by design not tied to any specific project, it is virtually impossible to evaluate. Indeed, judged by its own terms of reference, it is impossible to demonstrate failure for any policy reform loan or grant. After all, if conditions improve after a government accepts policy reform aid, lenders can take credit for the changes; if conditions deteriorate, lenders can argue that things would have been still worse but for their intervention. (This fact may not have escaped prospective recipients, and may help to explain why this particular type of aid is in such demand today.) But if a policy reform loan cannot be shown to fail, it is correspondingly impossible to demonstrate success.

Yet there is one indirect indicator of the efficacy of policy reforms by governments that have accepted money for this undertaking. This is the price of their debt on the "secondary market"—i.e. the amount that private purchasers are willing to pay for a given dollar of outstanding commercial debt obligations contracted by a sovereign government. The price of a government's debt on this secondary market speaks to the credibility of its policies in the eyes of those who are not directly involved in accepting or dispensing policy reform aid.

Almost all of the governments whose bonds are traded in this secondary debt market have been recipients of structural adjustment loans or other types of policy reform aid at some point during the past decade. Despite these agreements, and infusions, the overall price of secondary sovereign debt dropped drastically during the 1980s. By 1989, the unweighted average for these issues was down to barely a third of their nominal face value. (Prices have improved a bit over the past three years; some portion of this improvement, however, may be due to the stimulating effects of lower international interest rates on *all* bond markets, including this one.)

Despite the generally poor performance of sovereign debt in the secondary market, certain issues have witnessed a vigorous recovery in recent years. Mexican debt's secondary price, for example, has risen steadily since early 1989, after having fallen for years. The date of the turnaround is significant: it coincided with the assumption of power by a new president. Under the previous president, Mexico had attempted to muddle through its economic crisis with a series of pseudo-reforms. Confidence in Mexican debt issues grew only as the international business community gradually concluded that his successor was both intent on, and capable of, leading his country to economic health.

Is Boris Yeltsin willing and able to do for Russia what Carlos Salinas de Gortari has been doing for Mexico? The question is central to the efficacy of the policy reform aid pending for the CIS. What is equally apparent, unfortunately, is that the former Soviet Union suffers by comparison with contemporary Mexico in a number of significant respects.

A Long Road to Recovery

For one thing, the road to economic health is vastly longer for Russia and the other CIS states than it was for Mexico in 1989. Their economies are far more distorted, and they lack the civil-legal infrastructure which even Mexico could take for granted. For another, it is not yet clear that Russia's leadership is ready to confront the enormity of the effort that will be required to establish a competitive market economy.

To date, Russia's "privatization" program has been almost entirely talk; there has been almost no action. Despite its huge burden on society, the military industries continue their activities, the civilian government's determination to decommission or convert them notwithstanding. A host of restrictions continues to discourage international trade. High taxes and a hostile regulatory atmosphere discourage foreign entrepreneurs from risking investment in Russia. Enormous subsidies are still being granted to money-losing, state-owned enterprises.

Nor do the forensics of the reform process inspire confidence that the Russian regime is ready to take the steps necessary to make its economy viable. In the spring of 1992, when it finally seemed clear that the West would soon be granting the CIS a major aid package, the Yeltsin government did not redouble its efforts at transformation. Quite the contrary: it restricted the portfolio of the adviser perhaps most closely associated with radical reform, Yegor Gaidar; it backtracked on price decontrols; and it granted further subsidies to money-losing state ventures.

Offer Experience, Not a Bailout

To make . . . government-to-government loans today would be to make payments for the management of Russia's misery by propping up the sterile economic forces of the state.

We can do better. From the dawn of the industrial revolution to the advent of the lap-top, we have a rich reserve of experience to offer the former Soviet Union on the pitfalls, success and mysteries of democratic capitalism. So instead of blinding the Russians with bailouts, let's open their eyes to the promise of the market.

John Seymour, debate before the U.S. Senate, July 2, 1992.

Moreover, as the *New York Times* (July 13, 1992) put it, "Russia let its budget deficit and inflation rate soar in the second quarter [April-June 1992] after having slashed them in the first quarter [January-March 1992]." At this writing, Western observers guess Russia's budget is now running at about 17 percent of GNP—back up, in other words, to the level that characterized the economy in the last days of the Gorbachev era. As for monetary policy, the only firm program to date has been raising the denomination of the country's currency: a new 5,000 ruble note has just been introduced, and the word is out that a 10,000 ruble note is already being planned.

Ultimately, this reversal may prove to be akin to Lenin's *peredyshka*: a tactical retreat for "breathing space" while the government gathers strength to push its true program forward. So we may certainly hope. Yet, however events may unfold, such temporizing only underscores a simple but basic fact about aid for policy reform: depending on the disposition of the government in question, such funds may be used either for financing the reform process, or for postponing it.

The preceding review should not be taken to suggest that *all* forms of state aid to Russia and the other CIS republics would be wasteful or unwise. Humanitarian aid—temporary relief during famines or after natural disasters—has an impressive record of saving endangered lives. If a catastrophe were to strike within the CIS, Western aid could certainly help to contain its human toll and suffering.

Political aid or security assistance could also serve useful purposes. At the moment, for example, the United States is providing a program of limited aid to help dismantle outmoded Soviet nuclear warheads. And at the July 1992 economic summit in Munich, the G-7 leaders agreed to assist (both technically and financially) in the clean-up of nuclear and toxic chemical sites in the former Soviet Union. Further aid and cooperation of this general nature is easy to imagine. . . .

Differences in Aid

But humanitarian aid and security assistance, we must remember, are motivated by very different considerations—and evaluated by very different criteria from those of development assistance. Humanitarian aid reflects the Western view that life is precious and that it be protected. Political and security aid, for their part, are meant to further the international policy, and enhance the safety, of the states and citizens dispensing it. Neither form of aid needs to be justified by its prospective impact on the economic health or the pace of material advance in the recipient state.

Secretary of State James Baker calls the prospective U.S. economic assistance package for Russia "an investment in America's security now and in the future." His reluctance to describe the package as a "development assistance" effort is understandable. Unlike humanitarian aid and security assistance, development assistance must be justified on economic grounds. Until Russia's business climate is favorable, rates of return cannot be high on physical or human capital—or for that matter, on official development assistance offered by well-meaning foreign friends.

Barring changes in legal and commercial arrangements which only the Russians—and other CIS populations—can make, the economic assistance programs now under consideration in the West may not only prove to be wasteful, but may even ultimately retard reform worthy of the name.

"An investment in democracy in Russia today is better than paying trillions later for defense against her."

U.S. Aid Would Reduce Russia's Military Threat

James A. Baker

James A. Baker has served as secretary of state and chief of staff in the Bush administration. In the following viewpoint, Baker argues that American aid can help Russia establish a strong democracy and a vital economy. Baker believes that without aid, Russia and the other former Soviet republics may resort to authoritarian governments that could threaten America's security.

As you read, consider the following questions:

1. Explain what the FREEDOM Support Act will accomplish, according to Baker.
2. Why does Baker believe that Americans will be willing to aid Russia?
3. What does the author mean when he refers to the "two peace dividends"?

From James A. Baker, "From Cold War to Democratic Peace," *U.S. Department of State Dispatch*, June 29, 1992.

Nothing so defined the Cold War—or so revealed its terror—as the nuclear arms competition. Future generations will find it difficult to understand how pervasive the threat of nuclear war was, not only in our foreign policy but in our daily lives. There was always the fear—not on the surface, perhaps, but always just beneath it—that the next crisis might be the terrifying last. For my generation, that fear was there at night when we put our children to bed, and there in the morning when we read about the latest flare-up over Cuba, Berlin, or the Middle East. Americans lived at Ground Zero.

There were those who told us that we would have to accept the threat of nuclear war as a horrifying but inevitable fact of life. They said that agreements could only slow the arms race, never halt or reverse it.

But President George Bush made his first priority as Commander in Chief to reduce the threat to America and the danger to Americans. Working with a democratic Russia and the other new states of the former Soviet Union, we have pursued a comprehensive and integrated approach that in less than 10 months has radically reduced the nuclear danger:

• All tactical nuclear weapons have been consolidated in Russia;

• By 2003 and, hopefully, by the year 2000, Russia and the United States will cut our strategic nuclear weapons by two-thirds, reducing our inventories to no more than 3,500 warheads each;

• Russia and the United States will eliminate all multiple warhead land-based missiles, the most destructive and destabilizing weapons in the history of humanity;

• Byelarus, Kazakhstan, and Ukraine—still host to a fourth of Soviet strategic forces—will responsibly forswear the nuclear option and become parties to the Non-Proliferation Treaty; and

• Finally, we will put in place the most intensive and extensive verification regimes ever developed.

We have gone far in putting 40 years of fear behind us. We have moved far from Ground Zero and nuclear confrontation.

But another task has just begun: We must create a real, enduring peace with Russia and the other states of the former Soviet Union. . . .

A Democratic Peace

A democratic peace is a real and enduring peace: a peace rooted in a shared commitment to democratic government; a peace nurtured by the prosperity that only the free market can provide.

It is a peace based on the same values upon which our own great nation is founded: responsible representative government, respect for human rights, the rule of law, and private property.

The peace we hope to build with Russia and the other new and independent states is the peace that we enjoy today with Western Europe and Japan—a peace that has let us flourish as no other nations in history, attaining unprecedented peace and prosperity. It's a peace that makes even the idea of war between the United States and its allies the stuff of fantasy.

Building a democratic peace with Russia and the other new and independent states will not occur overnight. Neither did the peace we enjoy today with old enemies like Germany and Japan.

And building a democratic peace will not be easy. But neither was re-creating a world from the ruins of World War II.

Our task today—to extend democracy to Russia and the other new and independent states—is no less daunting. Our success will depend on developments there—above all, on the political and economic transformation of the states of the former Soviet Union. Only then can these nations become full members in the world's democratic community. And only then can they successfully integrate into the world economy and share in—and add to—its abundance.

President Yeltsin and other brave democrats have put their political lives—and more—on the line to achieve that transformation. They've asked not for charity but for our partnership.

The FREEDOM Support Act

The FREEDOM [Freedom for Russia and Emerging Eurasian Democracies and Open Markets] Support Act is our answer. The act directly addresses the military, political, and economic transformation of Russia, Ukraine, Kazakhstan, Byelarus, and the other new states. It supports threat reduction, defense conversion, non-proliferation, and nuclear safety. It strengthens democratization and people-to-people programs. And it encourages free markets through technical assistance, trade and investment promotion, and macroeconomic stabilization.

Let me explain the act—what it is and what it's supposed to do:

First, the FREEDOM Support Act supports freedom by bolstering reform. With the International Monetary Fund, Russia has embarked on a broad, bold program to free prices, privatize property, and create a convertible currency. President Yeltsin and other reformers are attempting to build modern, free-market economies from the ground up. Their efforts are hampered by political turmoil, economic hardship, and the simple fact that no one has ever done what they are trying to do.

Our help is no hand-out. The reformers must take the hard decisions. They must do the hard work. But we, and all who want to see this courageous experiment in freedom prevail, can help them succeed.

Second, the act will underpin America's share in an international effort—our fair share. The problems of the former Soviet Union are too huge for any one country to tackle. In January 1992, President Bush convened a coordinating conference in Washington to forge a broad coalition of more than 50 nations and international institutions to support reform in Russia, Ukraine, Kazakhstan, Armenia, and the other new and independent states. That coalition is at work today.

And this is only right. Both we and our partners will all benefit from a democratic peace. And together we must share the responsibility of helping make it a reality.

From Enemy to Ally

Russia has shed the Soviet empire, dissolved the Soviet Union, agreed to sweeping cuts in conventional and nuclear forces, reduced military spending significantly, cast off the yoke of totalitarianism, and installed a democratically elected government.

As a result, Russia no longer can be considered America's enemy. It is not yet, of course, an ally. Russia's leaders are taking a fresh look at the world, redefining Russian national security while at the same time struggling to keep their new democracy afloat. If they succeed, a new Russia can emerge. It can be a democratic Russia fully integrated into the West. If they falter, an assortment of ex-communists, ultra-nationalists, and disgruntled military officers seems ready to return Russia to the militarism of the past seventy years.

It thus is in America's interests to help Russia, the world's newest nuclear superpower, safely to make the transition from enemy to ally.

Jay P. Kosminski and Leon Aron, The Heritage Foundation *Backgrounder*, March 23, 1992.

Third, the act creates economic opportunity—there and here. The current hardship in Russia, Ukraine, Armenia, and the other new states of the former Soviet Union obscures their great economic potential. These nations straddle two continents and stretch across 11 time zones. They possess vast material and human resources, much of it still untapped. Russia and the other new states comprise one of the world's largest markets—one that today cries out for American goods, American services, American technology. Visionary American investors and traders are already on the scene doing business.

By catalyzing the private sector, the FREEDOM Support Act will help create opportunities for Russians, Ukrainians, Kazakhs, Byelarussians, for all the people of the former Soviet Union—and for Americans and American business.

Fourth, and most importantly, the act is an investment in America's security, now and in the future. There are two peace dividends. The first is financial and important. The second is human, and it is critical: The freedom from fear that we wish for all Americans.

Let there be no doubt: If Russia and the other new democracies fail, if democracy collapses and authoritarianism returns, we stand to lose both dividends. Defense budgets could rise again, and the fear we knew during the Cold War could return. We could find ourselves setting back the clock and putting forward the time when we can consign the nuclear nightmare to a memory.

In sum, the FREEDOM Support Act represents our part in a partnership for a democratic peace—and a chance to seize a historic opportunity.

A Moment of Opportunity

For decades, Soviet communism not only enslaved peoples but kept change itself captive. In the Soviet Empire and the petty tyrannies it spawned in Eastern Europe, communism froze economic and political development. Abroad, it locked the world into a dangerous contest known as the Cold War.

Now Soviet communism is gone. Change, suddenly, is everywhere we look, sweeping empires and ideologies before it, shaping a new era even as we watch.

Such moments are rare. They have occurred only twice before in this century, and they are precious. Because such moments offer us a unique opportunity to create a better world. But they do not last.

Today, we stand at such a moment. President Bush and the Administration have acted. . . . We can begin to close forever the tragic chapter of the arms fear. But, no less importantly, we can press forward with the FREEDOM Support Act to build a democratic peace. By doing so we begin to open a new chapter—a chapter of hope. . . .

Times here at home have been tough. The budget is tight, and it is an election year. There should be no wonder, then, when we hear arguments against support for Russia and the other states of the former Soviet Union. But all these arguments reduce to one excuse: America can't afford it.

To which I say: We can. Because we, as a people, are rich in the best sense of the word:

- Rich in the courage it takes to put partisanship aside to do what is right for our country;

• Rich in the common sense it requires to see that an investment in democracy in Russia today is better than paying trillions later for defense against her;

• Rich in the generosity it takes to foster abroad the very values upon which our own great nation was founded; and

• Above all, rich in the imagination it requires to seize a once-
in-a-lifetime opportunity to ensure that our children and grandchildren will never know the uncertainty and fear of another
Cold War. . . .

Learning from History

History is not something that happens to men and women, but
something that men and women make happen. . . .

After World War II . . . we seized the historic opportunity and
forged the great alliance that would fight the Cold War and finally prevail.

Today, we face a similar challenge, a similar choice. We must
act and, by acting, leave to future generations of Americans an
inheritance of hope, not a legacy of "what ifs." If we fail, history
will judge us harshly: not just the history of textbooks, but the
human history that will be read in the lives of our children and
grandchildren—a history that we today, by our decisions, have
already begun to write.

VIEWPOINT

> *"[Aid] measures . . . ignore the need to rapidly reduce the enormous threat (both internal and external) posed by the ex-Soviet military forces."*

U.S. Aid Will Not Reduce Russia's Military Threat

Christopher Cox and Jack Wheeler

The former Soviet republics, especially Russia, still possess huge armies that threaten America's security, Christopher Cox and Jack Wheeler argue in the following viewpoint. The authors maintain that aiding the republics will only help support these armies and increase the risk to the United States. Cox is a Republican member of Congress from California. Wheeler is president of the Freedom Research Foundation, a conservative think tank in Malibu, California.

As you read, consider the following questions:

1. How did the Marshall Plan fail, in the authors' opinion?
2. What criticisms do Cox and Wheeler make about IMF aid?
3. How can the United States help demobilize the former Soviet military, according to the authors?

Christopher Cox and Jack Wheeler, "The Right Way to Assist Russia," *Human Events*, April 11, 1992. Reprinted with permission.

The $24-billion U.S.-led aid program for Russia is a mistake. It is at once too much and too little. The misplaced emphasis on government-to-government giving is destined to fail, while the inattention to the enormous military threat posed by ex-Soviet military forces renders the entire approach inadequate.

Led first by former President Richard Nixon's calls for massive U.S. foreign aid to Russia's government, and given impetus by Arkansas Gov. Bill Clinton's criticism of the Bush Administration for its failure to act, the move toward a huge Western-led Russian welfare program has now become a juggernaut.

In the process, the generally correct perception of our strong American interest in Russian recovery and stability has led to the non sequitur of massive U.S. foreign aid to Russia's government.

Certainly Mr. Nixon is correct to point out that America has a strong interest in supporting the development of democracy and free enterprise in the former Soviet Union. He is even more compelling in arguing that, if chaos reigns in place of communism, the military forces of the former Soviet Union could once again pose a serious threat to our national security.

Red Army Threat

Indeed, the nightmarish vision of a renewed threat from Red Army soldiers is already becoming reality. As the rioting by Soviet soldiers at the Baikonur space center underscores, a disintegrating Soviet military poses an immediate threat not only to the region but the entire world. The fact is, the world's largest army no longer has a country. This is a sure-fire recipe for disaster.

The 300,000 Soviet soldiers in the Baltic states are refusing to leave. The Soviet 14th Army has just reconstituted itself as the armed forces of a hard-line Communist "Dneister Republic" attempting to secede from Moldavia. Soviet forces in eastern Germany are selling entire planeloads of weapons to Russian criminal gangs, and rumors are circulating of impending sales of nuclear material to a number of Third World nations.

These problems will only multiply in the coming months. We must act quickly to head off a potentially explosive situation.

How, then, can the U.S. help to eliminate this military threat and complete the transformation of the Soviet system to one of peaceful, multinational free enterprise and democracy?

The answer is certainly *not* through a multi-billion-dollar program of direct U.S. aid to the governments of Russia and the other formerly captive nations of the Soviet Empire, or multilateral financial aid through organizations such as the International Monetary Fund and the World Bank.

Such measures will do little to help establish free enterprise in place of communism, and they ignore the need to rapidly reduce the enormous threat (both internal and external) posed by the ex-Soviet military forces.

Many who advance the billion-dollar bailout approach are fond of citing the "success" of the Marshall Plan. Unfortunately, a nostalgic fog now colors our recollection of the plan. While the massive transfer of funds certainly played a role in Europe's reconstruction, it failed miserably in many respects.

For instance, Great Britain received the lion's share of Marshall Plan aid, yet remained an economic disaster throughout most of the 1950s because of the government's refusal to denationalize the economy. Far less aid flowed to Germany, which in 1948 began its ascent into the ranks of the economic elite by adopting the radical free market policies advanced by Ludwig Erhard.

The difference is staggering when one looks at the figures. According to IMF data, Britain's Gross National Product grew by 31 per cent between 1950 and 1960. Germany's increased by 129 per cent. Germany chose to make the hard choices almost overnight. The U.K. clung to outdated and inefficient Socialist policies throughout the decade.

Similarly, aid from the IMF will do little to help move the nations of the Commonwealth of Independent States (CIS) toward market economies. As they say, the proof is in the pudding, and the IMF's track record leaves much to be desired.

Most recipient nations have nothing to show from the billions showered upon them by the IMF. As Doug Bandow from the free market Cato Institute has pointed out, the countries which have been given the most IMF assistance over the past 30 years are the very nations who today top the list of the economically destitute.

Who could argue that Tanzania, Uganda, Zaire, India, or Sudan are much better off now than they were in the 1950s?

Aid Prevents Progress

The central problem with IMF aid is that it is most frequently given directly to governments which tend to be far more interested in prolonging their own rule than advancing the free market.

Thus, it is likely that IMF aid for Ukrainian President Leonid Kravchuk and Russian President Boris Yeltsin and the leaders of the other CIS nations would only postpone the hard choices—choices which are essential if their economies are to show any progress.

Until the Communist bureaucracies and infrastructure are dismantled, until commercial codes are established, until ownership of land is legalized, and until private banking and private business transactions are protected by law, granting aid would be "like pouring water into the desert," as one former Soviet official noted.

Ironically, the current push for new financial aid comes only months after it was discovered that the West's $50 billion in aid to Gorbachev had disappeared. The National Security Council's Ed Hewett states flatly that "no one is quite sure where it went." Gorbachev even admitted that he had "no idea" where his $2.9 billion in cash aid from Germany ended up.

Asay, by permission of the *Colorado Springs Gazette Telegraph*.

Not much has changed. Richard Pipes of Harvard notes that "there are no structures there ready to absorb large-scale aid. It's absolutely useless. Right now the money will just be stolen."

Instead, the nations of the West must focus on what is achievable, and what will do the most significant long-term good for our own national security: dissipating once and for all the military threat from ex-Soviet forces.

Specifically, the U.S. should lead the way to a carefully planned and supervised *demobilization* of at least 80 per cent of the Soviet, or "CIS," military. The remaining 20 per cent would be taken up by the national armed forces of the newly independent republics. This would require demobilizing approximately two million troops, some 400,000 of whom are officers.

Achieving this will require (1) providing lump-sum severance pay to the demobilized soldiers, together with (2) a "homestead" program to grant land for the construction of private homes to former troops returning to Russia and the other former captive nations.

The focus of the demobilization program should be on the officers. The 1.6 million conscripts to be demobilized were private citizens as recently as a few months or a year ago. It should be sufficient to provide them each with $100 in hard currency (*valuta*)—equal to almost a few years' pay—and return them to their homes. The cost would be $160 million.

To entice the officers—especially the senior officers—to retire will require an offer they find hard to refuse. The average salary of a junior officer in the Soviet/CIS army is 2,000 rubles per month. At a conservative exchange rate of 120 rubles to the dollar, that is $200 a year. This means a lump-sum severance payment of $2,000 is equivalent to *10 years' salary* for these officers. Double this for senior officers.

Using an average severance payment of $2,000 per officer (ranging from $500-$1,000 for NCOs, to $10,000 for generals), it would cost $800 million to provide 10 years' salary in the form of severance pay to retire 80 per cent of the Soviet/CIS officer corps.

Help from NATO

In other words, for less than $1 billion, the Soviet/CIS Armed Forces can be effectively demobilized. What's more, any money devoted to this purpose should come from all NATO countries, so that the U.S. share would be far less.

The second component of the program, however, is equally important. The reason, constantly cited, that former Soviet soldiers cannot leave eastern Germany or the Baltics is: they have no place to go, no home or apartment in which to live. Housing —or rather, the lack of it—is the central conundrum.

While Germany has found the resources to bribe the army to leave, nations such as Poland, Estonia, Latvia and Lithuania are already strapped for cash for their own reforms, let alone CIS housing projects.

U.S. Housing and Urban Development Secretary Jack Kemp urged Yeltsin to initiate a "homesteading" program in Russia.

For starters, Russia could begin such a program by offering returning troops a parcel of land as a reward for faithful service. Using the demobilization money to build new housing on their own property, the former soldiers could create real wealth and new lives for themselves.

At the same time, their arrival on the scene in large numbers would help spur the development of private construction companies, a title insurance industry, mortgage firms and the entire panoply of businesses that operate in the housing market.

By stimulating investment in the nascent private economy, the severance pay-cum-homesteading plan would yield collateral dividends that are likely to exceed all the general aid, commodity credits, and IMF and World Bank loans the West could muster.

Most importantly, however, it would precisely target a much smaller amount of American aid at our true national security objective: dismantling the awesome military threat that has been the principal reason for our $300-billion annual defense budget.

The American Example

The late Eric Hoffer wrote that "There is an American hidden in the soil of every country and the soul of every people. It is our task to help common people everywhere discover their America at home."

We should not permit the American example of free enterprise at home to be lost upon our Russian neighbors as we extend enormous new government funding to the inadvertent support of the corrupt Communist bureaucracy, much of which continues to hold the reins of power in Russia.

Nor should we fail to recognize that the purposes of American foreign aid and American security policy should be one. That is why our aim now should be to extinguish once and for all the military threat that for most of this century has terrorized not only the captive nations of the Soviet Empire, but the entire free world. In so doing, we can help make America more secure, and assist the people of Russia to discover their own America at home.

"Links between the United States and Russia can best be established in the military sphere."

The U.S. Should Form a Military Alliance with Russia

Fred Charles Iklé

For more than forty years, the United States and the Soviet Union were fierce military rivals. Now that that rivalry has ended, it is time for the two nations to become military allies, Fred Charles Iklé asserts in the following viewpoint. Iklé maintains that a military alliance would make it easier for both nations to disarm their nuclear weapons, thereby reducing the likelihood of nuclear war. In addition, the author argues that the power of a U.S.-Russian military alliance would bring peace to the world by acting as a deterrent to other nations considering war. Iklé, a distinguished scholar for the Center for Strategic and International Studies, a Washington, D.C., think tank, was undersecretary of defense for policy in the Reagan administration.

As you read, consider the following questions:

1. What were the "three chronic diseases" that caused the collapse of the Soviet Union, in Iklé's opinion?
2. What does the author believe should be the common goal of a U.S.-Russian military alliance?
3. Why would a civilian-controlled Russian military be beneficial to the world, according to the author?

From Fred Charles Iklé, "New Comrades in Arms?" *New Times*, August 1992. Reprinted with permission.

In 1991, the Union of Soviet Socialist Republics expired, and the autopsy revealed that it died of three chronic illnesses. Most visible in the last few months was its death by terminal imperialism. The world's last empire could no longer hold its independent-minded nationalities together. The second chronic illness was communism. As the world's first "socialist" state, the USSR was afflicted for over seventy years—longer than any other country—with the economic inefficiency, political stultification, and human cruelty of the communist system of government. The third cause of the USSR's demise was militarism. No other industrialized state in the world has for so long spent so much of its national wealth on armaments and military forces. Soviet militarism, in harness with communism, destroyed the Soviet economy and thus hastened the self-destruction of the Soviet Empire.

Militarism Poses Threat

Of the Soviet Union's three mortal illnesses, militarism poses the greatest danger of being passed on to the successor states; not because Russians (and Ukrainians, etc.) are a particularly militaristic people, but because militarism has become so entrenched in society. Both figuratively and literally it is cemented into the landscape.

The American-Russian military relationship, therefore, presents the greatest challenge for statesmanship. By contrast, economic relations will have much less sway, either to hurt or to help. To help, American economic assistance can play only a small role, since conditions on both sides preclude "another Marshall Plan." To hurt, economic relations are too crushingly one-sided. We need not fear the day when "Russia-bashers" in Congress accuse Russia of flooding the American market with automobiles or computers. The main economic controversy will be about Russia's debt, while lesser trade conflicts might arise as they do with Brazil, India and other nations.

Mistakes in diplomacy could bring a new Cold War only if accompanied, or followed, by moves in the military sphere—such as Russian security guarantees or arms shipments to an aggressor nation, Russian covert military assistance to terrorists or troublemakers, hints from Moscow of nuclear blackmail, or an outright attack by Russian forces on another nation.

While the military interaction between America and Russia in the coming years is pregnant with danger, paradoxically, it also offers the most promising opportunity for building a solid structure of peaceful cooperation. The new, friendly links between Washington and Moscow are still fragile, without roots in the two governments and overly dependent on changing personnel in positions of leadership. For improved relations to become enduring, they must be anchored in institutions that are endowed with steadiness, influence and continuity. On the Russian side, only the military institutions can currently meet this requirement, while the trade and financial institutions for the post-communist market economy have yet to emerge from the vortex of change.

Proposals for joint activities and common structures between the American and the Russian military establishments do not have to sail against the wind these days. President George Bush proposed to Moscow cooperation on storage, transportation, and destruction of nuclear warheads, and discussions on nuclear command and control arrangements. He also foreshadowed proposals for cooperation on early warning against ballistic missiles. Former president Mikhail Gorbachev generally endorsed these ideas and mentioned specifically creating a joint system "to avert" nuclear missile attacks. Senior members of Congress have recommended a joint program for destroying nuclear, chemical and other weapons, and US assistance on converting Soviet arms plants to civilian production. Representatives from Soviet military industries have approached American government officials and business executives for joint ventures to facilitate such conversion. Representatives from the Soviet space program are exploring cooperation with the US strategic defense initiative. And so on.

Goal: Ending Confrontation

In the present atmosphere of good will between the two militaries there is no lack of ideas for joint projects. Lacking is a sense of direction—or, more to the point, a sense of destination. Without an agreed destination, all these joint projects will merely provide occasions for good fellowship between American and Russian military people. Without institutional links animated by a common purpose, these fraternal relations offer scant protection against a new enmity. One is reminded of those yellowed photographs from around 1910, depicting German and French, Russian and Austrian generals enjoying lavish picnics together while watching through binoculars their splendidly dressed troops executing a joint manoeuvre—the better to kill each other in the First World War.

A clear and ambitious destination should guide the United States and the new Russia in shaping their military relationship. The common goal should be to eradicate the adversarial confrontation throughout the two military establishments. This endeavour will take many years, moving forward step by step through changes in the deployment of forces, their armaments, their exercises and training, and in each side's preparation for war. Great strides have already been made; most significantly, the dismantling of the military confrontation in the center of Europe and, recently, the reductions on both sides in nuclear forces that are kept on alert.

To describe the destination of the evolving military relationship as a "defense community" serves to evoke a useful analogy with the "economic communities" that began to link former enemies in Europe forty years ago, starting with the Coal and Steel Community launched in May 1950 to promote lasting reconciliation between France and Germany. The analogy, of course, must not be pushed too far; and like all enterprises that seek to shape international affairs, the attempt to create an American-Russian defense community might fail.

Strengthen U.S.-Russian Ties

During the Cold War, exchanges of military personnel and other institutional links between U.S. and Soviet military forces were little more than public relations gimmicks. With the Soviet state committed to enmity with the West, Soviet military officers in contact with American counterparts were closely watched by the KGB, and many were themselves disinformation specialists and Communist Party loyalists. Today, however, this sort of contact can have real effect. With a Russian civilian leadership predisposed toward cooperation with America and eager to democratize Russian society, there is an opportunity over time to reverse the deep institutional animosity toward America that still exists among many former Soviet officers and soldiers and to help transform the former Soviet military into a law-abiding institution under political control.

Jay P. Kosminsky and Leon Aron, The Heritage Foundation *Backgrounder*, March 23, 1992.

Failure, though, is more likely for a policy that would cling to the tried and old. Denied a constructive long-term goal, such a policy would lack the calendar to force a process of step-by-step improvement. America and Russia, in their security relationship, would sail ahead without a compass, bobbing and weaving between partnership and confrontation, anxiously focused on some quivering balance of armaments, forever undecided whether to live with each other as friend or foe.

Nuclear Treaties Established Precedent

The nuclear arsenals on both sides will provide the lever and the fulcrum to create a defense community. On nuclear arms, Washington and Moscow are accustomed to the idea of cooperation, and America's allies favor, or at least do not oppose, such cooperation. Prudent policy-makers will continue to be burdened with the threat to national survival that lurks behind the continuing "balance of terror." And from time to time, incidents will occur to stir up public anxiety about nuclear war.

The idea that some day, somehow, this latent threat of massive nuclear destruction should be "abolished" is neither new nor the brainchild only of pacifists and left-wingers. When the nuclear age was only nine years old and proliferation had not yet started, even a realist like John Foster Dulles could speak of "nuclear abolition" as at least a distant possibility. Today, in a literal sense, abolition appears to have become impossible. But the political transformation in Moscow has now opened the door to other solutions—although it may not stay open for long. While the United States and Russia cannot abolish nuclear weapons, they can overcome their nuclear confrontation; and in doing so, they will go a long way toward establishing a defense community.

Too much has been made of reducing the numbers of nuclear weapons, and not enough of the need to reduce the adversarial postures of the strategic forces on both sides. Without a fundamental change in these postures, even the most drastic reductions in the number of weapons would still leave America and Russia in a potentially mortal confrontation. Senior defense officials correctly keep reminding us that Soviet missiles could destroy our nation in thirty minutes. This would still be true if the 4,900 nuclear missile warheads permitted by START were halved or even reduced tenfold.

Toward a Community

To overcome this confrontation, both sides must abolish the hair-trigger launch procedures of their strategic forces and abandon their constant readiness to unleash nuclear cataclysm. Presidents Bush and Gorbachev have agreed to take a fraction of their missile forces off alert status, a step decidedly in the right direction. Much more can and must be done. Reductions in alert status already begun can be expanded. Both sides could implement a series of specific measures, in a coordinated fashion, that would make large-scale nuclear attack impossible—short of a clearly verifiable remobilization that would take weeks or months to carry out. The joint warning system suggested by Presidents Bush and Gorbachev would complement such measures. A welcome byproduct of reducing the readiness of strategic forces will be the added protection from civil disturbances in the former Soviet Union that might endanger deployed nuclear weapons.

Nuclear planners schooled in Cold War theories will reject as heresy a nuclear strategy that would be without its thousands of missiles, primed to retaliate instantly against an enemy first strike. The American-Russian defense community, by bringing about a wide range of military reforms, will make the abolition of the nuclear confrontation both safe and psychologically acceptable. At the end of this road, the remaining, restructured nuclear forces of the United States and Russia will coexist side by side—much like the French and British nuclear forces—without the adversarial concern about the "stability" of mutual deterrence. Are any French generals worried whether their nuclear forces are up to the task of deterring perfidious Albion from launching a first strike against France? . . .

Conventional Forces

The scope of a defense community linking America and Russia should not be confined to bilateral nuclear issues and to issues raised by the global proliferation of weapons of mass destruction. The community must also serve to develop a constructive relationship between the conventional forces of both sides. To this end, continued progress in reducing military secrecy is essential, and progress here can have mutually reinforcing benefits. If the two nations no longer see each other as potential enemies, the need for military secrecy between them could nearly vanish; and if military secrecy between them is nearly eliminated, they will have removed a key source of military tension that could cause a new enmity.

A particularly inspiring purpose of the defense community, both for Americans and for the new democratic forces in Russia, is the promotion of democratic practices and traditions for civilian control of the military. These days, such an effort will find open doors in Russia. Most of the military officers now in charge there want their nation to become a modern state with stable civilian control of the armed forces, and the political authorities in Moscow today, of course, share this objective. For the sake of the Russian people, for the sake of world peace, Russia must not become a "giant Burma"—a huge country with a backward civilian economy and a brutal, highly armed military dictatorship.

To construct meaningful institutional links in the military sphere, Washington and Moscow will have to design projects that can benefit from intensive cooperation and, at the same time, are important for the security of both sides. Some of these projects may be temporary (such as the safe disposal of nuclear weapons) and will be followed by new common tasks. Other joint missions will grow in importance and be long-lasting (such as coping with the continuing proliferation of new technologies for mass destruction).

The common military projects that, collectively, will constitute the defense community must not be confused with contrived clusters of bureaucrats, forever in search of a real purpose but always busy with organization charts and acronyms. A sense of urgency in tackling the most dangerous problems will have to be complemented by a sense for organic evolutionary growth. When the European Coal and Steel Community was created, the founders did not seek to establish a common monetary system—it will be forty years later when (and if) such a system materializes.

Enduring Benefits

As the U.S. moves into the post-Soviet era, no foreign policy or national security issue is as important as the transformation of Russia from enemy to ally. Now, as Russia prepares to build its own armed forces, the president can work closely with the Yeltsin government in assuring that the Russian defense establishment serves the cause of peace and stability. It may be, given the volatile situation in Russia, that America cannot forestall a return of militarism. But given the enduring benefits of success, for America and for Russia, the president cannot afford to offer anything less than his best shot.

Jay P. Kosminsky and Leon Aron, The Heritage Foundation *Backgrounder*, March 23, 1992.

At this time, four broad missions of the defense community can be identified. First, eliminating the adversarial confrontation of nuclear forces—above all, the hair-trigger posture of these forces. Second, gradually abolishing secrecy between the two military establishments. Third, balancing measures against proliferation with the need to respect the legitimate sovereignty and independence of all nations. Fourth, cultivating responsible civilian control of the Russian military and—in both militaries—a sense of dedication to make the community serve the interests of both nations. . . .

Military Equality

After World War II, meaningful links between France and Germany could best be established in the economic sphere; after the Cold War, links between the United States and Russia can best be established in the military sphere. Economically, Russia is a supplicant. By contrast, in a military concordat with the United States, Russia can play a global role constructively. However, the national interests that the two nations could now pursue in common through a defense community remain strictly limited. When Russia's economic relations with the outside world gain in importance, its principal partners are likely to be Germany and Japan, not the United States. It is inconceivable that the United States and Russia would ever be seized by a convergent imperialist frenzy, to form a Washington-Moscow axis for global hegemony.

The purpose of the American-Russian defense community will not only remain limited, it will remain fully supportive of the enduring national interests of America's allies. Russia and America will want to eliminate the risk of global nuclear war—the paramount interest of every nation in the Northern Hemisphere. And their new military relationship will also serve to prevent military developments between them that would either threaten America's allies or Russia's national interests and territory. These purposes cannot be achieved by some vast multilateral conglomerate, such as the CSCE or the UN.

America's Atlantic and Pacific alliances have emerged from the Cold War as viable and valued security structures for the new era, linking old allies as well as enemies that fought each other in World War II. America's and Russia's armed forces have never fought a war against each other; they fought together as allies in two world wars. Their day has come to work together for the sake of both their nations and the world at large.

"The germinating U.S. military alliance with the former Soviet Union must be examined."

The U.S. Should Not Form a Military Alliance with Russia

Robert W. Lee

In the following viewpoint, Robert W. Lee contends that U.S. and Russian leaders are conspiring to unite the two nations' militaries as part of a plan to create a world military force under the direction of the United Nations. Lee opposes such a force, believing that it would leave the United States defenseless and at the mercy of the U.N. Lee is the author of the book *United Nations Conspiracy* and a frequent contributor to the conservative periodical *The New American*.

As you read, consider the following questions:

1. Why does the author fear the coming of a "New World Order"?
2. Why does Lee disapprove of U.S.-Russian disarmament agreements?
3. What does the author believe will happen if the U.N. is given the authority to inspect nations for nuclear weapons?

Robert W. Lee, "The U.S.-Russian Military Merger," *The New American*, May 4, 1992. Reprinted with permission.

On January 31, 1992, leaders of the 15 countries that currently constitute the United Nations Security Council met at UN headquarters in New York City for the first-ever Security Council summit. Among other things, the confab pledged to expand the UN's role as world "peacekeeper" by strengthening the world body militarily. British Prime Minister John Major, at whose behest the summit was convened, told his fellow internationalists: "We should send a clear signal that it is through the U.N. and its Security Council that we intend to deal with threats to international peace and security."

The 15 leaders ratified a non-binding declaration which, among other things, asked UN Secretary-General Boutros-Ghali to submit to the Security Council recommendations for enhancing the UN's capacity for "preventive diplomacy, for peace-making and for peace-keeping," which could, as reported by Associated Press, "include creating a standing U.N. army."

Blueprint for Betrayal

It is within the context of this accelerating United Nations "peacekeeping" power, and the receding military proficiency of individual nations (including the U.S.), that the germinating U.S. military alliance with the former Soviet Union must be examined. On September 15, 1959, then-Soviet Premier Nikita Khrushchev outlined to the United Nations a three-stage program calling for the pooling of national armies under UN control. Two years later, on September 25, 1961, President John F. Kennedy presented a shockingly similar U.S. plan to the UN. Subsequently printed as State Department Publication 7277, entitled *Freedom from War: The United States Program for General and Complete Disarmament in a Peaceful World*, the scheme called for the "disbanding of all national armed forces . . . other than those required to preserve internal order and for contributions to a United Nations Peace Force" and the "elimination of national arsenals of all armaments . . . other than those required for a United Nations Peace Force and for maintaining internal order." The goal was to create a situation in which "no state would have the military power to challenge the progressively strengthened U.N. Peace Force."

On April 18, 1962, the Kennedy Administration submitted an outline for a formal treaty to a disarmament committee convened in Geneva. Entitled *Blueprint for the Peace Race*, it reiterated that parties to the treaty "would progressively strengthen the United Nations Peace Force . . . until it had sufficient armed forces and armaments so that no state could challenge it."

This scheme for creating an all-powerful United Nations, originally outlined in *Freedom from War*, remains the policy of the U.S. government. On May 11, 1982, the General Council for the

213

U.S. Arms Control and Disarmament Agency confirmed in writing to a member of Congress that "the United States has never formally withdrawn this proposal [*Blueprint for the Peace Race*]."

And on January 16, 1991, when announcing the commencement of the Persian Gulf war (in which our participation was predicated on UN directives and guidelines), President George Bush asserted that in the war's wake would follow "a real chance at this new world order, an order in which a credible United Nations can use its peacekeeping role to fulfill the promise and vision of the UN's founders." He further stated that "out of the horror of combat will come the recognition that no nation can stand against a world united."

Remember Katanga

During its first 42 years, the UN instigated only 13 "peacekeeping" operations, perhaps the most memorable of which was its bloody war of aggression against the anti-communist Congolese province of Katanga in the early 1960s. From 1988 to 1992, it intervened in eight other troublespots, in one instance (Cambodia) seizing complete control of a country. As syndicated columnist Samuel Francis has suggested, "If you're going to have a New World Order, you'd also better get a New World police force to keep it orderly." The reality, he warns, "is the construction of an army under U.N. control that can force sovereign nations and their citizens to do what the United Nations (or whoever runs it) wants them to do."

Once the UN globalists have their standing army, Francis points out, "they can strangle nationalism in its cradle and keep their own transnational, bureaucratic empires on permanent life-support. Since the United Nations has no population, revenues or territory, it can muster the New World army only from the taxes and citizens of its member states, which means that Americans in particular may soon be paying for and fighting in wars that have nothing to do with them and their interests."

The Spring 1991 issue of *Foreign Affairs*, the influential quarterly of the Council on Foreign Relations (CFR), included an important article entitled, "The U.N. in a New World Order," by Bruce Russett (Dean Acheson Professor of International Relations and Political Science at Yale University) and James S. Sutterlin (former director of the Executive Office of the UN Secretary-General). The "new world order" envisioned by President Bush and then-Soviet President Mikhail Gorbachev, the authors agree, entails "the possibility of military enforcement measures by the United Nations." Indeed, the Gulf war was the vehicle by which the Security Council demonstrated "that it has the capacity to initiate collective measures essential for the maintenance of peace in a new world order."

The article concludes with a call for a permanent UN capability to carry out its "peacekeeping" functions, with the Security Council given authority "to mobilize a force to serve under U.N. command for enforcement purposes. That capacity may be virtually indispensable in an emergent world order. The chance to achieve it should not be missed."

Comrades at Harvard

In addition to its many other pro-UN facets, the Gulf war served as the excuse to have U.S. and Soviet soldiers work side-by-side as UN "peacekeepers." In one instance, a Soviet officer was assigned to train and send U.S. soldiers into the field.

Once the war was over, the April 9, 1991 *Los Angeles Times* reported that the U.S. Defense Department was "struggling to cast aside more than four decades of suspicion" by "exploring ways to help the Soviet Union and the newly independent Baltic countries by offering technical and organizational advice to their armed forces." On September 10, 1991, the Associated Press reported that "Soviet defense officials have begun restructuring their nation's military, not under the gold domes of the Kremlin but inside the red brick walls of Harvard University." AP asserted that 28 "Soviet colonels, generals and admirals will be lectured by the likes of U.S. Joint Chiefs of Staff Chairman Colin Powell [CFR] and Gen. John Galvin [CFR], supreme Allied commander in Europe."

One week later, the *New York Times* reported that "the Defense Department is considering giving technical and organizational help to Moscow's armed forces and those of the newly independent Baltic countries." The *Times* revealed, "Senior American and Soviet officers have regularly exchanged visits since 1989," and that Secretary of Defense Dick Cheney (CFR) had invited his Soviet counterpart to visit Washington, while Joint Chiefs of Staff Chairman General Colin Powell had written his counterpart "to reaffirm the United States' commitment to the military exchanges." During the year, the Pentagon had spent about $1 million to sponsor 30 officials from Poland, Czechoslovakia, and Hungary to "attend American military colleges to study English and learn how to make their armies conform to those under reliable civilian leadership."

Brain Drain

During the January UN summit, Russian President Boris Yeltsin asserted that he "considers the U.S. and the West not as mere partners but rather as allies." He reiterated a proposal that he had made in December of 1991 that Russia and the U.S. collaborate to create a global antimissile shield similar to the Strategic Defense Initiative (SDI) that could, among other things, provide work for Russia's unemployed nuclear scientists to preclude their "drifting abroad and spreading dangerous technologies.". . .

Star Wars Secrets

At the conclusion of the UN summit, Boris Yeltsin attended a private dinner at the Federal Reserve Bank of New York, where he met with some 80 representatives of U.S. government, business, and banking, including Federal Reserve Board Chairman Alan Greenspan (CFR) and Treasury Secretary Nicholas F. Brady (CFR). Among other things, he called for an end to U.S. restrictions on technology transfers to Russia.

On February 18th, 1992, Russia and the U.S. announced that they would indeed cooperate on an SDI-type ballistic missile defensive system, beginning with a joint center to monitor ballistic missile launches worldwide. U.S. officials described the joint center agreement as "the first move to create a precedent for defense cooperation," and traced the genesis of the proposed warning system to former President Ronald Reagan's statements about sharing missile defenses and technology with the Soviets.

A U.S.-Russian Partnership

George Bush and Mikhail Gorbachev wanted the UN to assume responsibility not only for keeping UN-style peace internationally, but for using UN force within the borders of nations. And the wielder of this force in our part of the world will be a Russian socialist who, like Gorbachev, was a communist only yesterday.

The United Nations remains a growing threat to national sovereignty and personal freedom. . . . The new world order isn't something we might have to worry about in 50 years. It's being built right before our eyes—today.

John F. McManus, *The New American*, June 15, 1992.

One U.S. official asserted that, while the center would integrate and display information from existing early warning radars and satellites, it was possible that the two countries would jointly develop new devices. Secretary of State James Baker said that other members of the Commonwealth of Independent States, and also members of NATO, could join the center, along with any other nations "that would want to participate in a responsible way." Details of the proposed center were not made available, but they reportedly could include electronic data links, paper-sharing, and joint space operations.

Secretary Baker told Yeltsin that the U.S. would help Russia build a depot to store plutonium and uranium removed from nuclear weapons. U.S. experts had been skeptical about the plan, but a senior official was quoted as saying that Baker had discussed with Yeltsin "how we can cooperate with them in the construction of a facility and paying a lot of the costs." According to the official, the U.S. was willing to help turn the nuclear material into fuel for atomic power stations.

It was also revealed that the U.S. would provide Russia with 25 railroad cars designed to safely transport nuclear weapons, as well as 250 large containers to hold nuclear weapons during transit, and sundry other containers for nuclear weapons parts. Following a three-hour meeting in Moscow, Secretary of State Baker and President Yeltsin further announced that, to give the Soviet nuclear scientists something to do other than build atomic weapons for Third World countries, Russia, the United States, and Germany would create an international center to put them to work solving global problems. The center, which is to be situated in Moscow, will cost U.S. taxpayers at least $25 million. . . .

Russian Spying

On February 1st, 1992, Presidents Bush and Yeltsin chatted for over three hours during an informal "summit" at the presidential retreat at Camp David, Maryland. The two leaders signed a joint declaration asserting, among other things, that "Russia and the United States do not regard each other as potential adversaries. From now on, the relationship will be characterized by friendship and partnership founded on mutual trust and respect and a common commitment to democracy and economic freedom."

Nonetheless, in testimony to the House Foreign Affairs Committee on February 25th, CIA Director Robert Gates revealed that the old Soviet Union is continuing to produce and deploy new strategic missile systems. He also asserted that the Russian Foreign Intelligence Service (Boris Yeltsin's successor to the KGB) still has as its top priority the illegal acquisition of high technology and equipment from the United States.

On March 5th, the Associated Press reported that the FBI had concluded that Russian spying on the U.S. was, in the words of Wayne R. Gilbert, assistant director of the bureau's Intelligence Division, "a formal intelligence operation directed from Moscow." According to Gilbert, both the GRU military intelligence service and the new Foreign Intelligence Service are active in Washington. He predicted that the Russians will be focusing on scientific and high-technology secrets from both civilian companies and the military. He also told AP that the FBI was preparing for spying by some of the other former Soviet republics that are, with the help of former KGB operatives, establishing their own intelligence services.

And then there are the biological weapons. On March 22nd, AP reported that the old Soviet Union had "denied it had a germ-warfare program," but that the "United States didn't believe that then, and wants Russia to come clean now." Specifically, the U.S. wants Yeltsin . . . "to reveal the full scope of former and current biological-weapons programs." On March 3rd, the *Washington Times* had reported that U.S. intelligence "has identified 16 sites in the former Soviet Union where 'offensive' biological weapons are thought to be stored."

Yeltsin had admitted during his major disarmament speech on January 29th that there had indeed been a "lag" in Soviet implementation of the 1975 Biological and Toxin Weapons Convention, which bans offensive biological arms. According to the *Times*, Yeltsin's admission "could lead to new disclosures that support U.S. charges that an outbreak of pulmonary anthrax at Sverdlovsk in 1979 was caused by a biological weapons accident. Soviet authorities said the disease outbreak was caused by the consumption of tainted meat" and the military "covered up the incident, which caused at least 70 deaths, according to recent accounts in the Russian press."

Treaty Noncompliance

It appears that the Yeltsin regime has also been following typical communist strategy by violating its treaty commitments (it is exclusively responsible for past Soviet treaty obligations). Six U.S. senators implored the White House to send Congress a report on the former Soviet Union's arms control compliance that was three months overdue. The senators specifically requested that the report include details about such possible recent violations as:

• The December 20, 1991 launch of an SS-190 ICBM from Kazakhstan that used coded test data transmissions, a procedure precluded by the START treaty which President Bush and then-Soviet President Gorbachev signed during their Moscow summit. The treaty is pending in the Senate, which has postponed the ratification debate until all four of the nuclear-armed CIS states (Russia, Ukraine, Belarus, and Kazakhstan) sign it.

• Construction of a network of radars around the CIS, which may be illegal under the 1972 ABM treaty.

• Failure to totally disassemble the controversial and illegal ABM radar complex near Krasnoyarsk in Siberia.

• Continuation, as noted above, of treaty-banned offensive biological weapons production.

• Failure to notify the U.S. in advance of missile launches.

Parade Magazine's "Intelligence Report" for March 22nd noted that the Gulf war had given "the UN Security Council the power to inspect sites in Iraq for nuclear weapons," that the UN was trying to "stop North Korea from building nuclear weapons," and that it had the "obvious goal" of stopping "the spread of the Soviet Union's nuclear arsenal. . . ." The United States, *Parade* suggested, could use its sophisticated surveillance capability to "tell the UN what to look for and where to look. The real test will be whether its inspectors are allowed in. World peace may depend on it."

Needless to say, if the United Nations is given the unprecedented global military monopoly that champions of the new world order clearly have in mind, it will not be a question of whether or not a country allows UN "inspectors" in, as the UN will have the military clout to force its way in.

The escalating military alliance between Russia and the United States is part of a grand design to, among other things, implement the terrifying terms of the long-standing State Department Publication 7277 and its sister *Blueprint for the Peace Race*, without the formality of Senate debate and ratification.

The late Dr. Medford Evans, who was from 1944 to 1952 administrative officer on the atomic energy project, once observed: "World Authority with a monopoly of nuclear weapons would be a greater object of terror than an arms race between nations."

a critical thinking activity

Evaluating Sources of Information

When historians study and interpret past events, they use two kinds of sources: primary and secondary. Primary sources are eyewitness accounts. For example, the memoirs of former secretary of state James A. Baker III, in which he details his talks with the Soviet foreign minister, would be a primary source. A history book that quotes Baker's memoirs would be a secondary source. Primary and secondary sources may be decades or even hundreds of years old, and often historians find that the sources offer conflicting and contradictory information. To fully evaluate documents and assess their accuracy, historians analyze the credibility of the documents' authors and, in the case of secondary sources, analyze the credibility of the information the authors used.

Historians are not the only people who encounter conflicting information, however. Anyone who reads a daily newspaper, watches television, or just talks to different people will encounter many different views. Writers and speakers use sources of information to support their own statements. Thus, critical thinkers, just like historians, must question the writer's or speaker's sources of information as well as the writer or speaker.

While there are many criteria that can be applied to assess the accuracy of a primary or secondary source, for this activity you will be asked to apply three. For each source listed on the following page, ask yourself the following questions: First, did the person actually see or participate in the event he or she is reporting? This will help you determine the credibility of the information—an eyewitness to an event is an extremely valuable source. Second, does the person have a vested interest in the report? Assessing the person's social status, professional affiliations, nationality, and religious or political beliefs will be helpful in considering this question. By evaluating this you will be able to determine how objective the person's report may be. Third, how qualified is the author to be making the statements he or she is making? Consider what the person's profession is and how he or she might know about the event. Someone who has spent years being involved with or studying the issue may be able to offer more information than someone who simply is offering an uneducated opinion; for example, a politician or layperson.

Keeping the above criteria in mind, imagine you are compiling materials for a book on the history of U.S.-Soviet relations. You decide to cite an equal number of primary and secondary sources. Listed below are several sources that may be useful for your research. *Place a P next to those descriptions you believe are primary sources. Place an S next to those descriptions you believe are secondary sources.* Next, based on the above criteria, *rank the primary sources, assigning the number (1) to what appears to be the most valuable, (2) to the source likely to be the second-most valuable, and so on, until all the primary sources are ranked. Then rank the secondary sources, again using the above criteria.*

P or S | | Rank in Importance

_____ 1. Boris Yeltsin's account of the August 1991 _____ coup in the Soviet Union.

_____ 2. A *New York Times* report of U.S. aid to the _____ former Soviet republics.

_____ 3. A documentary in which Ukrainians de- _____ scribe their feelings about their republic's newly gained independence.

_____ 4. Nancy Reagan's autobiography, in which she _____ describes her visits with Raisa Gorbachev.

_____ 5. A *Newsweek* article discussing Bill Clinton's _____ plans for aid to the Soviet republics.

_____ 6. An "ABC News" report on the Pentagon's _____ plans for post-cold war defense cuts.

_____ 7. Mikhail Gorbachev's book *Perestroika and _____ Soviet-American Relations.*

_____ 8. An interview in which former U.S. president _____ Ronald Reagan discusses his administration's policies toward the Soviet Union.

_____ 9. The diary of an American reporter stationed _____ in Moscow during the cold war.

_____ 10. A made-for-TV movie dramatizing the _____ August 1991 Soviet coup.

_____ 11. A *Science* article describing the possibility of _____ a future joint U.S.-Soviet space venture.

_____ 12. The travel section of a newspaper explaining _____ how American tourists can best enjoy the architecture of St. Petersburg.

Periodical Bibliography

The following articles have been selected to supplement the diverse views presented in this chapter.

James A. Baker III	"America and the Collapse of the Soviet Empire: What Has to Be Done," *Vital Speeches of the Day*, January 1, 1992.
Jonas Bernstein	"Aid: The Best Way Up?" *Insight*, March 9, 1992. Available from 3600 New York Ave. NE, Washington, DC 20002.
Abraham Brumburg	"Changes in Russia and the American Right," *Dissent*, Winter 1992.
Congressional Digest	"Aid to the Former Soviet Union," August/September 1992.
Lawrence Eagleburger	"A Democratic Partnership for the Post-Cold War Era," *U.S. Department of State Dispatch*, July 8, 1992.
Nicholas Eberstadt	"Wrongheaded Aid to Russia," *The Wall Street Journal*, September 1, 1992.
Steven Erlanger	"In Russia, a Familiar Chill in the Political Air," *The New York Times*, August 9, 1992.
Henry A. Kissinger	"The New Russian Question," *Newsweek*, February 10, 1992.
Jay P. Kosminsky and Leon Aron	"Transforming Russia from Enemy to Ally," The Heritage Foundation *Backgrounder*, March 23, 1992. Available from 214 Massachusetts Ave., Washington, DC 20002.
Bruce W. Nelan	"Is the West Losing Russia?" *Time*, March 16, 1992.
Nicolai N. Petro	"Russian-American Relations: Looking for a New Agenda," *Global Affairs*, Summer 1992. Available from Subscription Services Dept. GLA, PO Box 3000, Denville, NJ 07834-9792.
Dimitri K. Simes	"America and the Post-Soviet Republics," *Foreign Affairs*, Summer 1992.
Boris Yeltsin	"Social Reforms in Russia: A Plea to Pass the Freedom-Support Act," *Vital Speeches of the Day*, July 15, 1992.

Glossary of Acronyms

ABM   Antiballistic missile; a missile designed to intercept and destroy other missiles.

AID   Agency for International Development (also referred to as USAID, the United States Agency for International Development); the U.S. government agency that carries out economic assistance programs for developing countries.

AIDS   Acquired immunodeficiency syndrome; a life-threatening depression of the immune system believed to be caused by **HIV**.

ASDF   Air Self-Defense Force; Japan's air force.

CIS   Commonwealth of Independent States; an alliance of some of the nations that were part of the former Soviet Union.

CSCE   Conference on Security and Cooperation in Europe; an organization comprised of the United States, Canada, all European nations, and the former Soviet republics. The organization aims to prevent military conflict and to promote cooperation between member states.

FREEDOM   Freedom for Russia and Emerging Eurasian Democracies and Open Markets; legislation passed by the U.S. Congress providing foreign aid to the former Soviet republics.

G-7   Group of Seven; an organization of the world's major industrialized nations that works to promote economic cooperation. Members include the United States, Great Britain, France, Japan, Germany, Italy, and Canada.

GRU   An intelligence agency of the former Soviet Union that dealt with national affairs.

GSDF   Ground Self-Defense Force; the ground forces of Japan's military.

HIV   Human immunodeficiency virus; believed by most scientists to be the cause of **AIDS**.

KGB   The primary intelligence agency of the former Soviet Union that dealt with international affairs.

ICBM   Intercontinental ballistic missile.

IMF   International Monetary Fund; an international organization that aims to promote monetary cooperation and currency stabilization and to expand international trade. The IMF loans money to nations as a way to stabilize economies and encourage free enterprise.

LDP   Liberal Democratic Party; the most powerful political party in Japan, the LDP has ruled the nation almost without interruption for more than four decades.

MFN Most-favored nation clause; a trade agreement clause that requires one member of a trade agreement to extend equal trade benefits to all other members of the agreement.

MSDF Maritime Self-Defense Force; Japan's navy.

MST Mutual Security Treaty; the 1951 defense treaty signed by Japan and the United States in which the United States agreed to protect Japan in exchange for the right to base U.S. military troops there.

NATO North Atlantic Treaty Organization; A strategic alliance established in 1949 that now includes the United States, Canada, Belgium, Denmark, Iceland, Italy, Luxembourg, the Netherlands, Norway, Portugal, the United Kingdom, Germany, Greece, and Turkey.

PLO Palestine Liberation Organization; the primary representative of the interests of the Palestinian people in their dispute with Israel over Israeli-occupied territories. The PLO, which consists of several Palestinian guerrilla, political, and refugee groups, is controversial because some of its factions have been involved in terrorist activities.

SALT Strategic Arms Limitation Talks; a series of discussions between the United States and the Soviet Union during the 1970s in which the two nations sought to reduce the number of strategic weapons.

SDF Self-Defense Forces; Japan's military.

SDI Strategic Defense Initiative; a plan to create a defensive shield in space that would protect the United States from enemy missiles.

START Strategic Arms Reduction Talks; a series of discussions between the United States and the Soviet Union during the 1980s in which the two nations sought to reduce the number of strategic weapons.

UN United Nations; an international organization of countries, established in 1947 to promote cooperation and peace.

Organizations to Contact

The editors have compiled the following list of organizations that are concerned with the issues debated in this book. All have publications or information available for interested readers. For best results, allow as much time as possible for the organizations to respond. The descriptions below are derived from materials provided by the organizations. The list was compiled upon the date of publication. Names, addresses, and phone numbers of organizations are subject to change.

American Defense Institute (ADI)
1055 N. Fairfax St., 2d Fl.
Alexandria, VA 22314
(703) 519-7000

The goal of ADI is to educate young Americans about foreign threats to freedom and the need for a strong defense. The institute sponsors internships, fellowships, and programs that emphasize the preparation of young people for leadership in defense policy-making. It believes that NATO is still vital for the security of Europe and the United States. ADI publishes the quarterly *ADI Newsletter*.

American Enterprise Institute for Public Policy Research (AEI)
1150 17th St. NW
Washington, DC 20036
(202) 862-5800

AEI is a conservative research and education organization that studies national and international issues, including American foreign policy. It promotes the spread of democracy and believes the United States should continue to be a world leader. The institute publishes the monthlies *American Enterprise* and *AEI Economist*, the bimonthly *Public Opinion*, and various books on America's foreign policy.

American Friends Service Committee
1501 Cherry St.
Philadelphia, PA 19102
(215) 241-7000

The committee is a Quaker organization that seeks better international relations through peacemaking and pacifism. It opposes U.S. intervention in other nations' affairs. Its purpose is to relieve human suffering and to find new approaches to world peace through nonviolent social change. The committee publishes the monthly magazine *Friends Journal*.

Asia Resource Center (ARC)
PO Box 15275
Washington, DC 20006
(202) 547-1114

ARC is an educational corporation formed in 1971 to bring the concerns of Asian people to the American public. It opposes enlarging the Japanese military. ARC provides publications and audiovisual resources, and distributes *AMPO*, a progressive Japanese-Asian quarterly review.

The Asia Society
725 Park Ave.
New York, NY 10021-5088
(212) 288-6400

The Asia Society is a nonprofit public education organization dedicated to increasing Americans' understanding of Asia and its growing importance to the United States and to world relations. Publications include briefing papers on Japan, Korea, India, China, and other Asian countries. In addition to the journal *Focus on Asian Studies*, the society publishes books and other materials on U.S.-Asia relations.

The Brookings Institution
1775 Massachusetts Ave. NW
Washington, DC 20036-2188
(202) 797-6000

The institution, founded in 1927, is a liberal think tank that conducts research and education in foreign policy, economics, government, and the social sciences. It publishes the quarterly *Brookings Review*, the biannual *Brookings Papers on Economic Activity*, and various books, including *In Search of a New World Order: The Future of U.S.-European Relations*.

Cato Institute
224 Second St. SE
Washington, DC 20003
(202) 546-0200

The institute is a libertarian public policy research foundation dedicated to stimulating foreign policy debate. It publishes the triannual *Cato Journal*, the periodic *Cato Policy Analysis*, and a bimonthly newsletter, *Cato Policy Review*.

Center for Initiatives
3268 Sacramento St.
San Francisco, CA 94115
(415) 346-1875

The center, formerly the Center for U.S.-U.S.S.R. Initiatives, works to strengthen relations between Americans and the peoples of the former Soviet republics. It sponsors agricultural, environmental, and economic programs to assist the republics in creating better societies. The center publishes three bimonthly newsletters and a variety of brochures.

Center for Teaching International Relations
University of Denver
University Park
Denver, CO 80208
(303) 871-3106

The center works to promote international and foreign policy studies in elementary and high school classrooms. It publishes extracurricular teaching materials on America's foreign relations.

Council on Foreign Relations
58 E. 68th St.
New York, NY 10021
(212) 734-0400

The council is a group of individuals with specialized knowledge of foreign affairs. It was formed to study the international aspects of American political and economic policies and problems. It publishes the renowned journal *Foreign Affairs* five times a year.

Delegation of the Commission of the European Communities
2100 M St. NW, 7th Fl.
Washington, DC 20037
(202) 862-9500

The delegation is concerned with explaining to Americans the nature and goals of European integration and how this integration will affect American-European relations. It offers scholarly analyses on the topic and publishes the monthly magazine *Europe* and a variety of booklets.

Foreign Policy Association
729 Seventh Ave.
New York, NY 10019
(212) 764-4050

The association is an educational organization that provides nonpartisan information to help citizens participate in foreign policy decisions. It publishes the monthly *Foreign Policy Preview*, the quarterly *Headline Series*, and the annual *Great Decisions*.

The Heritage Foundation
214 Massachusetts Ave. NE
Washington, DC 20002
(202) 546-4400

The foundation is a conservative public policy research institute dedicated to the principles of free, competitive enterprise, limited government, and individual liberty. Its scholars write numerous articles on foreign policy issues. Among its publications are the periodic *Backgrounder* and the monthly *Policy Review*.

Hudson Institute

PO Box 26919
Indianapolis, IN 46226
(317) 545-1000

The institute studies public policy aspects of national and international economics. It supports the view that the United States must continue to lead the world economically and politically. Publications include the quarterly *Hudson Institute Report*, research papers, and books.

Institute for Policy Studies

1601 Connecticut Ave. NW, Suite 500
Washington, DC 20009
(202) 234-9382

The institute's national security program provides factual analyses and critiques of America's foreign policies. Its goal is to provide a balanced view of international relations. The institute publishes books, reports, and briefs.

Liberty Lobby

300 Independence Ave. SE
Washington, DC 20003
(202) 544-1794

Liberty Lobby is a populist political organization. It opposes American entanglement in international affairs. Publications include the weekly *Spotlight* newspaper, books, and pamphlets.

National Committee on American Foreign Policy

232 Madison Ave.
New York, NY 10016
(212) 685-3411

The committee is composed of Americans from varied backgrounds who are interested in foreign policy and want to encourage citizen participation in foreign policy decisions. It also organizes fact-finding missions that meet with top political and economic leaders. Publications include the bimonthly *American Foreign Policy Newsletter*, monographs, and books.

Reason Foundation

3415 S. Sepulveda Blvd., Suite 400
Los Angeles, CA 90034
(310) 391-2245

The foundation promotes individual freedoms and free-market principles. It contends that the United States should avoid the extremes of isolationism and interventionism in its foreign policy. Publications include the monthly *Reason* magazine, newsletters, research reports, and books.

Russian-American Exchange Program
345 Franklin St.
San Francisco, CA 94102
(415) 563-4731

The Russian-American Exchange Program is an organization that seeks
to further cooperation between the United States and Russia. To accomplish this goal, it sponsors exchange programs for professionals, seminars for the American public, and informal dialogues between U.S. and
Russian scientists, political leaders, and scholars. The organization publishes materials about its programs and brochures and pamphlets on
strengthening U.S.-Russian relations.

The Spartacist League
Box 1377 GPO
New York, NY 10116
(212) 732-7860 or 267-1025

The Spartacist League is an international organization that advocates
revolutionary, socialist political theories. It publishes the periodic journal *Spartacist*, the biweekly tabloid *Workers Vanguard*, and monographs.

Trilateral Commission
345 E. 46th St., Suite 711
New York, NY 10017
(212) 661-1180

The commission encourages closer cooperation among North America,
Western Europe, and Japan. It works to develop proposals for joint ac-
tion among the three regions. Publications include the annual magazine
Trialogue, the semiannual *Triangle Papers*, books, and brochures.

United Nations Association of the United States of America
(UNA-USA)
485 Fifth Ave., 2d Fl.
New York, NY 10017
(212) 697-3232

UNA-USA is a nonpartisan, nonprofit research organization dedicated
to strengthening the United Nations and U.S. participation in it.
Publications include the bimonthly newspaper *The Interdependent* and
reports such as *Pulling Together: A Program for America in the United
Nations* and *Washington and the World: Organizing Economic Cooperation
in an Age of Global Competition*.

U.S. Department of State
Office of Public Communications, Public Information Service
Bureau of Public Affairs
Washington, DC 20520
(202) 647-6575

The Department of State advises the president in the formulation and execution of foreign policy. It publishes speeches and testimonies by government officials. Write or call for a list of publications.

United States Institute of Peace (USIP)
1550 M St. NW, Suite 700
Washington, DC 20005-1708
(202) 457-1700

The institute is an independent, nonpartisan organization established by Congress to support and promote the peaceful resolution of international conflict. Publications include the monthly *In Brief* and *Journal* newsletters.

U.S.-Japan Culture Center (USJCC)
2600 Virginia Ave. NW, Suite 711
Washington, DC 20037
(202) 342-5800

USJCC serves as a resource center on Japan and its relations with the United States. It maintains a library of Japanese and American books and periodicals, sponsors exchange and research programs, and provides seminars and language classes. It sponsors an essay contest on relations between the United States and Japan and publishes winning essays. The center's bimonthly publication *News* describes its activities.

Women's International League for Peace and Freedom (WILPF)
1213 Race St.
Philadelphia, PA 19107-1691
(215) 563-7110

WILPF is an international network of women activists, with one hundred branches in the United States. The league opposes militarism and U.S. intervention in other nations' affairs. WILPF publishes the bimonthly magazine *Peace and Freedom* and the book *The Women's Budget*, which proposes a 50 percent cut in military expenditures and proposes redistributing those funds to social programs that benefit women and children.

World Policy Institute
777 United Nations Plaza
New York, NY 10017
(212) 490-0010

The institute, affiliated with the New School for Social Research in New York City, is a public policy research organization that studies national security issues and foreign affairs. Publications of the institute include the quarterly *World Policy Journal*, books, monographs, and pamphlets.

Bibliography of Books

Graham Allison and Gregory F. Treverton, eds.	*Rethinking America's Security*. New York: Norton, 1992.
The Aspen Strategy Group	*Facing the Future: American Strategy in the 1990s*. Lanham, MD: University Press of America, 1991.
Thomas Bodenheimer and Robert Gould	*Rollback! Right-Wing Power in U.S. Foreign Policy*. Boston: South End Press, 1989.
Linda Brady	*The Politics of Negotiation: America's Dealings with Allies, Adversaries, and Friends*. Chapel Hill: The University of North Carolina Press, 1991.
Henry Brandon, ed.	*In Search of a New World Order*. Washington, DC: The Brookings Institution, 1992.
Philip J. Briggs	*Making American Foreign Policy: President-Congress Relations from the Second World War to Vietnam*. Lanham, MD: University Press of America, 1991.
The Carnegie Endowment National Commission on America and the New World	*America and the New World*. Washington, DC: The Brookings Institution, 1992.
Ted Galen Carpenter, ed.	*America Entangled: The Persian Gulf Crisis and Its Consequences*. Washington, DC: Cato Institute, 1991.
James Chace	*The Consequences of Peace: The New Internationalism and American Foreign Policy*. New York: Oxford University Press, 1992.
Noam Chomsky	*Deterring Democracy*. New York: Verso, 1991.
Michael Clough	*Free at Last? U.S. Policy Toward Africa and the End of the Cold War*. New York: Council on Foreign Relations, 1992.
Angelo Codevilla	*Informing Statecraft: Intelligence for a New Century*. New York: The Free Press, 1992.
John Dumbrell	*The Making of U.S. Foreign Policy*. Manchester, England: Manchester University Press, 1990.
Nicholas Eberstadt	*U.S. Foreign Aid Policy: A Critique*. Ithaca, NY: Foreign Policy Association, 1990.
Cynthia Enloe	*Bananas, Beaches, and Bases: Making Feminist Sense of International Politics*. Berkeley: University of California Press, 1990.
John Lewis Gaddis	*The United States and the End of the Cold War: Implications, Reconsiderations, Provocations*. New York: Oxford University Press, 1992.

Jeffrey E. Garten	*A Cold Peace: America, Japan, Germany, and the Struggle for Supremacy*. New York: Oxford University Press, 1992.
Robert A. Goldwin and Robert A. Licht, eds.	*Foreign Policy and the Constitution*. Washington, DC: The AEI Press, 1990.
Louis Henkin	*Constitutionalism, Democracy, and Foreign Affairs*. New York: Columbia University Press, 1990.
Seymour M. Hersch	*The Samson Option: Israel's Nuclear Arsenal and American Foreign Policy*. New York: Random House, 1991.
Paul Hollander	*Anti-Americanism: Critiques at Home and Abroad, 1965-1990*. New York: Oxford University Press, 1991.
Robert Jervis and Seweryn Bialer, eds.	*Soviet-American Relations After the Cold War*. Durham, NC: Duke University Press, 1991.
Paul M. Kennedy, ed.	*Grand Strategies in War and Peace*. New Haven, CT: Yale University Press, 1991.
Richard J. Kerry	*The Star-Spangled Mirror: America's Image of Itself and the World*. Savage, MD: Rowman & Littlefield, 1990.
Michael Ledeen	*Superpower Dilemmas: The U.S. and the U.S.S.R. at Century's End*. New Brunswick, NJ: Transaction Books, 1992.
Jonathan Samuel Lockwood	*The Soviet View of U.S. Strategic Doctrine 1954-1992*. New Brunswick, NJ: Transaction Books, 1992.
Geir Lundestad	*The American "Empire" and Other Studies of U.S. Foreign Policy in a Comparative Perspective*. Oxford, England: Oxford University Press, 1991.
George C. McGhee, Peter F. Krogh and Kenneth W. Thompson, eds.	*National Interest and Global Goals*. London: University Press of America, 1989.
Thomas E. Mann, ed.	*A Question of Balance: The President, Congress, and Foreign Policy*. Washington, DC: The Brookings Institution, 1990.
Constantine C. Menges	*The Twilight Struggle: The Soviet Union v. the United States Today*. Washington, DC: The AEI Press, 1990.
Joshua Muravchik	*Exporting Democracy: Fulfilling America's Destiny*. Washington, DC: The AEI Press, 1991.
Donald E. Neuchterlein	*America Recommitted: United States National Interests in a Restructured World*. Lexington: The University Press of Kentucky, 1991.

Richard Nixon	*Seize the Moment: America's Challenge in a One-Superpower World*. New York: Simon & Schuster, 1992.
Don Oberdorfer	*The Turn: From the Cold War to a New Era—The United States and the Soviet Union, 1983-1990*. New York: Poseidon Press, 1991.
Felix E. Oppenheim	*The Place of Morality in Foreign Policy*. New York: Lexington Books, 1991.
Robert A. Pastor	*Whirlpool: U.S. Foreign Policy Toward Latin America and the Caribbean*. Princeton, NJ: Princeton University Press, 1992.
Daniel Pipes and Adam Garfinkle	*Friendly Tyrants: An American Dilemma*. New York: St. Martin's Press, 1991.
Matthew Polesetsky and William Dudley, eds.	*The New World Order: Opposing Viewpoints*. San Diego, CA: Greenhaven Press, 1991.
John E. Rielly, ed.	*American Public Opinion and U.S. Foreign Policy 1991*. Chicago: The Chicago Council on Foreign Relations, 1991.
Nicholas X. Rizopoulos, ed.	*Sea-Changes: American Foreign Policy in a World Transformed*. New York: Council on Foreign Relations, 1990.
Brad Roberts, ed.	*U.S. Foreign Policy After the Cold War*. Cambridge, MA: The MIT Press, 1992.
John Spanier	*American Foreign Policy Since World War II*. 12th ed. Washington, DC: CQ Press, 1991.
Martin Staniland, ed.	*Falling Friends: The United States and Regime Change Abroad*. Boulder, CO: Westview Press, 1991.
John D. Steinbruner	*Restructuring American Foreign Policy*. Washington, DC: The Brookings Institution, 1988.
Robert W. Tucker and David C. Hendrickson	*The Imperial Temptation: The New World Order and America's Purpose*. New York: Council on Foreign Relations, 1992.
George Weigel	*American Interests, American Purpose: Moral Reasoning and U.S. Foreign Policy*. Washington, DC: Center for Strategic and International Studies, 1989.
Carol Wekesser, ed.	*America's Defense: Opposing Viewpoints*. San Diego, CA: Greenhaven Press, 1991.

Index

237